مراقي الفلاح بامداد الفتاح
شرح نور الايضاح و نجاة الارواح

Maraqi al Falah bi imdaad al Fatah
Sharh Nur al Idah Wa najat al-Arwah

The Steps to Success with the Help of al-Fattah
A Commentary of,
The Light of Clarification and the Salvation of Souls

Imam Allama Sheikh Hasan Bin Ammar Bin Al-Shurunbalaali Al-Hanafi

Dar Ul Thaqafah

www.twitter.com/darulthaqafah

2020 CE – 1441 H

Translation of the Qur'ān

It should be perfectly clear that the Qur'ān is only authentic in its original language, Arabic. Since perfect translation of the Qur'ān is impossible, we have used the translation of the meaning of the Qur'ān throughout the book, as the result is only a crude meaning of the Arabic text.

Qur'ānic verses appear in speech marks proceeded by a reference to the Surah and verse number. Sayings (*Hadith*) of Prophet Muhammad ﷺ appear in inverted commas along with reference to the Hadith Book and its Reporter.

ﷺ - صلى الله عليه وسلم (Peace be upon him)
ﷻ - سبحانه وتعالى (Glory to Him, the Exalted)

Contents

Introduction

Praise is to the One who honoured His elect slaves to inherit from His choicest one, the best of His slaves. He helped them with His Divine Providence. Consequently, they excelled in worshipping him, preserved His Sacred Law, and conveyed it to His slaves.

I testify that there is no god except Allah, al-Malik[1], al-Barr[2], al-Rahim[3]. I testify that our master Muhammad is His slave and His messenger - he is the noble prophet who said, *"Study knowledge, and study with it tranquillity and gentleness."* Blessings and peace on his family and companions who gave victory to this religion in times of war and peace.

Hasan ibn 'Ammar ibn 'Ali, al-Shurunbulali, the Hanafi – Allah forgive him his sins, cover his faults, and be gentle with him in all his affairs, whether open or hidden; may He do good to his parents, his teachers, his offspring, those who love him, and himself; and may He cause His favours to continue to flow freely, both internally and externally, on them and him – the lowly slave, hopeful of the pardon of his Lord, al-Jalil[4] says,

This is a book that is small in size, yet rich in knowledge and its rulings are correct. It contains knowledge by which the five pillars of worship can be elucidated and corrected. The proofs for it come from the Honourable Book, the exalted sunna, and consensus. Through it, the hearts, sight and hearing of the believers attain happiness.

---

[1] Al-Malik is the owner of the universe, of the whole creation – the absolute Ruler.

[2] Al-Barr is the perfect Doer of Good.

[3] Al-Rahim is the source of infinite mercy and beneficence, who rewards with eternal gifts the ones who use His bounties and beneficence for the good.

[4] Al-Jalil is the Lord of Majesty and Might.

In this book, I have put together my commentary on the primary text, after having been asked to do so by men of virtuous character. The book is an introduction for students and is there to facilitate success on the path to the place of return. I have named it, "The Steps to Success with the Help of al-Fattah[5]", being the commentary to, "The Light of Clarification and the Salvation of Souls".

I ask Allah, al-Karim[6], and supplicate to Him through His beloved, the chosen one, that He benefits the community by it, and that, by His grace, He accepts it and protects it from the evil of those who are not worthy of it. Indeed, His acceptance is the most sublime of favours and the greatest blessing. I, again, ask Allah that He benefits His slaves through it, and causes this benefit to perpetuate. He is able to do whatever He wants, and is able to respond.

Allah, accept my prayer.

---

[5] Al-Fattah is the Opener and the Solver, the Easer of all that is locked, tied and hardened.
[6] Al-Karim is the Generous One.

Taharah (Purity)

Section 1 - Waters

The words 'book' and 'writing' both in Arabic language mean 'collection'. However, in Islamic terminology, the term 'book' may be used to cover a group of legal issues that can be treated independently or addressed as a single entity.

Tahara is the verbal noun of 'the thing is pure', meaning it is clean. *Tihara* is the tool. *Tuhara* is the remains of that by which purification is performed. However, in Sacred Law, *tahara* means a ruling that affects those parts of the body and places of prostration pertaining to the prayer, and the agent used to purify them.

Purification precedes the prayer itself as it is a condition of the prayer. The means of removing ritual impurity, by agreement, is water. *Miya*[7] and *amwa*[8] are both plurals of water. Water is a clear liquid, from which the life of every living, growing thing is derived. In terms of pronunciation, the word *ma* can be elongated, but sometimes it can be shortened.

The types of water with which it is valid, to perform purification are seven. The first is rainwater based on His statement, *"Have you not seen that Allah has sent down water from the sky and has caused it to penetrate the earth as water springs?"*[9] This is purifying based on His statement, *"that He may purify you with it."*[10] This is understood to refer to rainwater as 'sky' is anything that is above and provides shade. Hence, the ceiling of a house is a 'sky'. Furthermore, dew is purifying, according to the correct position.

---

[7] This plural refers to any number from three to infinity.
[8] This plural refers to any number from three to nine.
[9] al-Zumar 21.
[10] al-Anfal 11.

Secondly, salty sea water is permitted based on his statement, upon him be peace and blessings, *"its water is purifying, and its dead creatures are lawful."*[11]

Thirdly, river water, such as Sayhun, Jayhun, the Euphrates and the Nile which are all from Paradise.[12]

The next three are well water, and the water that melts from snow and hail. This excludes water that melts from salt, which does not purify, despite being able to do so before becoming salt; it melts in the winter and solidifies in the summer, as opposed to water.

Finally, fountain water that flows on the ground emanating from springs.

The genitive construction in all of these waters is for classification and not for restriction. The difference between the two is that it is permitted to call the first type water as opposed to the second. Thus, it is not permitted, for example, to refer to rosewater as water without mentioning rose. However, this is permitted with well water.

Waters can also be subdivided into the following types, each having its own specific quality.

The first type is pure and purifying, but not offensive. This is absolute water that has had nothing mixed with it that would restrict it to any of the below categories.

---

[11] This is recorded by Abu Dawud 83; Tirmidhi 69; Nasai'i 59; Ibn Majah 386 to 388 and Malik, Book of Purity, 12.

[12] This is recorded by Muslim 7161. Furthermore, Imam Lucknowi has mentioned in his notes on *Hidaya* that this tradition has been recorded by Ahmad as a raised tradition.

The second type is pure and purifying, but slightly offensive to use, according to the most correct position. This is that which an animal such as a domestic cat and others like it such as free-range chickens, predatory birds, snakes, and rats have drunk from. These animals all cause the water to become slightly offensive because none of these avoid impurities. The explanation for the Prophet, upon him be peace and blessings, tilting the container for the cat[13] was that at that moment he was aware that there was nothing impure on the cat. This category of water only becomes *slightly offensive* after having been drunk, if it is small in quantity, the definition of which will soon come. The leftover water of a wild cat is impure.

The third type is pure in itself but non-purifying for ritual impurity, as opposed to filth. This is that which has been used on the body, or has touched it without intention, to remove ritual impurity, or intended for a righteous act. Examples of righteous acts include an ablution with intention, in another place, whilst already in a state of ablution, as an approach to Allah to make it an act of worship. However, if the second ablution is in the same place, it is offensive, and the water used for ablution is not regarded as used water. Washing the hands before and after eating is also regarded as a righteous act, based on his statement, upon him be peace and blessings, "*The blessings of food is in washing the hands before and after it.*"[14] Hence, if it is used to wash away dirt, whilst in a state of ablution and without intending a righteous act, it does not become used, for example, when washing a garment, or an animal lawful to eat.

Water only becomes used when it separates from the body, even if it has not settled at a place, according to the correct position. The rule of usage is not applicable before separation because of the necessity of purification. After the separation there is no necessity.

---

[13] This is a reference to the tradition narrated by Abu Dawud 75 and 76 and Tirmidhi 92.

[14] This statement is a portion of a tradition narrated by Abu Dawud 3761 and Tirmidhi 1846.

Ablution is not valid with liquid from trees or fruits because of its complete mixing which causes it not to be absolute. This is the case even if it comes out by itself without being pressed, like drops from vines, according to the most apparent position. By this, the claim "that it is not permitted with liquid that drops by itself" is excluded, because the drops that come out without being pressed have no effect in negating the restriction[15] and the validity of negating the name[16] from it.

It is valid to join cleansing liquids with absolute water for the purification of intrinsic impurity because of the presence of the required condition in cleansing liquids. This condition is the removal of the impurity when being washed. This condition, however, is absent in the case of legal impurity, because there is no tangible impurity on the limbs of the affected person. Ritual impurity is a matter dictated by Sacred Law. It carries the rule of being an impurity thereby preventing the affected person from praying. The Lawgiver has chosen a specific tool for the removal of ritual impurity, and no other tool can be used in its place.

Nor is ablution valid with water whose nature has been removed, which is to be fine and fluidic, able to quench thirst, and cause vegetation to grow, through cooking the likes of chickpeas and lentils. This water when it becomes cold thickens. The same is the case when water is cooked with some cleaning agent, such as *sidr*[17], and becomes thick. However, in both instances, if it remains fine ablution is permitted.

Water becomes restricted by one of two methods. The first method is by complete mixing, through absorption of the vegetation or through cooking. This method has been mentioned previously. The second

---

[15] of being non-purifying.

[16] i.e. absolute water.

[17] Lote tree leaves.

method is the dominance of the mixing substance over the water. However, because determining dominance will differ depending on the mixing substance, the scholars have set guidelines.

Dominance in the mixing of water with pure solids is attained when the water loses its fineness, thus being no longer able to drip from clothes, and its fluidity, thus no longer being able to flow on the limbs in the normal manner of water. However, if the fineness and fluidity remain there is no harm, i.e. it does not prevent the ablution being valid, even if all its characteristics change. Examples include solids such as saffron, fruits, or leaves mixing with it, other than by cooking. This is based on the narrations from Bukhari and Muslim *that the Prophet, upon him be peace and blessings, ordered that the one who had been thrown off and killed by his camel whilst in ihram be washed with water and sidr.*[18] *He also ordered Qays ibn Asim, on becoming Muslim, to perform the ritual bath with water and sidr. On occasions, the Prophet, upon him be peace and blessings, performed the ritual bath with water that had traces of dough in it.*[19] *The Prophet, upon him be peace and blessings, used to perform ritual bath and wash his hair with khitmi*[20] *whilst in the state of major ritual impurity, and would suffice with that.*[21]

Dominance in the mixing of liquids is attained by the appearance of a single characteristic, such as colour alone or taste, in liquids having only two characteristics. An example of this is milk that has colour and taste alone. If these two are not present ablution is valid. However, if one appears ablution is not valid. The same is the rule if the mixing substance has one characteristic and that characteristic appears, such as certain types of melons that have only one characteristic.

---

[18] This is recorded by Bukhari 1266; Muslim 2891 to 2901; Abu Dawud 3238 to 3241; Tirmidhi 951 and Nasa'i 2856 to 2861.
[19] This is recorded by Nasa'i 241and Ibn Majah 378.
[20] *Khitmi* is marshmallow.
[21] This is recorded by Abu Dawud 256.

Dominance is attained by the appearance of two characteristics in liquids having three characteristics, such as vinegar that has colour, taste and odour. Any two characteristics appearing will prevent the ablution from being valid. However, one characteristic does not harm, being too insignificant.

Dominance in the mixing of liquids that have no characteristics that would make it differ to water by way of colour, taste and odour, such as used water or rose water that has lost its smell, is determined by weight. After being used, the taste, colour and odour do not change, and, according to the correct position, it is pure. Weight is used to determine, because there is no way of determining by the other characteristics as they are not present. Thus, if two *ritl*, for example, of used water or rose water that has lost its smell mix with one *ritl* of absolute water ablution is not permitted due to the dominance of the restricted water. But the opposite, where the majority is absolute water means ablution is permitted. The ruling for when the two are equal is not mentioned in the primary narrations.[22] The scholars say that rule takes the rule of the dominated[23], out of caution.

The fourth type of water is impure. This is stagnant water that is small in quantity in which an impurity has entered, and it is known to have entered with certainty or high probability. This is with an impurity other than horse or donkey droppings, which are exempted, as we shall mention.

Small is defined as that body of water whose surface area is less than ten by ten arm lengths.[24] The word arm is both masculine and feminine. Thus, if it is small and an impurity touches it, it becomes impure, even if no trace of the impurity appears.

---

[22] These are the six books in which Imam Muhammad Shaybani gathered the legal statements of Imam Abu Hanifa.

[23] This water is pure and non-purifying.

[24] One arm length is equivalent to 46 centimeters.

However, if it is a rectangular fountain that measures ten by ten arm lengths, or circular that measures thirty six arm lengths, and its depth is such that on taking a handful of water no earth is present, according to the correct position, it does not become impure even at the point where the impurity entered unless a characteristic of the impurity appears. It is also said that the depth is an arm length or a hand span. The Balkh scholars have taken this position to make ease for people. However, the estimation of ten by ten arm lengths is the fatwa.

There is no problem in performing ablution or drinking from a large vessel whose mug is in the corner of the house, as long as it is known that no impurity has entered. The same is the case with a pond, in which it is feared, without confirmation, that impurity is present. It is not necessary to ask about this. The same also applies to a well in which dirty bucks are lowered, having been carried by children and slaves and touched by farmers with soiled hands, unless the impurity is known for certain.

Water is also impure if it is flowing and the trace of impurity appears in the flowing water. Trace is the taste, colour or odour of the impurity. The presence of the trace indicates the impurity itself is present.

The fifth type is water in which there is doubt over its purifying ability, but not in its purity. It is water that has been drunk by a donkey or a mule. The mother of the mule is a donkey and not a mare, because the consideration is by the mother, as we will mention in Section 2 - Leftover Water, God willing.

Section 2 - Leftover Water

A small body of water - which we have defined as being less than ten by ten arm lengths -that is not flowing, when drunk by an animal can fall under one of four categories. Whatever remains after having been drunk is known as leftover water, or *su'r*, the plural being *as'ar* – its *'ayn* letter in the trilateral root is *hamza*. The word is also employed to refer to leftover food. The verb is *as'ara*, which means to leave behind something after having drunk from it. The active participle is *saa'ar*. However, this deviates from the rule, which dictates that the active participle should be *mus'ir*. A parallel example of this is the verb *ajbara*, which has the active participle *jabbar*.

The first type is pure and purifying leftover water. By agreement, there is no offence in using it. It is that which a human whose mouth has no impurities on it has drunk from. This is based on the narration from Muslim, that 'Aisha said, *"I used to drink whilst menstruating. I would pass the drink to the Prophet, upon him be peace and blessings, who would drink where I had drunk from."*[25] There is no difference in this rule between young and old, Muslim and non-Muslim, and the menstruating woman or the person in the state of major ritual impurity.

However, if a person's mouth becomes impure and water is immediately drunk the leftover water is impure. If, however, the saliva has circulated a number of times and is then spat out or swallowed before drinking, the leftover water does not become impure, according to Abu Hanifa and Abu Yusuf. The leftover water, though, is *offensive* to use, because of Muhammad's stance that saliva does not purify an impurity.

---

[25] This is recorded by Muslim 692; Abu Dawud 259; Nasa'i 280 to 283;and ibn Majah 643.

The leftover water of a horse is pure without any *offence* by agreement, according to the correct position.

Water that an animal lawful to eat, such as camels, cows, sheep and goats, have drunk from is also pure and purifying. There is no offence in using its leftover water, unless it eats *jalla* (animal droppings). Originally, *jalla* referred to camel, sheep or goat droppings. However, it can also be used to describe human faeces. If the animal does eat *jalla* then its leftover water is of the third type, which is offensive.

The second type of leftover water is severely impure, although it is said to be slightly impure. Purification is not valid with it and can only be drunk in absolute need, as with the eating of carcass. It is that water which a dog has drunk from, irrespective of whether the dog is a hunting dog, a shepherd dog or any other type of dog. This is based on the narration of Daraqutni, that Abu Hurayra narrated, *"from the Prophet, upon him be peace and blessings, that a container a dog licks should be washed three, five, or seven times."*[26]

The water that a pig has drunk from is also impure, because of the intrinsic impurity of the pig. This is based on His statement, *"for that assuredly is foul."*[27]

The water that a predatory animal has drunk from is also impure. This excludes predatory birds, whose ruling will come. A predatory animal is any animal that is voracious and aggressive by nature, such as a cheetah, wolf, hyena, tiger and monkey. The impurity is because its saliva is a product of its flesh which is impure. The same is true of its milk.

---

[26] This is recorded by Daraqutni. Similar narrations have been mentioned by Muslim 648 to 658; Abu Dawud 81 to 84 and Tirmidhi 91.

[27] al-An'am 145.

The third type of leftover water is slightly offensive to use for purification, in the presence of other water that is not offensive. However, because it is pure it is not offensive to use when there is no such water available. Thus, it is not permitted to perform dry ablution in its presence. It is the leftover water of a domestic cat. The ruling of impurity does not apply to the cat, by agreement, due to the cats' movements. This is textually documented by his statement, upon him be peace and blessings, *"It is not impure. It is from amongst those that move in your midst."* – Tirmidhi has classified this as a fair-sound tradition.[28] However, its leftover water is slightly offensive, according to the most correct position, because it does not avoid impurities. The incident of the Prophet, upon him be peace and blessings, tilting the container for a cat is interpreted as having occurred at a moment when the Prophet, upon him be peace and blessings, was aware that no impurity was present on the cat's mouth.

The above rule is the case with water that a child has dipped its hand in. It is offensive to pray after a cat has licked the palm of a person's hands without washing it. It is also offensive to eat the leftover food that a cat has eaten from, if the person is rich and has other food. However, if the person is poor it is not offensive, out of necessity. The leftover water of a wild cat is impure because the cats' movements no longer remain an issue.[29]

The leftover water of a free-range chicken[30] that moves about in dirt is also slightly offensive. This is because the purity of its beak cannot be ascertained with certainty. However, if this is not the case there is no offence, for example, by being caged thereby preventing its beak from touching any dirt.

---

[28] This tradition is recorded by Tirmidhi 92. The tradition has also been mentioned by Abu Dawud 75 and 76.

[29] Thus, the rule reverts back to the original which is one of impurity.

[30] Chicken or *dajaja* with the *dal* three ways and its *ta* for singularity not femininity. *Dajaj* is common to between male and female but *dajaja* is exclusively female. Thus, if he swears that he will not eat *dajaja* meat he has not broken it by eating rooster meat. Maraqi Falah.

The leftover water of predatory birds such as a hawk, falcon, kite, vulture or raven is offensive, because this category of birds consume carrion and other impurities. In this, they resemble free-range chickens. Again, if it is known with certainty that there is no impurity on its beak its leftover water is not offensive. Analogical deduction necessitates that the leftover water should be impure because its flesh is unlawful, as with predatory animals. However, the leftover water is pure by hidden analogical deduction because it drinks with its beak, which is a pure bone. Predatory animals, on the other hand, drink with their tongues which are moistened by their impure saliva.

The leftover water of creatures having flowing blood that inhabit dwellings, such as rats, snakes and lizards, is offensive, because of their movement and their impure flesh. The leftover water of scorpions, dung beetles, crickets and cockroaches is not offensive, because they are not impure.

The fourth type is water that is doubtful in being regarded as purifying. Thus, it cannot be regarded as being purifying with certainty. However, at the same time, the possibility cannot be rejected outright. This is the leftover water of a donkey – the word donkey can be used for both the male and female – and a mule, whose mother is a donkey. Its saliva is pure, according to the correct position. However, the doubt is due to the apparent contradiction between the two reports on the permissibility of its flesh. The mule is an offspring of the donkey, thereby taking its rule.

If a person in the state of ritual impurity cannot find water other than the leftover water of a mule or donkey, ablution should be performed with the water along with dry ablution. The best is to perform the ablution first, because of Zufar's position that it must performed first. The safest is to make intention, because of the disagreement over the necessity of making intention when performing ablution with the leftover water of a donkey. Then prayer is performed. The prayer is valid with certainty because the ablution, if it is valid, is not harmed by the dry ablution, and vice versa.

The claim of some of our scholars that "the leftover water of the stallion is impure because it smells urine thereby causing its lips to become impure" is not correct. It is based on speculation, because it is not a regular occurrence. Thus, this speculation does not have any affect in removing certainty.

It is recommended to wash the limbs afterwards to remove the traces of the doubtful and offensive water.

Section 3 - Investigation[31]

If a set of containers, most of them being pure but some impure, become mixed, a person must investigate before performing ablution or ritual bath. However, if the pure and impure containers are equal in number dry ablution must be performed. In this case, it is best to mix them or to pour them away and then perform the dry ablution. By this, the purifying water is no longer present for certain.

If three men were to find three containers, one of which is impure, and each one, after investigating, arrives at a different conclusion, their prayer would be valid individually.

If the containers are predominantly pure, before drinking from the containers the person must investigate to find the pure containers. Here, the minority is treated as though it does not exist.

If two containers become mixed and the person does not investigate but instead performs ablution with both containers, praying is valid as long two separate places, and not the same place, are wiped when wiping the head. If the first ablution was with pure water the ritual impurity would have been removed. The second ablution, though, would subsequently have made the limbs impure. This though is immaterial because the person who has no purifying water prays even with impurity present. But, if the first ablution was with impure water the second ablution would cleanse the impurity from the limbs. This would only be the case if two different parts of the head are wiped. If the same part is wiped with both waters it would be valid if the first ablution was with the pure water, but invalid if the second ablution was with the pure water – here, the wetness would become impure at the moment of contact. Hence, out of caution, due to the presence of doubt the ablution is not regarded as being valid.

---

[31] The investigation here is to determine pure from impure.

If most of the containers are impure investigation is only required for drinking. Here, all of the containers are regarded as impure, based on the majority. Thus, according to most scholars, the containers should be poured away and dry ablution performed. Imam Tahawi holds that the water should be mixed and given to animals to drink.

As for clothes that have been mixed, a person must investigate whether the majority are pure or not. There is no substitute for clothes to cover nakedness, whereas earth acts as a substitute for water in removing ritual impurity.

If the person has only two set of clothes available and prays in one of them, after having investigated for the impure clothes, and then prays another prayer but, in this instance, the investigation results in a different conclusion, the original prayer is not valid. Personal deduction cannot be negated by itself, except in determining the direction of prayer. The direction of prayer can possibly change to another direction through investigation because it is a matter determined by Sacred Law. Impurity, though, is a tangible matter that does not change state and become pure by investigation. Thus, all prayers must be repeated if impurity becomes clear after investigation with clothes and containers. Hence, if through personal deduction one set of clothes are taken to be pure it cannot be made impure through another personal deduction. As a result, every prayer prayed with the initial investigation becomes invalid, but is valid with the resulting investigation.

If two just persons disagree over the permissibility of meat, such that one of the two claims that the meat has been slaughtered by a Zoroastrian while the other claims that a Muslim has slaughtered it, it is not permitted to eat. It remains in its original state of impermissibility due to the conflict in the reports. Conversely, if a person is informed about water, and again there is a conflict between two just persons over its purity, the water remains in its original state of purity.

Section 4 - Wells

The rules relating to wells centre on impurity entering wells whether it is animal droppings, an animal itself, a drop of blood or something similar.

The water of a small well – which is less than ten by ten arm lengths – is drained if an impurity enters, however small that impurity may be, such as a drop of blood or alcohol. A small amount of impurity makes a small body of water impure, even if no traces of the impurity appear. The exception to this is animal droppings.

The well is also drained if a pig falls in and its mouth has not touched the water, even if it emerges alive, because of its intrinsic impurity.

The well is drained by the death of a dog within it. Here, the condition is its death because it is not intrinsically impure, according to the correct position. Thus, if it does not die and emerges alive without having touched the water, the water is not impure.

It is also drained by the death of a sheep or a human being in it. Zamzam water was drained after a man had died in it on the instruction of ibn 'Abbas and ibn Zubayr in the presence of a group of companions without any objection being raised[32].

The well is also drained if an animal dies and then swells in it, even if the animal is small. The swelling causes impurity to spread.

It is necessary to drain the well by removing two hundred average-sized buckets that are normally used at that well, if the well cannot be drained. It is recommended to increase this by one hundred buckets. Muhammad, Allah have mercy upon him, estimated the figure of two hundred buckets upon seeing the wells of Baghdad having plentiful

---

[32] This is recorded by Daraqutni 62 to 63.

water due to the proximity of the Tigris. The soundest approach is to base the estimation on the testimony of two men experienced in dealing with water – this is the most correct position.

The well becomes pure when the last bucket passes the mouth of the well, with them both. However, with Muhammad, it is when the last bucket separates from the water, even if, in the process, some water falls back in to the well, out of necessity. He[33] stated, "Separation is a condition because without separation it will remain connected through the water falling back."

If the necessary amount is drained over a period of days, or an impure cloth is washed over a period of days, it becomes pure.

If a chicken, cat or something resembling them in size dies in a well without swelling forty buckets must be drained, after having removed the animal. This figure of forty buckets for a chicken has been narrated from Abu Sa'id Khudri. Any animal similar in size takes its rule. It is recommended to increase this to fifty or sixty buckets, based on the narrations from 'Ata and Sh'abi.

If a rat or something resembling it, such as a small bird, dies in a well without swelling twenty buckets must be drained, after having removed the animal. This is based on the response of Anas to the question, "A rat dies in a well and is immediately removed?"[34] It is recommended to increase this to thirty buckets because of the possibility that the buckets mentioned in the tradition are larger than the estimated average-sized buckets.

It has been narrated from Abu Yusuf and Hasan that the draining of the well acts as purification for the well, the bucket, the rope, the pulley and the hand of the person drawing the water. All of these are impure due to the impurity of the water. Thus, they all become pure

---

[33] i.e. Imam Muhammad.
[34] The response being, "Twenty buckets must be removed".

when the water becomes pure, thereby removing any difficulty. Other examples of this include the bottle becoming pure when wine changes to vinegar, or the jug handle becoming pure by the purity of the hand if held every time the hand is washed.

It is narrated from Abu Yusuf that four rats is equivalent to one rat, five to nine rats is equivalent to a chicken and ten rats is equivalent to a sheep. However, Muhammad held that three to five rats is equivalent to a cat and six rats are equivalent to a dog – this is the primary narration. Anything between a rat and a cat has the rule of the rat. Anything between a cat and a dog has the rule of the cat. Finally, if a rat and a cat both fall in they are treated as a cat. The smaller animal is overridden by the larger animal.

The well does not become impure through camel, sheep and goat droppings (*b'ar*), or horse, mule and donkey droppings (*rawth*) or cow droppings (*khithy* – the plural of which is *akhtha'*).

According to the correct position, there is no difference between urban and rural wells. There is also no difference between moist and dry or whole and broken droppings, according to the primary narrations. Necessity covers all these types, and thus they do not make the well impure.

The above is only the case if the droppings are not abundant. Abundant is that which the observer regards as being abundant, and sparse is that which the observer regards as being sparse – this is the position that is relied upon. Abundant could also be such that no bucket is free of droppings – this opinion has been authenticated in *Mabsut*.

The water does not become impure by pigeon droppings (*khar'* is the singular of droppings – the plural of which is *khur'*). Nor does it become impure by the droppings of small birds that can be eaten, other than chicken and geese. The purity of pigeon droppings is based on hidden analogical deduction, because the Prophet, upon him be peace and blessings, thanked pigeons by saying, *"It built a nest over the mouth of the cave until I was safe. Therefore, Allah rewarded it with the mosque as its abode."* This tradition is an evidence of the purity of all that emanates from it. In addition, ibn Mas'ud wiped away pigeon droppings with his finger. Hence, the preference in many books of the school is that it is pure. There is a difference in authenticating the purity of droppings from birds that cannot be eaten – its impurity is slight.

Water or liquids do not become impure by the death of an animal that has no blood, whether it is terrestrial or maritime, such as fish and frogs. Terrestrial animals that have blood make the water impure. However, maritime animals that have blood, such as crayfish, beavers, otters and water hogs do not make the water impure

Bedbugs – pungent-smelling insects similar to ticks, flies[35] and lice do not make water impure if they die in it. The Prophet, upon him be peace and blessings, said, *"When a fly falls in a person's drink let him dip it and then remove it, for indeed in one of its wings is a disease and in the other is a cure."*[36] The narration of Abu Dawud continues, *"For indeed it protects with the wing that has the disease."* He, upon him be peace and blessings, also said, *"Salman, every food or drink that an insect, having no blood, falls and dies in is lawful to eat, drink and perform ablution with."*

The water does not become impure if a human or a lawful animal, such as a camel, cow, sheep or goat, fall in, if they emerge alive and there is no definite impurity on its body. The thighs of these animals, despite seeming to be covered in urine, are not considered.

---

[35] Flies in Arabic are known as *thubab* because whenever they are repelled (*thubba*) they return. Maraqi Falah.

[36] This is recorded by Bukhari 3320; Abu Dawud 3844; and ibn Majah 3504 and 3505.

Nor does the water become impure if a mule, donkey or predatory birds, such as a hawk, falcon or kite, fall in. It also does not become impure if a wild animal, such as a predatory animal or a monkey, fall in, because their bodies are pure. It is also said that it is necessary to drain all the water because the wetness of the animal is linked to that of its saliva.

If the saliva of the creature that falls in touches the water, the water takes the rule of the saliva, be it pure, impure or *offensive* – the details of these have been covered in Section 2 - Leftover Water. Here, it would be necessary to drain the impure and doubtful cases. However, it is recommended to drain the offensive cases with a number of buckets – it is said that the number of buckets is twenty.

If a dead animal is found in a well and it is not known when it fell in, with the Imam[37], the well is considered impure for a period of twenty four hours or a period of seventy two hours if the dead animal has swelled, out of caution. The swelling is an indicator of the length of time having passed. Hence, all prayers over this period must be repeated if ablution or ritual bath were performed with this water whilst in a state of ritual impurity. Equally, if clothes have been washed without any impurity on them no prayer is repeated by consensus. If clothes that had impurity were washed with this water but ablution was not performed then the clothes must be washed, according to the correct position. This is because the moment when the impurity touched is not known. By agreement, no prayer is repeated, according to the correct position.

Abu Yusuf and Muhammad hold that the water is considered impure from the moment it is known to have become impure. Thus, it is not obligatory to repeat any prayers or to wash off any water used before it was known when the water became impure.

---

[37] The phrase "the Imam" in books of the Hanafi school is a reference to Abu Hanifa, Allah reward him profusely.

If this water has been used to make dough, it is said that the dough should be thrown to dogs or given as fodder to grazing animals. Some have suggested that it be sold to a Shafi'.

If sperm is found on clothes all prayers are repeated from the last sleep taken. However, with blood nothing needs to be repeated, because blood usually comes from an external source.

Section 5 - Cleansing Oneself

Cleansing oneself is the removal of impurity with the likes of water. Removal can also be attained by reducing the impurity with the likes of stones.

A man must[38] clear his front orifice until all trace of urine has stopped. The aim is to clear the front orifice of any trace of dripping.

The traces of urine are only regarded as having stopped when wetness no longer appears on a stone placed on the front orifice. Only then can a man be satisfied that the urine has completely stopped.

A woman does not need to do this. She is merely required to wait a little and then cleanse herself.

For a man, clearing the orifice can be completed in any manner normal to him. This may include walking, clearing the throat, inclining to the left side, moving the feet, striking the ground with the feet or gently squeezing the penis. The manner of clearing the orifice is not restricted to any one way because of the difference in the way people do this.

Beginning ablution is not valid until a person is satisfied that the dripping of urine has completely stopped. Any wetness that reappears at the head of the penis is considered the same as flowing urine. Thus, this prevents subsequent ablution from being valid.

Cleansing oneself is an emphasised sunna for both men and women as it was regularly performed by the Prophet, upon him be peace and blessings. However, it is not *necessary* because he, upon him be peace and blessings, did leave it on occasions. He, upon him be peace and

---

[38] The term 'must' has been used because it is stronger than necessary. If an obligatory action is not performed, any conditional action becomes invalid. If a necessary action is not performed any conditional action remains valid.

blessings, said, *"Whoever cleanses oneself should do so an odd number of times. Whoever does so has done well, but whoever does not there is no harm."*[39] Some have mentioned that cleansing oneself falls under other categories, including obligatory. However, this has been done merely to simplify matters for people.

Cleansing oneself only applies to impurity. Therefore, cleansing oneself after having broken wind is an innovation, because wind, according to the correct position, is pure. Cleansing oneself is an emphasised sunna whether or not the impurity comes from the front or rear orifice. Thus, if either the front or rear orifice is touched by an impurity from an external source, even if it be puss or blood emanating from the veins, cleansing oneself purifies the orifice. This would be done in the same manner as following emissions from either orifice. Prayer is valid if either puss or blood flows from the veins because there is a consensus amongst the latter scholars that, should the puss or blood soil the body or garment more than the size of a dirham, it does not prevent the prayer being valid. However, if that same person were to sit in a small body of water, the water would become impure.

Cleansing oneself is only sunna if the impurity does not spread across the rear orifice. However, if it does spread across the orifice and is the size of a dirham it is no longer considered as cleansing oneself. It is now necessary to remove the impurity with water or a liquid, the action now falling under the category of the removal of an impurity, as opposed to the cleansing of oneself. Hence, wiping the impurity away with stones will not suffice.

If the impurity that has spread is more than the weight of a dirham, and is a solid, or the size of a dirham, and is a liquid, it is obligatory for it to be washed away either with water or liquid.

It is obligatory to wash any impurity in the rear orifice when performing ritual bath from sexual impurity, menstruation or postnatal

---

[39] This is recorded by Abu Dawud 35 and Ibn Majah 337.

bleeding with absolute water, even if the impurity be small, so as to fulfil the obligatory washing of ritual impurity.

It is sunna to cleanse oneself with a cleansing stone, neither so rough as to cause damage nor so smooth as to not allow cleansing, because cleansing is the aim.[40] Something similar to a cleansing stone may also be used. It must be pure, not valuable or respected and remove impurity without causing harm.

Washing with absolute water is best because with it purity is attained by agreement. Also, by using absolute water the sunna is established in the most comprehensive manner. Using stones merely reduces the amount of impurity present, whilst there is a difference of opinion over using other than absolute water for purification.

The best method, in all ages, is to wipe and then wash, in that order. Hence, first the impurity coming out from the orifice is wiped away, and then the orifice is washed. Allah has praised the people of Quba for washing with water after having used stones. Thus, using both is a sunna in all ages, according to the correct position, which is the fatwa.

It is valid to use water alone. This is second to using both water and stones in preference. To use stones alone is the least preferable. The sunna is attained by this, as the ultimate purpose is achieved, although the most preferable method carries the most reward.

It is recommended to use three stones, because of his statement, upon him be peace and blessings, *"Whoever cleanses oneself should do so an odd number of times."*[41] This tradition indicates permissibility as opposed to necessity. Thus, the number is recommended and not an emphasised sunna. The tradition continues further, and is conclusive in providing an option, by his statement, upon him be peace and blessings, *"Whoever cleanses oneself should do so an odd number of times. Whoever*

---

[40] An example of a rough stone is baked brick and an example of a smooth stone is carrelion.

[41] This is recorded by Abu Dawud 35 and Ibn Majah 337.

does so has done well, but whoever does not there is no harm."[42] Hence, it is recommended to cleanse oneself with three stones if purification is attained with less.

The aim of cleansing oneself is to cleanse the orifice as thoroughly as possible. The recommended manner mentioned below is preferred because cleanliness is attained in the most comprehensive manner.

The man begins by wiping the rear orifice with a stone from the front to the back. A second stone is then used to wipe from the back to the front. A third stone is then used to wipe from the front to the back a second time. This order is used if the testicles are sagging, whether it is summer or winter, from fear of soiling them. However, if they are not sagging the man should cleanse initially from the back to the front and proceed from there. This order is preferred because it is a more thorough manner of cleansing.

The woman begins by wiping from the front to the back from fear of soiling her external genitals and proceeds from there.

After wiping in the above manner, the hands are washed with water to avoid the body having to absorb impure water at the beginning of cleansing oneself. The area is then rubbed with water with the pulp of one or two fingers at first, or three fingers if need be. The man raises the middle finger above the others from the beginning of cleansing oneself so that the impure water flows away without spreading over the body. After washing for a little while the ring finger is raised, followed by the little finger, and, if needed, the index finger. This enables cleansing to be performed thoroughly. One finger alone should not be used because it can possibly produce an ailment and it does not cleanse thoroughly.

---

[42] This is recorded by Abu Dawud 35 and Ibn Majah 337.

The woman should raise the middle finger and the ring finger together from the beginning from fear of attaining pleasure if only one finger was used. This could possibly require her to perform a ritual bath without her even realising. The virgin should cleanse herself with the palm of her hand and not with her fingers from fear of possibly breaking her hymen.

The person cleansing oneself should persist in cleaning until the bad odour has been removed. There is no estimate for the number of times for this because the correct position is to leave this to the individual until convinced that they are clean.

The following are less strong positions
- Someone afflicted with constant doubt should limit the washing to seven or three times.
- Three times for the front orifice and five times for the rear orifice.
- Nine times.
- Ten times.

Whilst cleansing oneself, the person should strive to loosen the rear orifice so that as much impurity as possible can be removed from the anus, provided one is not fasting. The person fasting, however, should not do so to prevent the fast from being coming invalid. Likewise, the person fasting should avoid inserting a wet finger because it invalidates the fast.

After cleansing oneself with water the hands are washed a second time and the rear orifice is dried before standing. This will prevent the rear orifice from gathering water thereby breaking the fast. It is also recommended so as to protect the garment from being wetted with used water.

Section 6 - Etiquettes of Cleansing Oneself

It is not permitted to expose the nakedness whilst cleansing oneself. It is unlawful and there is wrongdoing involved in it. Hence, it should not be done in order to establish a sunna.

The orifice is wiped from beneath the garment with the likes of stone. However, if it is left the prayer is still valid.

If the impurity spreads beyond the orifice and the amount spread is more than a dirham, in weight, if it is solid, or in size, if it is liquid, prayer is not valid. It is more than the amount exempted from cleansing by water or another liquid.

The person should, in this case, attempt to remove the impurity without exposing the nakedness, assuming the possibility of being seen, and thereby avoiding committing an unlawful act.

However, if the impurity is more than a dirham only after including the amount in the rear orifice, there is no harm in leaving it. Only that which has spread beyond the orifice is taken into account.

Cleansing oneself with any of the following is deemed offensive
- Bones or *rawth*[43], because of his statement, upon him be peace, *"Do not cleanse yourself with rawth or bones for they are the provision of your brethren amongst the jinn."*[44] When the jinn find bones, the bones become as if they have not been eaten and thus they can eat them. Likewise, the *rawth* becomes barley and straw for the animals of the jinn. This all occurs as a miracle granted to him, upon him be peace and blessings. The prohibition in the tradition necessitates the ruling of severe offence.

---

[43] *Rawth* has been defined in Section 4 – Wells, page 2.
[44] This is recorded by Muslim 1007; Abu Dawud 36 to 39; and Tirmidhi 18.

- Food for humans or animals, because of the Prophetic prohibition of contempt for and waste of food.
- Baked brick as, rather than cleaning the area, using it would be harmful.
- Pebbles as rather than cleansing, using them would soil the hand.
- Coal as it would create mess.
- Glass or plaster, as it would be harmful to the area.
- Anything that is respected for its value, such as a piece of silk brocade or cotton. Using these to cleanse would result in poverty through destruction of wealth.
- The right hand, because of his statement, upon him be peace and blessings, "*When one of you urinates, he should not touch his penis with his right hand. When he excretes he should not wipe with his right hand. When he drinks he should not drink in one breath.*"[45] However, if there is a problem with the left hand, cleansing oneself is performed either through a servant pouring water or with flowing water.

It is recommended to enter the toilet with the head covered, left foot first. This is from the honour given to the right side, as the toilet is a dirty place with devils present. Thus, before exposing the nakedness and before entering the toilet, a person seeks refuge with Allah. Before even seeking refuge, the person mentions the name of Allah because of his statement, upon him be peace and blessings, "*The screen between jinn and the nakedness of people on entering the toilet is to say 'In the name of Allah.*"[46] In addition, he, upon him be peace and blessings,

---

[45] This is recorded by Bukhari 153; Muslim 613 to 615; Abu Dawud 31; Tirmidhi 15; Nasa'i 47 and 48; and ibn Majah 310.

[46] This is recorded by Tirmidhi 606 and ibn Majah 297. Tirmidhi mentions that the tradition is singular and its chain is not strong. However, Munawi responds by saying that none of the narrators in the chain have been discredited, and a person would be correct in saying that the chain is sound.

said, "*Indeed these toilets[47] are occupied by jinn. Therefore, when one of you enters the toilet say, 'I take refuge in Allah from demons, male and female.'*"[48]

The word *shaytan* is derived from *shatana yashtunu* meaning 'to be distant'. *Shatana* and *shaytana* are other verbal forms used. It is also suggested that the word is derived from *shata yashitu* meaning 'to be destroyed'. The rebel is destroyed by his rebellion. It is possible that the word is a noun on the form *fulan* because of his extreme efforts to destroy others. *Rajim* means 'being repelled by curse'. The meaning of jinn occupying toilets is that they lie in ambush waiting to harm people. However, after the person has finished, the jinn return to the open spaces they abide in.

The person should sit, inclining to the left side, whilst slightly spreading their legs. This allows them to relieve themselves easily. A person should not then speak, unless there is a necessity, because that person is deemed repugnant by doing so.

It is considered severely offensive to have one's front or rear towards the direction of prayer, even if indoors, because of his statement, upon him be peace and blessings, "*When you relieve yourself, do not have your front or rear towards the direction of prayer, but face east or west.*"[49] This is prohibited without exception. However, *if a person sits with the front towards the direction of prayer forgetfully and then remembers and turns away, out of reverence for the direction of prayer, that person does not rise from that place until all sins have been forgiven.*[50]

---

[47] *Hushush* is the plural of *hushsh* and *hashsh*. The original meaning is 'a garden of palm trees'. However, it began to be used to mean any place where a person excretes. Maraqi Falah.

[48] This is recorded by Abu Dawud 6 and Ibn Majah 296.

[49] This is recorded by Bukhari 144; Muslim 609; Abu Dawud 9; Tirmidhi 8; Nasa'i 21 and 22 and Ibn Majah 318.

[50] Although, in the text of *Maraqi Falah* this has been mentioned as being related by Tabarani, this has actually been related by Imam Tabari as a raised tradition.

There is a difference of opinion about having one's front towards the direction of prayer whilst cleansing. Tumurtashi has chosen the position that it is not offensive.

It is offensive to hold a child towards the direction of prayer to urinate.

It is offensive to have one's front:
- Towards the direction of the sun or the moon because they are two mighty signs of Allah.
- Where there is wind because that which comes out could come back and soil the person.

Equally, it is offensive to urinate
- In water, even if it is flowing.
- Near to a well, river or pond.
- At a place that people take shade.
- At an animal hole because of the harm to whatever may dwell therein.
- At a road because of his statement, upon him be peace and blessings, *"'Beware of the two that curse.' They said, 'What are the two that curse, Messenger of Allah?' He said, 'The one that excretes in public roads or in the shade.'"*[51]
- At the graveyard.
- Beneath a fruit tree because of the damage that will be caused to the fruit.
- Whilst standing, unless there is an excuse such as back pain, as this would normally result in the person's contamination by the urine.
- At the place where ablution is performed because this could create doubts in the mind of one performing ablution.

---

[51] This is recorded by Muslim 618 and Abu Dawud 25.

It is recommended to enter the toilet with clothes other than the ones used for prayer. However, if the same clothes are worn, care must be taken to avoid any impurity.

It is offensive to enter the toilet with anything that has the name of Allah or Koranic verses written on it.

It is prohibited to
- Expose the nakedness standing.
- Remember Allah. Thus, "al-hamdulillah" is not said in response to someone sneezing.
- Respond to "as-salamu 'alaykum".
- Reply to the muezzin.
- Look at the nakedness.
- Look at the urine or faeces.
- Spit.
- Blow one's nose.
- Clear one's throat.
- Move about excessively.
- Fidget.
- Raise one's sight to the heavens.
- Remain sitting for too long because of the possibility that it could produce haemorrhoids or a liver ailment.

The person steps out of the toilet with the right foot first. This is the most appropriate foot to begin with by way of thanking Allah for the favour of having removed the harmful elements and of having left the presence of devils. After leaving, the person says, "Praise is to Allah who rid me of the hurt", by the removal of the toxic residue, "and gave me health", by the nutrients remaining. Had the harmful impurity remained, or the sustenance been removed, it would lead to death. Hence, *the Prophet, upon him be peace and blessings, would also say on leaving the toilet, "Your forgiveness."*[52] This is an expression by which we

---

[52] This is recorded by Abu Dawud 30; Tirmidhi 8; and ibn Majah 300.

accept our shortcomings in giving true thanks for the favour of having sustenance provided in the first instance, followed by having the nutrients retained and the harmful elements removed without any difficulty. Through this, our bodies remain healthy. Equally, it could be in recognition of our inability to remember Allah with the tongue at the moment of excretion.

Section 7 - Ablution

Wudu and w*adu* are both verbal nouns that mean ablution. However, *wadu* also refers to that with which ablution is performed. In Arabic language, the word ablution is derived from purity, excellence and cleanliness. Thus, it is said *'wadua al-rajul'*, to mean the man has become clean.

In Sacred Law, ablution is defined as a specific cleanliness. This contains the linguistic meaning, in that the person performing ablution is excelling towards the limbs washed in the ablution by cleansing them in this world, and in the afterlife, by the limbs of ablution being brightened as reward for fulfilling service of the Master.

Ablution precedes ritual bath because Allah has mentioned it first in the Koran.

The integrals of ablution, which are its obligatory components, are four.

1. Washing the face

This is obligatory because of His statement, *"wash your faces."*[53]

Ghasl is the verbal noun of *'ghasaltuhu'*[54]. *Ghusl* is the noun. *Ghisl* is that which is used to wash with, e.g. soap.

Washing is defined as making water flow on the area such that the water drips. The minimum number of drops is two, according to the correct position. Making the water flow without drops trickling does not suffice.

---

[53] al-Ma'idah 6.
[54] *'Ghasaltuhu'* means 'he washed it'.

The face is that which faces a person. The boundary of the face is from the beginning of the top of the forehead, whether the person has hair or not, to the bottom of the chin, in length. The forehead is that which is between the two temples. The chin is the point at which the both jawbones meet. In breadth, the boundary of the face is between the two ear lobes. A portion of each limit is included within the obligation of the face because it is connected to the face. It is obligatory to wash the clear space between the beard and ear, according to the correct position. However, according to Abu Yusuf, the requirement is dropped by the beard growth.

2. Washing both hands with the elbows

Washing one of the elbows is obligatory by the explicit meaning of the text. The mention of plural with the plural necessitates singular with the singular. Washing of the second elbow is obligatory by the inferred meaning of the text, because both elbows are exactly the same, and by consensus. The elbow is the meeting point of the upper arm and forearm, and in Arabic language, although it is known as *mirfaq*, it can also be said as *marfiq*.

3. Washing both feet with the ankles

This is obligatory because of His statement, *"and your feet"*.[55] The reading of this with the genitive case is due to proximity. The Prophet, upon him be peace and blessings, after washing his feet said, *"This is the ablution of the one from whom Allah does not accept a prayer without it."*[56]

Washing of the ankles is obligatory because the limit is included in with that to which the limit is set.

---

[55] al-Ma'idah 6.
[56] This is recorded by ibn Majah 419.

The ankles, which in Arabic language are *k'aban*, are the elevated bones on either side of both feet. The word is derived from elevation, which is highlighted in examples such as Kaaba and *ka'ib*, being the buxom woman whose breasts are developing.

4. Wiping a quarter of the head

This is obligatory because the Prophet, upon him be peace and blessings, wiped his forelock.[57]

The area that is wiped is above the ears. Thus, wiping a quarter of this area is valid. It is not valid to wipe any hair that descends beneath the ears. Therefore, it is not valid to wipe any plaits that are tied on the head.

The claim that the obligatory amount to be wiped is three fingers is rejected, even if it has been authenticated.

In Sacred Law, wiping is defined as touching a limb with a wet hand, even if the hand is wet after washing a limb. However, it is not valid if the hand is wet after wiping a limb or with wetness taken from a limb. If water or rain falls on the obligatory amount it suffices.

The cause[58] of ablution is to make lawful, i.e. to want that which is not lawful without it, such as prayer, touching the Koran and circling the Kaaba. This is its rule in relation to this world. As for its rule in relation to the afterlife it is the attainment of reward if performed with intention, as is the case with any act of worship.

There are eight conditions of obligation, i.e. for a person to be regarded as legally responsible, for the ablution.

---

[57] This is recorded by Abu Dawud 147 and ibn Majah 564.
[58] Cause here means that which leads to a thing without affecting it.

1. Intellect, without which there is no divine injunction.
2. Maturity, because there is no legal responsibility for a legal minor by divine injunction.
3. Islam, because the requirements of Sacred Law are not addressed to the non-Muslim.
4. The ability of the legally responsible person to use purifying water. The absence of water or having need of water negates it legally. Therefore, there is no ability without water sufficient for use on all the limbs once. Anything other than this is regarded as non-existent.
5. The presence of ritual impurity. Therefore, an ablution upon an ablution is not required.
6. The absence of menstruation and postnatal bleeding by their having ceased, as defined by Sacred Law.
7. Shortage of time, because at that point the divine injunction becomes restricted. However, at the beginning of the prayer time the divine injunction is extended.

These above conditions can be summarised as one condition: the ability of the legally responsible person to purify with water.

There are three conditions of validity for the ablution.

1. All the skin to be covered with purifying water, such that if the size of a pinhead remains from any part that is obligatory to be washed without water touching it the ablution is not valid.
2. The cessation of ritual impurity whilst performing ablution because the ablution is not valid by appearance of urine or the flow of anything that invalidates the ablution.
3. The removal of anything that prevents water reaching the body due to the density of the barrier, such as wax or fat. The substance must have density because oil fat or something similar does not prevent the water reaching the body due to the absence of any barrier.

These three conditions can be summarised as one condition: purifying water, as determined by Sacred Law, covering all the skin.

Section 8 - Further Points on Ablution

It is obligatory to wash the surface of a thick beard, according to the most correct fatwa from those that have been authenticated. A thick beard is that beard through which the skin beneath cannot be seen. Washing the surface of the beard suffices because the beard takes the place of the skin and thus the obligation passes on to it. Those who held the position that a third or a quarter of a thick beard suffices or wiping all of it or similar statements have turned away from these statements.

It is obligatory to pass water to the skin beneath a sparse beard, according to the chosen position. With a sparse beard, the skin still faces a person and there is no difficulty in washing it. However, it is said that the obligation is dropped, because the skin does not completely face a person due to the growth on it.

It is not obligatory to wash the hair of the beard that extends beyond the face, because this hair is not part of the face itself nor is it a substitute for any part of the face.

It is not obligatory to wash the part of the lips that cannot be seen when the lips are closed normally. The part of the lips that can be seen is considered as being from the mouth, according to the correct position, and the part of the lips that appear is considered as being from the face. Nor is it obligatory to wash the eyes, even if ritual bath is being performed, because of the potential harm that could be caused. The inside of an ulcer that has healed but has not separated from its shell does not have to be washed, because of the necessity. The exception is the cut from which puss flows.

If fingers join in such a manner that water cannot naturally flow between them, or finger nails and toe nails grow in such a manner that they cover the finger tips and toe tips respectively and prevent water reaching beneath it is obligatory to wash beneath. Equally, if there is anything that prevents water reaching the skin, such as dough, wax and sleep around the eyes when closed, on any part that is obligatory to be washed it is obligatory to wash beneath it after having removed the barrier. However, dirt beneath the nails does not prevent water, whether the person is a villager or a city dweller, according to the correct position. Therefore, washing is valid with it present. Flea or fly droppings do not prevent water reaching the body because water can penetrate through the droppings due to their being miniscule and not being sticky. Whatever paint is on the nails of a painter does not prevent the validity of the ablution because of the necessity, according to fatwa.

It is necessary to loosen a tight ring, according to the chosen view of the two positions. A tight ring clearly does prevent water reaching the finger. *The Prophet, upon him be peace and blessings, when performing ablution would loosen his ring.*[59]
Likewise, it is necessary to loosen any earring, because of the tightness present. High probability suffices in attempting to determine whether water has reached the earring hole. Thus, a person does not have to pass something fine through the hole to ensure the water has entered, due to the difficulty involved.

If washing cuts on the feet is harmful it is valid to pass water over the ointment that has been used, because of the necessity,

After cutting hair, it is not required to rewash the hair, even if the original washing was due to sexual impurity, or to wipe the hair again, after having performed ablution, because of the absence of any fresh ritual impurity. For the same reason, after clipping the nails or trimming the moustache, rewashing is not required. However, in all the above instances, rewashing is recommended.

---

[59] This is recorded by ibn Majah 449.

Section 9 - Sunnas[60] of Ablution

There are eighteen[61] actions that are sunna whilst performing ablution.

1. Washing both hands to the wrists[62]

This is sunna at the beginning of the ablution, whether or not the person has just woken from sleep. However, there is stronger emphasis for the person who has just woken, because of his statement, upon him be peace and blessings, *"When one of you wakes from his sleep he should not insert his hand in the container until he has washed them."*[63] The wording of Muslim continues, *"until he has washed them thrice, for he does not know where his hand has been."*

If a person who has impurity on the hand cannot tilt the container, the fingers of the hand that is free of impurity is entered and the water collected is poured on the other hand until it is cleansed. The other hand is then inserted in order to wash the first hand. However, if this is done more than is necessary and the whole hand is inserted the water will become used.

2. Mentioning the name of Allah at the beginning

---

[60] In Arabic language, sunna is a path, even if it be an evil path. However, in Islamic terminology, sunna is a path that is consistently followed in religion, without being compulsory. It is an emphasised sunna if the Prophet, upon him be peace and blessings, left it occasionally, and is recommended if he, upon him be peace and blessings, did not perform it consistently. It becomes *necessary* if there is mention of the threat of punishment for the one who leaves it.

[61] This number has been mentioned to simplify matters for students. However, in reality, the number of sunna acts is more than this.

[62] The word for wrist in Arabic language is *rusgh*. This word can also be used for ankle, as is stated in *Misbah Munir*.

[63] This is recorded by Bukhari 162; Muslim 643 to 647; Abu Dawud 103 to 105; Tirmidhi 24 and ibn Majah 393 to 395. The wording is from Muslim.

If a person forgets this but remembers whilst performing and then mentions the name of Allah the sunna has not been attained. This differs to the rule for eating because ablution is a complete act whereas every morsel eaten is an individual act. The Prophet, upon him be peace and blessings, said, *"Whoever performs ablution and mentions the name of Allah the whole of his body is cleansed. However, whoever performs ablution and does not mention the name of Allah only the parts of ablution are cleansed."*[64]

The wording of this that has been transmitted from the early Muslims - and it is said, from the Prophet, upon him be peace and blessings – is, "In the name of Allah the Most Great. Praise is to Allah for the religion of Islam." It is also said that the best is to say, "In the name of Allah the Most Merciful the Very Merciful", because of the general nature of his statement, upon him be peace and blessings, *"Any significant matter that does not begin with 'In the name of Allah the Most Merciful the Very Merciful' is severed."*

The name of Allah is also mentioned prior to cleansing oneself and exposing the nakedness, according to the most correct position.

3. Using the tooth stick[65]

This is sunna because of his statement, upon him be peace and blessings, *"Were I not to cause difficulty on my community I would have ordered them to use the tooth stick at every prayer,"*[66] or *"with*

---

[64] This is recorded by Daraqutni 228 to 230; Bayhaqi 1:199 to 201 and ibn Abi Shayba, Section on Mentioning the Name of Allah with the Ablution, who mentions the tradition as interrupted at Abu Bakr, Allah be pleased with him.
[65] Tooth stick, in Arabic language, is known as *siwak* or *miswak*. However, the word *siwak* is equally used for the act of using the tooth stick.
[66] This is recorded by Bukhari 887 and Muslim 589.

every prayer."[67] It has also been narrated that, "*every prayer with it is superior to seventy prayers without it.*"[68]

It is preferred that the tooth stick is from the arak tree[69], soft, being a finger in thickness, a hand span in length and straight with few knots.

With us, using the tooth stick is from the sunnas of ablution and not from the sunnas of prayer. Therefore, the virtues of the tooth stick are attained with every prayer performed with an ablution in which the tooth stick had been used.

The moment when it is sunna to use is at the beginning of the ablution. According to the statement of the majority, however, the sunna is on rinsing the mouth. Others have said that time is before ablution.

It is further recommended to use the tooth stick when
- The mouth odour has changed.
- Waking from sleep.
- Intending to pray.
- Returning home.
- People have gathered.
- Reading Koran or traditions.

This is because of the statement of the Imam, "It is from the sunnas of the religion." In addition, the Prophet, upon him be peace and blessings, said, "*Using the tooth stick is a purification for*

---

[67] This is the ending as mentioned in the narration of Bukhari.

[68] This tradition has been recorded by Haythami in *Majm'a Zawaid,* Section on That Which has Come on Using the Tooth Stick, where he traces the tradition to Ahmad, Bazzar and Abu Y'ala. He further states that Hakim has authenticated it.

[69] The arak tree is a citrus tree that has fruits resembling grapes.

the mouth and pleasing to the Lord."[70] This indicates that the use of a tooth stick is equal in all situations.

In the absence of a tooth stick, the virtue is attained if a finger or a coarse cloth is used, because of his statement, upon him be peace and blessings, *"The fingers suffice for the tooth stick.*"[71] Also, Ali, Allah be pleased with him, has said, "Moving with the index finger or the thumb is using the tooth stick." For women, mastic replaces the tooth stick because of the soft nature of their gums.

The sunna in holding the tooth stick, as has been narrated by ibn Mas'ud, is to place the small finger beneath it, the ring and index finger above it and the thumb beneath its head. It should not be grasped, because it could possibly cause haemorrhoids. It is offensive to be used reclining, because it could possibly cause inflammation of the spleen.

The knower of Allah, the ascetic, Shaykh Ahmad has gathered the virtues of using the tooth stick in a work entitled *Tuhfa Sullak fi Fadha'il Siwak.*[72]

4. Rinsing the mouth

In the Arabic language, this means a movement. However, in Islamic terminology, it means to cover all the mouth with water.

It is sunna that this is done thrice, because he, upon him be peace and blessings, *"performed ablution, rinsing his mouth thrice and nose thrice. Each time, he took fresh water.*"[73]

---

[70] This is recorded by Nasa'i 5. Bukhari has mentioned this as a suspended tradition in the Chapter on Fasting, Section 27.

[71] This is recorded by Bayhaqi 1:177 and 178.

[72] This means "Gift to the Travellers on the Virtues of Using the Tooth Stick."

[73] This tradition has been mentioned by Zayla'i in *Nasb Raya,* 7 where he states that Tabarani has narrated this tradition.

If rinsing the mouth is performed with one handful the sunna of rinsing the mouth is accomplished, but not the sunna of repeating the rinsing.

5. Rinsing the nose

In Arabic language, rinsing the nose is *istinshaq* which comes from the word *nashq*, which means to draw water or its likes into the nose with the nose wind. In Islamic terminology, it means to take water into the nose cartilage.

Rinsing the nose is performed with three handfuls, because of the aforementioned tradition. It is not valid for the nose to be rinsed thrice with one handful of water, because the nose is not able to hold in the water, as opposed to when rinsing the mouth.

6. Exaggerating in rinsing the mouth and nose for the person not fasting

Exaggerating in rinsing the mouth is performed by taking water to the back of the throat, and exaggerating in rinsing the nose is performed by taking the water to the back of the nose. However, the person fasting does not do so, from fear of invalidating the fast. The Prophet, upon him be peace and blessings, said, *"Exaggerate in rinsing the mouth and the nose unless you are fasting."*[74]

7. Saturating the thick beard with a palm of water from the bottom

According to the most correct position this is sunna. This is the statement of Abu Yusuf, because of the narration of Abu Dawud

---

[74] This is recorded by Abu Dawud 142; Tirmidhi 788, Nasa'i 87 and ibn Majah 407. The phrase "rinsing the mouth" does not appear in the narrations of the Compilers of the Four Sunan.

from Anas that *the Prophet, upon him be peace and blessings, used to saturate his beard.*[75]

Saturation is to separate the hair, working from the bottom upwards. It is performed after the face has been washed thrice.

It is performed with a palm of water because the Prophet, upon him be peace and blessings, would, when performing ablution, take a palm of water from under his lower mouth and saturate his beard with it. He, upon him be peace and blessings, said, *"This is as my Lord, Mighty and Majestic is He, has ordered me."*[76]

Abu Hanifa and Muhammad prefer it, because it was not done consistently. Furthermore, it is performed to complete the obligation of washing the face and the inner part of the beard is not part of this obligation, as opposed to saturating the fingers.

In *Mabsut*, the author has favoured the stance of Abu Yusuf, because of the narration of Anas.

8. Saturating the fingers and toes

It is sunna to saturate between all the fingers, because of the order to do this[77] and because of his statement, upon him be peace and

---

[75] The wording of this tradition is not related by Abu Dawud on the authority of Anas. Rather, this wording has been related by Tirmidhi 31 and ibn Majah 430 on the authority of 'Uthman ibn 'Affan. Tirmidhi further adds that Muhammad ibn Isma'il (i.e. Bukhari) has commented that this is the most authentic tradition on this matter.

[76] This is recorded by Abu Dawud 145.

[77] For example, the tradition of the Prophet, upon him be peace and blessings, as narrated by the Compilers of the Four Sunan, *"When you perform ablution do so properly and saturate between the fingers."* This has been mentioned by Zayla'i in *Nasb Raya*, in the Section on the Traditions on Saturating the Fingers, where he has collated other traditions on the subject.

blessings, "*Whoever does not saturate between the fingers with water Allah will saturate between them with fire on Judgement Day.*"[78]

The manner of saturating the hands is to intermesh between the two sets of fingers, whilst the manner of saturating the toes is to use one finger. It suffices if the fingers and toes are put under flowing water or something similar.

9. Washing thrice

Whoever does more or less has overstepped the mark and done wrong, as has been related from the sunna[79], unless there is a necessity.

10. Wiping all of the head once

This is as was done by the Prophet, upon him be peace and blessings.[80] The wiping is performed once, as with wiping over a bandage and the dry ablution, because wiping has been ordained for ease.

11. Wiping the ears

Wiping can be performed even with water used for the head, because the Prophet, upon him be peace and blessings, took a handful of water and wiped his head and ears. It is fine if fresh water is taken, despite there being some remnants of wetness.

---

[78] This has been mentioned by Haythami in *Majm'a Zawaid*, in the Section on Saturation. He adds that in the chain is 'Ala ibn Kathir Laythi, about whom there is a consensus that he is weak.

[79] For example, the tradition of the Prophet, upon him be peace and blessings, as narrated by Abu Dawud 135, where, after showing a man how to perform the ablution, with each limb being washed thrice, he, upon him be peace and blessings, said, "*Ablution is like this. Thus, whoever does more than this or less has done bad and wrong - or done wrong and bad.*"

[80] This is a reference to Abu Dawud 129 and Tirmidhi 34.

12. Rubbing the limbs

This is sunna because the Prophet, upon him be peace and blessings, would do so[81], after washing the limbs, by running his hand over them.

13. Continuity

This is sunna because the Prophet, upon him be peace and blessings, consistently did so. Continuity is defined as washing the limbs before the previous limb has dried, assuming moderate body temperature, time and place.

14. Intention

In Arabic language, intention is the determination of the heart to perform an action. In Islamic terminology, it is the heart focusing on generating an act, with certainty.
The moment of the intention is before cleansing oneself, so that all of the action can be a righteous act.

The manner of intending is either to intend
- Lifting a state of ritual impurity.
- Establishing the prayer.
- Performing ablution.
- Obeying an order.

The place of the intention is the heart. The scholars have, in addition, recommended for a person to utter the intention, so as to unite between the action of the heart and tongue.

Intention is sunna for a person wanting to attain reward, because in the verse of ablution the only order mentioned is to wash and wipe.

---

[81] This is a reference to Daraqutni 329 and Bayhaqi 1:250 and 251.

Nor did the Prophet, upon him be peace and blessings, teach the Bedouin, despite his ignorance.[82]

Intention is obligatory in dry ablution, because dry ablution is performed with earth which is not a direct remover of ritual impurity.

15. Maintaining the order as stated in the Koran

This is an emphasised sunna, according to the correct position. It is not *obligatory*, because the *waw* in the order is there to indicate a general combination. The *fa* in his statement, *"wash your faces"*[83] indicates that mention of the limbs will follow.

16. Beginning with the right side

This is sunna for the hands and feet, because of his statement, upon him be peace and blessings, *"When you perform ablution, begin with your right side."*[84] The order is not regarded as *necessary*, because of the consensus that it is recommended due to the nobility of the right side.

17. Beginning with the fingertips and tips of the toes

This is sunna, because Allah has delineated the elbows and ankles as the limit of washing. Thus, these become the farthest point of the action. This was the manner in which it was performed by the Prophet, upon him be peace and blessings.

18. Beginning with the front of the head when wiping

19. Wiping the nape

---

[82] Refer to footnote 19 of this section.

[83] al-Ma'idah 6.

[84] This is a reference to Abu Dawud 4141 and ibn Majah 402.

This is sunna because the Prophet, upon him be peace and blessings, performed ablution and moved his hands from the front of his head until they reached the bottom of the nape.[85]
It is not sunna, but an innovation, to wipe the throat.

It is said that the last four are recommended. It seems that the basis for this is that these actions were not consistently performed. However, this is not accepted.

---

[85] The wording mentioned in the text is from Tabarani, as mentioned in *I'la Sunan*.

Section 10 - Etiquettes[86] of Ablution

There are fourteen main actions that are etiquettes of performing ablution. There are additional ones that will also be mentioned.

1. **Sitting at a raised seat**

By this, the person performing ablution can avoid used water.

2. **Facing the direction of prayer**

This is etiquette other than whilst cleansing oneself. Facing the direction of prayer is a state in which there is greater hope that supplication will be accepted.

3. **Placing a small container on the left side and a large container, from which the water is taken, on the right side**

4. **Performing ablution unassisted**

Worship is thereby performed alone without the help of anyone, unless there is a need to do so.

5. **Avoiding engaging in conversation**

---

[86] Etiquettes is defined as things being put in its correct place. It is also said that etiquettes are praiseworthy traits or godliness. In the commentary of *Hidaya*, it is mentioned as being that which the Prophet, upon him be peace and blessings, did not do consistently but once or twice. The rule for etiquettes is that there is reward entailed in performing it but no blame in leaving it. Sunna is that which the Prophet, upon him be peace and blessings, consistently performed but also left without any reason once or twice. The rule for sunna is that there is reward in performing it but blame and not punishment in leaving it.

Conversing whilst performing ablution, without any cause, distracts a person from reading the Prophetic supplications.

6. Uniting between the intention of the heart and the action of the tongue

This produces a determination to perform the action.

7. Reading the Prophetic supplications

These are the supplications that have been transmitted from the Prophet, upon him be peace and blessings, the companions and their students.

8. Mentioning the name of Allah and making intention on washing or wiping each limb

For example, on rinsing the mouth, whilst intending, a person says, "In the name of Allah. Allah, assist me in reciting the Koran, your remembrance, your thanks and worshipping you well." Also, when rinsing the nose, a person says, "In the name of Allah. Allah, permit me to smell the fragrance of Paradise and prevent me from smelling the stench of Hell." The same format is used with the remaining limbs.

The person also blesses the Prophet, upon him be peace and blessings, as is mentioned in *Tawdih*.

9. Inserting the little finger into the ear hole

This is in order to be thorough when wiping the ears.

10. Moving a loose ring

This is in order to be thorough when washing.

11. Rinsing the mouth and nose with the right hand

This is because of the nobility of the right side.

12. Blowing the nose with the left hand

This is because of the vileness of the left side.

13. Performing ablution before the prayer time has entered

This is etiquette in order for the person to hasten in performing an act of obedience. The exception here is the excused whose ablution, with us, is nullified by the end of the prayer time. According to Zufur, the ablution is nullified when the prayer time enters. Abu Yusuf regards that both the beginning and end of the prayer time nullifies.

14. Reading the two testimonies of faith after ablution, drinking from the remains of the water used in ablution standing and reading, "Allah, make me from those who repent and make me from those who purify themselves" after the ablution

This is read standing and facing the direction of prayer, because of his statement, upon him be peace and blessings, *"Any one of you who performs ablution properly and then says, 'I testify that there is no god other than Allah who is One having no partner and that Muhammad is His slave and messenger*[87] *will have the eight doors of Heaven opened, to enter by any one of them he wishes."*[88]

The Prophet, upon him be peace and blessings, also said, *"Whoever, on performing ablution, says, 'Glory be to You, Allah, and*

---

[87] In one narration, it is mentioned as, 'I testify that there is no god other than Allah who is One having no partner and that Muhammad is his slave and messenger.'
[88] This is recorded by Muslim 553; Abu Dawud 169 and 170 and Nasa'i 148.

with You is praise. I testify that there is no god other than You. I seek Your forgiveness and turn to You.' will have a stamp impressed for him that will be placed beneath the Throne and will be brought to the person on Judgement Day."[89]

Drinking from the remains of the water is etiquette, standing facing the direction of prayer or sitting. *The Prophet, upon him be peace and blessings, drank, standing, the remains of water used in his ablution and Zamzam water.*[90] He, upon him be peace and blessings, also said, *"None of you should drink standing. Thus, whoever forgets should vomit."*[91] There is a consensus amongst the scholars that the *offence* is *slight* on medical, and not religious, grounds.

The meaning of "make me from those who repent" is those who turn back from every sin. *Tawwab* is in the hyperbolic form. It is also said that it is the one who, whenever sin is committed, hastens to repentance. *Tawwab* is also one of the attributes of Allah, being the One who returns with His favour to every sinner by accepting repentance.

The meaning of "and make me from those who purify themselves" is those who remove themselves from indecency. Mention of the sinner precedes that of the person who purifies so as to eliminate despair and vanity.

Some additional etiquette includes
- Not using water warmed by the sun, because it may produce leprosy.

---

[89] This tradition has been recorded Nasa'i in *'Amal Yawm wa Layla* 81 to 83.

[90] This is a reference to Bukhari 1637 and 5615 to 5617; Tirmidhi 2694 and 2965 and ibn Majah 3422.

[91] This is a reference to Muslim 5243; Tirmidhi 1879 and ibn Majah 3423, where the narration states, *"that the Prophet, upon him be peace and blessings, prohibited drinking standing."*

- Not to reserve a container for oneself alone, because Sacred Law is true, simple and tolerant.
- Pouring water gently on the face.
- Not to dry the limbs. However, if a person were to wipe it should not be excessive.
- The container to be earthenware.
- Wiping the container handle thrice.
- Placing the container on the left.
- Placing the hand on the handle and not the mouth of the container whilst washing.
- Taking care to wash the inner corner of the eyes.
- Taking care to wash beneath any ring worn.
- Crossing the limits of the obligatory components so as to extend the brightness.
- Filling the container in preparation for the next prayer time.
- Reciting Sura al-Qadr thrice, because of his statement, upon him be peace and blessings, "*Whoever recites, after his ablution, 'We have sent it down on the Night of Influence' once is from the highest saints. Whoever recites it twice is listed in the register of the martyrs. Whoever recites it thrice is raised in the company of the prophets.*" – recorded by Daylami. This has also been mentioned by faqih Abu Layth in his *Muqaddima*.

Section 11 - Offensive Elements[92] of Ablution

There are six main actions that are offensive in performing ablution. However, this list does not limit the number because *offensive* elements also include the opposite of *recommended* etiquettes.

1. Wastage of water when pouring

This is because of his statement, upon him be peace and blessings, to S'ad, on passing him whilst he was performing ablution, *"What is this waste, S'ad?"* He said, *"Is there waste in ablution?"* He, upon him be peace and blessings, responded, *"Yes, even if you are at a flowing river."*[93]

2. Wiping thrice with new water

3. Being miserly in using water

This means making washing like wiping, which causes the sunna to be neglected. He, upon him be peace and blessings, said, *"The best matters are moderate ones."*

4. Striking the face with water

This is because striking the face is incompatible with the nobility of the face. Hence, when washing the face water should be poured on it gently.

5. Engaging in conversation

This distracts from supplications.

---

[92] Offensive element is defined as the opposite of desirable and etiquette.
[93] This is recorded by ibn Majah 425.

6. Seeking assistance from others, without any excuse

This is because of the statement of 'Umar, Allah be pleased with him, "*I saw the Messenger of Allah, upon him be peace and blessings, looking for water for his ablution. I hastened to find him some water. He, upon him be peace and blessings, said, "Stop, 'Umar, for I do not want anyone to assist me with my prayer.*"

This is the case if there is no excuse. However, if there is an excuse, because necessity makes prohibitions lawful, this is more so with something that carries no prohibition.

Imam Wabari mentions that there is no problem because a servant used to pour water for the Prophet, upon him be peace and blessings.

Section 12 - Types of Ablution

Ablution is of three types.

1. Obligatory

The meaning of obligatory here is that which is established unquestionably.

The verse of ablution was revealed in Medina, despite being made obligatory in Mecca.

Ablution is obligatory for the person in the state of minor ritual impurity who wishes to

- Perform prayer, even if it be optional, as has been ordered by Allah. This is because Allah does not accept any prayer without purification, as has been mentioned previously. The same applies to funeral prayer and prostration of recitation, which despite not being complete, are still prayer.
- Touch the Koran, even if it be a verse written on a coin or a wall, because of His statement, *"Which none may touch except the purified."*[94] This rule applies equally to the writing and to the blank spaces. Some of our scholars have said that it is only offensive for the person in the state of minor ritual impurity to touch the places on which there is writing and not the margins because that person has not touched the actual Koran. However, the correct position is that touching the margins is the same as touching the writing. By agreement, it is prohibited to touch the Koran even if it be in Persian, according to the correct position.

2. Necessary

---

[94] al-Waqi'ah 79.

This is ablution for circling the Kaaba, because of his statement, upon him be peace and blessings, *"Circling the Kaaba is like prayer other than you may speak in it. Thus, whoever does speak should only speak well."*[95]

However, because it is not an actual prayer its validity is not dependant on purity. Therefore, if a necessary circling is performed without purity sacrifice is necessary. If an obligatory circling is performed whilst sexually impure a camel is necessary. Charity is necessary if an optional circling is performed without ablution.

3. Recommended

There are many instances in which ablution is recommended. Included in these is touching Islamic books. Allowance has been made for a person in the state of ritual impurity in touching such books with the exception of Koranic commentaries, as has been mentioned in *Durar*. This statement necessitates the necessity of ablution for touching Koranic commentaries, thereby placing it in the second category.

Further instances include
- Sleeping in a state of purity.
- On waking from sleep.
- Renewing it to maintain it constantly, because of the tradition of Bilal, Allah be pleased with him.
- Ablution upon ablution, if the sitting has been changed, because it is light upon light. However, if there has been no change then it is wastage. Ablution alone is mentioned because ritual bath upon ritual bath and dry ablution upon dry ablution is pointless.
- After backbiting - which is mentioning your brother in his absence with that which he dislikes, lying – which is to

---

[95] This is recorded by Tirmidhi 960.

fabricate that which is not, and is not permitted except in the likes of war, rectifying where discord exists and pleasing the wife – and tale bearing – which is striving to convey information from one group of people to another seeking to cause dissension.

- After any sin and after reciting bad poetry, because ablution expiates minor sins.
- After laughing loud whilst not praying, because, in form, it is ritual impurity.
- After having washed and carried a deceased body, because of his statement, upon him be peace and blessings, "*Whoever washes a deceased body should perform ritual bath, and whoever carries a deceased body should perform ablution.*"[96]
- For every prayer time, because this is more befitting its state.
- Before the ritual bath, because this is the sunna.
- On eating, drinking, sleeping or repeating sexual intercourse for a sexually impure person.
- When angry, because ablution extinguishes the anger.
- When reciting Koran or reading and narrating traditions, out of respect for their nobility.

---

[96] This is recorded by Abu Dawud 3161 and 3162; Tirmidhi 993 and ibn Majah 1463. Abu Dawud has commented that this is abrogated and further states that he heard Ahmad ibn Hanbal, on being asked about performing ritual bath on washing the deceased body, say that ablution suffices. However, Tirmidhi, after mentioning the tradition, relates various opinions. He begins by stating that the people of knowledge have differed about the one who washes the deceased body. Some of the people of knowledge amongst the companions of the Prophet, upon him be peace and blessings, and others have said, "Ritual bath is upon the one who washes the deceased body." Others, however, hold that ablution is upon him. Malik ibn Anas has stated, "I prefer ritual bath on washing the deceased body. However, I do not regard it as obligatory." Shafi' has stated the same. Ahmad states, "I hope that ritual bath is not obligatory on whoever washes the deceased body. The least that holds is the ablution." Ishaq states, "Ablution is necessary." Finally, it is narrated from Abdullah ibn Mubarak that he said, "The one who washes the deceased body does not perform ritual bath or ablution."

- When studying knowledge of Sacred Law.

- On performing the azan, call to commence and sermon — even if it be a marriage sermon.

- When visiting the Prophet, upon him be peace and blessings, out of respect for his presence and for entering his mosque.

- On standing at 'Arafa, because of the nobility of the place and because Allah boasts to the angels about those standing at 'Arafa.

- On going between Safa and Marwa, so as to perfect the worship and because of the nobility of the two sites.

- After eating camel meat, because of the opinion that requires ablution after eating it and thereby removing oneself from disagreement.

- More generally, following from the previous point, to remove oneself from disagreement between all scholars, such as on touching a woman or on touching the genitals with the palm of the hand. By doing this, the worship will be valid by agreement thereby securing oneself in religious matters.

Section 13 - Nullifying Agents[97] of Ablution

The nullifying agents of ablution are twelve.

1. **Anything that comes from the front and rear orifice other than wind from the front orifice, according to the most correct position**

This nullifies the ablution even if it is small and even if it is not normal, such as tapeworm or a pebble.

Wind from the front orifice does not nullify because it is a convulsion and not wind. Even if it is wind there is no impurity involved. However, wind from the back orifice nullifies because it passes over impurity. The wind itself is pure. Therefore, according to most scholars, breaking wind does not make the wet garment of a person impure. Also, out of caution, the wind of the woman who urinates and defecates from one orifice nullifies.

Coming out of urine is determined by the appearance of wetness at the head of the orifice or the foreskin, if uncircumcised, according to the correct position.

2. **Giving birth without the appearance of blood**

In this instance, according to the statement of Abu Yusuf and the final statement of Muhammad, the woman is not considered to be in the state of postnatal bleeding. This is the correct stance because postnatal bleeding is connected to blood and here no blood is present.

---

[97] When nullifying is mentioned in connection to physical entities, such as a wall, destruction is meant. However, when it is mentioned in connection to concepts, such as ablution, removing it from its intended form is meant.

Abu Hanifa holds that she performs the ritual bath, out of caution, because giving birth is never free of even a small amount of blood. This has been authenticated in *Fatawa* and is the fatwa of Sadr Shahid, Allah have mercy with him.

3. Flowing impurity from other than the front and rear orifice, such as blood and puss

This is because of his statement, upon him be peace and blessings, *"Ablution is from all flowing blood."*[98] This is the school of the ten promised Paradise, ibn Mas'ud, ibn 'Abbas, Zayd ibn Thabit, Abu Musa Ash'ari, and other leading companions, as well as major figures amongst the students of the companions, such as Hasan Basri and ibn Sirin, Allah be pleased with them all.

Flowing in relation to the front and rear orifice is the appearance at the head of the orifice. However, in relation to other than the two orifices flowing impurity is the impurity crossing over to a point that needs to be washed, even if washing is merely recommended. Therefore, blood that moves from one point in the eye to another does not nullify the ablution. However, blood that flows at the back of the nose does nullify the ablution.

Blood and pus nullify ablution. In addition, water that seeps from the breast, navel or ear due to a medical ailment, according to the correct position, nullifies.

4. Vomiting a mouthful of food or water

Vomiting water nullifies even if the water has not changed. Furthermore, if on vomiting a black burnt substance or a yellow substance is brought up this too nullifies the ablution.

---

[98] This is recorded by Daraqutni 571.

With all of the above mentioned, the ablution is nullified if a mouthful is vomited. The ablution is nullified because these will have become impure as a result of coming in contact with that which is at the bottom of the stomach.

This is the school of the ten promised Paradise. In addition, the Prophet, upon him be peace and blessings, vomited and then performed ablution – Tirmidhi states that this is the most authentic tradition in this section.[99] Also, the Prophet, upon him be peace and blessings, said, *"Ablution is repeated from seven: urine drops, flowing blood, vomit, mouthful of vomit, sleeping on one's side, loud laughter of a man in prayer and emission of blood."*[100]

The definition of a mouthful is the amount that the mouth cannot hold without difficulty, according to the most correct explanation given. It is also said that it is the amount that prevents speech. If the vomit is in spurts the sum amount of all the spurts is considered if the cause is the same, according to Muhammad – this is the most correct position. Thus, if the total amount is a mouthful it nullifies. Abu Yusuf regards the factor as the place being the same.

The water from the mouth of a sleeping person is pure if it comes from the head, by agreement. The same is the case with water rising from the stomach, according to fatwa. It is said that if it is yellow or pungent then it is impure.

5. Blood in the mouth that dominates or is equal to the saliva

---

[99] This is recorded by Tirmidhi 87. The tradition continues by Abu Darda, the companion who narrated this tradition, mentioning, *"I met Thawban in Damascus mosque and mentioned that to him. He said, 'It is true. I poured the water for him."*
[100] This tradition has been mentioned by Zayla'i in *Nasb Raya*, in the Section on the Nullifying Agents of Ablution, where he traces the tradition to Bayhaqi in his *Khilafiyyat*. Zayla'i concludes that the tradition is weak because the chain contains Sahl ibn 'Affan and Jarud ibn Yazid who are both weak.

If the blood is equal to the saliva, out of caution, the ablution is nullified.

The level of blood is determined by colour. If the saliva is yellow the blood is not dominant. It is said that red is equal and deep red is dominant.

Blood that comes from the head nullifies because it has flowed, even if the amount is small, by consensus. The same is the case with fine blood rising from the stomach, which is the position held by most scholars.

6. Sleeping[101] such that the rear is not firmly seated on the ground

This can be, for example, if a person is sleeping lying on one's side, hip or back or turning onto one's face. This nullifies because the hold over the rear orifice has been removed. The nullifying agent is the ritual impurity, as indicated by his statement, upon him be peace and blessings, *"The eyes are the lace of the pouch. Thus, when the eyes sleep the lace is loosened."*[102] This tradition points out that the nullifying agent is not the sleep, because sleep is not ritual impurity. The ritual impurity that nullifies here is that which the sleeping person rarely avoids. However, the apparent cause takes its place.

A light nap, whereby the person can hear what is being said around them, does not nullify. If the person cannot hear anything then it is a heavy nap which nullifies.

---

[101] Sleep is defined as a natural state that occurs which prevents the external and internal limbs from working normally and prevents the intellect from being used.

[102] This is recorded by Bayhaqi 1:184; Daraqutni 587 and Darimi 722. However, they all record the word eye in the singular and not the dual as appears in the text. In addition, Abu Dawud 203 records, *"The lace of the pouch is the eyes. Thus, whoever sleeps should perform ablution."*

7. Lifting of the rear of a sitting sleeping person from the ground before waking up even if the person does not fall on the ground

This is the apparent position of the school. This nullifies because the rear has been removed from the ground.

8, 9 and 10. Becoming unconscious[103], insane[104] and intoxicated[105]

11. Loud laughing[106] by a waking adult praying a prayer containing bowing and prostration

This nullifies whether it is done intentionally or not. Laughing invalidates the prayer alone. Smiling[107] does not invalidate anything.

Loud laughing by a child does not invalidate the ablution, because children are not amongst those rebuked. It is also said that it does invalidate.

The loud laughing of a sleeping person praying does not nullify the ablution, according to the most correct position.

Loud laughing nullifies in a complete prayer, i.e. one that contains bowing and prostration even if by nodding. This nullifies whether

---

[103] Unconsciousness is defined as a sickness that removes strength and clouds the intellect.

[104] Insanity is defined as a sickness that removes the intellect and increases strength.

[105] Intoxication is defined as a lightness the effect of which is manifested by swaying and stuttering speech and the inability of the heart to benefit from the intellect because the person's controlling power has been removed by darkness on the chest.

[106] Loud laughing is defined as that laughing which can be heard by the next person, whereas laughing is that laughing which the person alone, and not the next person, can hear.

[107] Smiling is defined as that which produces no sound even if the teeth can be seen.

the person has performed ablution, dry ablution or ritual bath, according to the correct position, because nullifying occurs as a punishment. Thus, there is no need for the position whereby purity becomes fragmented. Loud laughing nullifies a complete prayer which excludes the funeral prayer and the prostration of recitation, because of the scriptural mention. Hence, the ablution is not invalid though the action is invalid.

Loud laughing nullifies in a complete prayer even if the person intends, by this laughing, to come out of the prayer after the last sitting with only the salaams remaining. At this point, the laughing nullifies because the person is still within the prayer, as is the case with the prostration of forgetfulness. The prayer is valid because the obligatory components have been completed, and is not deemed invalid because the necessary salaams have been left.

12. Sexual contact

This occurs when an erect penis touches a vagina or anus without a barrier that prevents body heat.

Sexual contact between two men or two women nullifies the ablution.

Section 14 - Non-nullifying Agents of Ablution

The non-nullifying agents of ablution are ten.

1. Appearance of blood that has not flown from its place

This does not nullify because it is not impure whether it is a solid or liquid, according to the correct position. Hence, it is non-nullifying.

2. Flesh coming away without blood flowing

This does not nullify because it is pure, and the separation of something pure does not require purity. An example of this is a pimple, as mentioned in *Fatawa Bazaziyya*.

3. Tapeworm coming from an injury, ear or nose

This does not nullify because it is not impure and there is little wetness involved, as opposed to tapeworm coming from the rear orifice.

4. Touching the penis, anus or vagina

This does not nullify without exception.

This is the school of the leading companions, such as 'Umar, 'Ali, ibn 'Abbas and Zayd ibn Thabit, as well as major figures amongst the students of the companions, such as Hasan, Sa'id and Thawri, Allah be pleased with them all. This does not nullify because *a man came to the Messenger of Allah, upon him be peace and blessings, who appeared to be a Bedouin. He said, "Messenger of Allah, What do you say about a man who has touched his penis in prayer?" He said, "Is it not a part of you, or a small piece of your flesh."* – Tirmidhi states that this tradition is the best and most authentic in this section.[108]

5. Touching a marriageable woman

This does not nullify because of the tradition reported in the Four Sunan from 'Aisha, Allah be pleased with her, *"The Prophet, upon him be peace and blessings, would kiss his wife and then pray without performing ablution."*[109]

Sexual intercourse is the meaning of touch in the verse[110], as is the case in His statement, *"If you divorce them before the marriage is consummated."*[111]

6. Vomit that is not a mouthful

This does not nullify because it comes from the top of the stomach.

7. Vomiting phlegm even if it is plentiful

This does not nullify because phlegm does not have impurity mixed in it and is thus pure.

8. Swaying of a sleeping person whose rear may have lifted from the ground

---

[108] This is recorded by Tirmidhi 85 as, *"Is it not a small piece of your flesh, or a part of you"* without mention of anything else. It is also recorded in Abu Dawud 172 and Nasa'i 165, with the wording similar to that in the text, and others.

[109] This is recorded by Abu Dawud 178 and 179; Tirmidhi 86; Nasa'i 170 and ibn Majah 502 and 503. In the narrations of Abu Dawud, Tirmidhi and ibn Majah the clear indication is that 'Aisha herself is the wife in question, because *'Urwa asked 'Aisha, "Who is she other than you?" upon which she laughed.*

[110] The verse referred to is al-Nisa 43, *"and if you be ill, or on a journey, or one of you comes from the privy, or you have touched women, and you find not water, then take clean earth and rub your faces and your hands. Surely Allah is Clement, Forgiving."*

[111] al-Baqarah 237.

This does not nullify because of the tradition reported in the Sunan of Abu Dawud, *"The companions of the Messenger of Allah, upon him be peace and blessings, would wait for 'isha until they would doze off. They would then pray without performing ablution."*[112]

9. Sleep firmly seated to the ground if the person is resting against something which if removed would cause the person to fall

This is the apparent position of the school of Abu Hanifa in this issue and the preceding one. This does not nullify because the person is firmly seated thereby being safe from the possibility of the emission of a nullifying agent. Abu Yusuf has narrated this from Abu Hanifa, and is the correct position. Most scholars hold this position. However, Quduri says that it nullifies. This stance has also been narrated from Tahawi.

10. Sleep of a person praying even if the person is bowing or prostrating in the sunna manner

This does not nullify if done in the sunna manner according to the apparent position of the school. The sunna manner of prostration is to keep the forearms apart from the sides and the stomach from the thighs. The Prophet, upon him be peace and blessings, said, *"Ablution is not necessary for the one who sleeps sitting, standing or prostrating until he lies down, because when he lays down his joints loosen."*[113] Equally, if a person sleeps outside of the prayer in this manner the ablution is not nullified, according to the correct

---

[112] This is recorded by Abu Dawud 200, with the phrase "the last 'isha" in place of "'isha".

[113] Tirmidhi 77 records that *ibn 'Abbas saw the Prophet, upon him be peace and blessings, sleep whilst prostrating such that he was snoring or breathing. He then stood up and prayed. I asked him, "Messenger of Allah, you were asleep?" He responded, "Ablution is only necessary for the one laying on his side, because when he lays down his joints loosen."*

position. If the person bows or prostrates but not in the sunna manner the ablution is nullified.

Section 15 - Necessitators[114] of Ritual Bath

Ritual bath is obligatory by one of seven things.

1. Emission of sperm[115] to the surface of the body after having separated from its source with desire through other than sexual intercourse

Sexual impurity is a state caused by the emission of sperm with desire. Thus, it is said *'ajnaba al-rajul'* when he satisfies his desire with a woman. The cause of ritual bath is to make lawful that which is not lawful with sexual impurity. The conditions of obligation and validity have already been mentioned in the Section 7 - Ablution. Its integral is to cover all that is possible, without difficulty, of the body with purifying water. Its rule is to make lawful what was not possible before it and to attain reward by doing it with the intention of approaching Allah.

Ritual bath is only obligatory when sperm has come to the surface of the body because until it has appeared no rule can apply to it. The source of sperm is the spine.

Examples of other than sexual intercourse include wet dream, even if it is the first time due to reaching puberty, according to the most correct position, looking, thinking or masturbating. Masturbating

---

[114] *Ghusl* is the noun from *ightisal,* being complete wash of the body. It is also used for the water with which the bath is performed. Most legal scholars have settled on *ghusl* despite *ghasl* being more eloquent and better known in the language. They have specified it for the ritual bath from sexual impurity, menstruation and postnatal bleeding.

[115] Sperm is defined as a white thick liquid that causes the penis to become limp after its emission and resembles the smell of the pollen of palm tree. The sperm of a woman, however, is a fine yellow liquid. This definition stems from the statement of the Prophet, upon him be peace and blessings, as recorded by ibn Majah 601.

is permitted, with no reward or sin, for a bachelor who needs to control his desire but not to induce it.

Mention of the condition of desire removes the need to mention surge because the two are inseparable. Thus, if desire is not present ritual bath is not needed, such as if a person carries a heavy object or is struck on the spine causing his sperm to be released without desire.

The same rule applies to women and men because of his statement, upon him be peace and blessings, *after being asked, "Is ritual bath on a woman who has had a wet dream?" "Yes, if she sees sperm."*[116]

The condition is that desire is present at the moment that sperm separates from the spine and not that the desire must remain until it emerges, as opposed to the stance of Abu Yusuf.

The difference manifests in the case of a man who holds his penis until his desire has passed, after which the sperm flows. According to Abu Hanifa and Muhammad, but not according to Abu Yusuf, he must perform ritual bath. The fatwa is with the position of Abu Yusuf in the case of a guest who is afraid of suspicion falling on him. If he is not able to hold himself he covers up by giving the impression of someone praying but without saying the prohibiting takbir or reciting.

Another instance where the difference manifests is the case of a man who performs ritual bath in a place and then prays, after which some remaining sperm flows. According to them both, but not according to him, he must perform ritual bath. However, the prayer is valid by agreement.

---

[116] This is recorded by Bukhari 282; Muslim 609 to 615; Tirmidhi 122; Nasa'i 197 and 198; ibn Majah 600 to 602 and Malik, Book of Purity, 84 and 85.

If sperm flows after having urinated, the penis having gone limp, sleeping or having walked many steps ritual bath is not needed by agreement.

Sperm, and everything mentioned in connection with it, is listed as the cause of ritual bath figuratively to make ease in teaching.

2. Disappearance of the head of the penis, or its size if the penis has been cut, in either one of the orifices of a living human

If the two involved are legally responsible then they are required to perform ritual bath. The adolescent is instructed to perform ritual bath as part of upbringing. Likewise, ritual bath is required after sex with a young girl who is not sexually desirable and who has not been penetrated because she has become someone with whom sexual intercourse can be performed, according to the correct position.

If a man wraps his penis with a cloth and penetrates without ejaculation, according to the most correct position, if he can feel the heat and pleasure of the vagina ritual bath is necessary, otherwise it is not necessary. However, in both cases, the safest is for ritual bath to be necessary because of his statement, upon him be peace and blessings, *"When the two circumcised parts meet and the head of the penis disappears ritual bath is necessary whether he ejaculates or not."*[117]

3. Ejaculation of sperm through intercourse with a corpse or an animal

---

[117] This is recorded by Bukhari 291; Muslim 783 and 784; Abu Dawud 216 and ibn Majah 611. The wording mentioned in the text occurs in the narration of ibn Majah but without the phrase "whether he ejaculates or not." The wording of Bukhari and Muslim, which is agreed upon, and Abu Dawud is, *"When he sits between her four parts and tires her out ritual bath is necessary."* Muslim also mentions a version that adds, *"even if he does not ejaculate."*

In this instance, ejaculation has been made a condition because the mere act of penetration does not necessitate ritual bath due to the limited desire produced.

4. Presence of thin liquid on arising from sleep without remembering a wet dream

This is the position of them both. However, Khalaf ibn Ayyub and Abu Layth both took the position of Abu Yusuf, which is the more logical, that the liquid is pre-ejaculation fluid.

However, they both base their position on the narration that he, upon him be peace and blessings, *was asked about the man who finds wetness but does not remember a wet dream. He said, "He performs ritual bath."*[118] Furthermore, sleep is a state of rest that stirs desire whilst sperm can possibly thin due to external factors. In addition, caution is necessary in worship.

This all applies if the penis was not erect before sleeping. However, if the penis was erect the liquid is taken to be pre-ejaculation fluid because erection is a cause of the release of pre-ejaculation fluid.

If the husband and wife find liquid between them without being able to remember who it came from or without there being any indicator to differentiate between them, such as its thinness, colour

---

[118] This is recorded by Abu Dawud 236; Tirmidhi 113 and ibn Majah 612. The complete version of the narration of Abu Dawud and Tirmidhi is, 'Aisha mentions, *"The Prophet, upon him be peace and blessings, was asked about the man who finds wetness but does not remember a wet dream. He said, "He performs ritual bath." "and about the man who remembers a wet dream but finds no wetness." He said, "There is no ritual bath upon him." Umm Sulaym then asked, "If a woman were to see that, is there ritual bath upon her?" He said, "Yes, for indeed women are partners of men."*- the wording is that of Abu Dawud.

or shape, ritual bath is upon both of them, out of caution, according to the correct position.

5. **Presence of wetness which is thought to be sperm after recovering from being intoxicated or unconscious**

This necessitates ritual bath out of caution.

6. **Menstruation and postnatal bleeding**

This is obligatory after becoming pure from their impurity by its cessation. Ritual bath from menstruation is based on text and from postnatal bleeding is based on consensus.

Ritual bath is obligatory by all the above necessitators if they are caused before becoming Muslim, according to the most correct position. This is because sexual impurity, etc, remains after becoming Muslim and the obligation of prayer and other acts cannot be performed in such a state. Therefore, because the person is now a legally responsible Muslim, purity is obligatory before prayer and the likes can be performed, according to the verse of ablution.

7. **Washing the deceased body of a Muslim, as a communal obligation**

This is the case of the deceased body of a Muslim who has not committed a crime that would remove the obligation of washing.

This discussion will be dealt with thoroughly in its place, God willing.

Section 16 - Non-necessitators of Ritual Bath

Ritual bath is not necessary from any of the following ten.

1. Pre-ejaculation fluid

Pre-ejaculation fluid can be pronounced as either *mathy* or *mithy*. The fluid is thin and white and is emitted at the time of desire and not due to desire. There is no surge associated with it and it does not cause the penis to become limp. It is also possible that the fluid can be emitted without the person realising. This fluid occurs more with women than men, and is called *qatha* in relation to women.

2. Urinary fluid

Urinary fluid is a grimy thick white fluid that has no smell. It is emitted after urinating but can sometimes precede it.

There is a consensus amongst the scholars that ritual bath is not necessary by the emission of pre-ejaculation or urinary fluid.

3. Wet dream without wetness

According to the primary narration, the woman is the same as the man because of the tradition of Umm Sulaym, as has been mentioned.

4. Giving birth without the appearance of blood, according to the correct position

This is the position of Muhammad and Abu Yusuf because of the absence of postnatal bleeding. However, the Imam has stated that ritual bath is upon her, out of caution, because giving birth is never free of even a small amount of blood, as has been mentioned previously.

5. Penetration with a cloth that prevents pleasure

This is according to the most correct position. However, we have already mentioned the necessity of ritual bath in this case, out of caution.

6. Injection

This does not necessitate ritual bath because it is used to remove excrement and not to satisfy desire.

7. Inserting a finger or something similar, e.g. a vibrator, into either of the two orifices

This is the chosen position because of the limited desire produced.

8. Intercourse with a corpse or an animal without ejaculation

This does not necessitate ritual bath because of the absence of the complete cause and nor does ejaculation usually occur in this instance for it to take its place.

9. Touching a virgin without removing her virginity and without ejaculating

This does not necessitate ritual bath because her virginity being intact will have prevented the two circumcised parts meeting.

If, however, his sperm enters her vagina without penetration no ritual bath is required as long as she does not become pregnant as a result.

Section 17 - Obligatory Components of Ritual Bath

Ritual bath has eleven obligatory components that must be washed. These, however, can all be referred back to one point: the water to cover as much as possible of the body without causing any difficulty. However, the obligatory components have been listed individually for educational purposes.

1 and 2. The mouth and nose once

This is a deductive obligation based on His statement, *"purify yourselves."*[119] In ablution, however, they are not obligatory because they do not fall within the definition of face as the inside of the mouth and nose is not faced. The hyperbolic form in His statement *"purify yourselves"*[120] includes them both and there is no difficulty involved.

3. The body once

This includes the external genitals, which resemble the mouth, and not the internal genitals, which resemble the throat.

Anything preventing water reaching the body must be removed, such as wax and dough. However, paint on the nail of a painter or anything between the finger nails, even of a city dweller, according to the correct position, such as flea or fly droppings, do not prevent water, as has been previously mentioned.

The obligatory component is to wash completely once because the order does not necessitate repetition.

---

[119] al-Ma'idah 6.
[120] al-Ma'idah 6.

4. **The inside of foreskin that can be pulled back with no difficulty**

This is according to the correct position. However, if this is difficult it is not necessary for the foreskin to be pulled back, as is the case with a hole that has sealed, due to the difficulty involved.

5. **The inside of a hollow navel**

This is considered to be from the external part of the body and there is no difficulty involved in washing it.

6. **A hole that has not sealed**

This is because there is no difficulty involved.

7. **The inside of the braided hair of a man without exception**

The man performing ritual bath must undo his braids. This washing, according to the correct position, is irrespective of whether water flows to the roots or not. This is the case because braids are not beauty for men thus there is no difficulty involved.

It is not obligatory for a woman to undo her braids if water does flow to her roots, by agreement, because of the tradition of Umm Salama, Allah be pleased with her, that she said, *"I said, "Messenger of Allah, I am a woman who ties her hair in braids. Do I undo them for ritual bath from sexual impurity?" He said, "It is enough for you to throw three handfuls of water on your head. Then pour water over the rest of your body and you will then be pure.""*[121]

However, if her hair is dense or thick she must undo it.

---

[121] This is recorded by Muslim 744 to 746; Abu Dawud 251 to 255 and ibn Majah 603 to 604.

It is not obligatory for water to reach within the hair, according to the correct position, as opposed to a man upon whom wetting all the hair is obligatory.

The cost of the water is upon the husband even if she is wealthy and even if her menstruation has ceased on ten days.

8. The beard

This includes washing the skin beneath the beard because of His statement, *"purify yourselves."*[122]

9 and 10. The moustache and the eyebrows

This includes the skin beneath them both.

11. The external genitals

This is because it resembles the mouth. The internal genitals are not washed because it resembles the throat, as has been mentioned.

---

[122] al-Ma'idah 6.

Section 18 - Sunnas of Ritual Bath

There are twelve sunnas in the ritual bath.

1. To begin by mentioning the name of Allah

This is because of the general nature of the tradition, *"Any significant matter"*[123].

2. To begin with intention

This will make the action as an approach to Allah which will be rewarded like the ablution.

Beginning with mentioning the name of Allah accompanies the intention because mentioning the name of Allah is connected to the tongue and the intention is connected to the heart.

3. Washing the hands to the wrists

This is done at the beginning as the Prophet, upon him be peace and blessings, did.[124]

4. Washing an impurity that is on the body

This is washed separately at the beginning and in order to ensure that it has been removed before it can spread over the body.

5. Washing the genitals

---

[123] This tradition has been mentioned in Section 9 – Sunnas of Ablution.
[124] This is recorded by Bukhari 238 and 239; Muslim 718 to 723; Abu Dawud 239 to 246; Tirmidhi 103 and 104; Nasa'i 253 and ibn Majah 573 and 574.

This is washed even if there is no impurity present as the Prophet, upon him be peace and blessings, did.[125] This washing ensures that water reaches the part of the genitals that would be hidden when standing but exposed when sitting.

6. Then to perform ablution in the manner of a normal ablution, thus washing thrice and wiping the head

Wiping the head is included in this ablution, according to the primary narration. However, it is said that it is not wiped because water will be poured over the head. The first is the most correct position because he, upon him be peace and blessings, performed the ablution of prayer before performing ritual bath.[126] In addition, ablution is the name given to the process of washing and wiping.

7. If a person whilst performing ritual bath is standing in a place where water gathers washing the feet is delayed

This is done to avoid the need to wash them again from the water used whilst washing.

8. Then pour water over the body thrice

With each washing the whole body should be covered, because of the tradition.

If the person performing ritual bath is immersed in flowing water or a large body of water and remained therein for the period of an ablution and ritual bath then the sunna has been completed because thoroughness has been attained, such as in washing thrice. The same rule applies if the person were to stand in the rain, even if it were for ablution alone.

---

[125] Refer to footnote 2.
[126] Refer to footnote 2.

9. To begin with the head when pouring water

This was done by the Prophet, upon him be peace and blessings.

10. Washing the right, then left, shoulder after washing the head

This is because of the preference of the right side, and is the position of *Shams A'imma* Halawani.

11. Rubbing the limbs of the body

This is sunna in the first washing so that the water will cover the body in the next two washings. Rubbing is not *necessary* in ritual bath except in a narration from Abu Yusuf because of the specific nature of the form *"purify yourselves"* as opposed to ablution which has the word *"wash"*.

12. Maintaining continuity when washing the body

Section 19 - Etiquettes of Ritual Bath

The etiquettes of ritual bath are the same as those of ablution, which have previously been mentioned.

The one exception is that the person performing ritual bath does not face the direction of prayer whilst performing ritual bath because ritual bath is normally performed with the nakedness exposed. However, if it is covered there is no problem.

It is recommended not to engage in speech, even if it be supplication because the person is at a place where dirt gathers and because it is offensive to do so with the nakedness exposed.

It is recommended to perform ritual bath in a place where no one who is not permitted to look at the nakedness could do so because of the possibility that it could be exposed whilst performing ritual bath or whilst dressing. This is based on his statement, upon him be peace and blessings, *"Allah is hayiyy sittir and loves the modest concealed person. Thus, when one of you performs ritual bath he should conceal himself"* – this is recorded by Abu Dawud.[127]

However, if the person cannot find anything to conceal with the place that conceals the most should be chosen. If a woman is in the presence of men she should delay her ritual bath. In all instances, the sin is upon the person looking and not on the person who has undressed for ritual bath.

---

[127] This is recorded, as mentioned in the text, by Abu Dawud 4012. In addition, it is recorded by Nasa'i 406 and 407. However, the wording of Abu Dawud mentions *"that the Messenger of Allah, upon him be peace and blessings, saw a man performing ritual bath in full view without a loincloth. He climbed the pulpit, praised and extolled Allah and then said, "Allah is hayiyy sittir and loves modesty and concealment. Thus, when one of you performs ritual bath he should conceal himself."* The wording of Nasa'i 406 is the same as that of Abu Dawud but adds the attribute *halim* – *"Allah is halim hayiyy sittir"* – meaning forbearing in the punishment of the guilty.

It is also said that it is permitted to completely undress for ritual bath alone and for a man to undress his wife for sexual intercourse if the house is the size of ten arm lengths.

It is recommended that two optional prayers be performed after ritual bath as with ablution because the ritual bath covers the ablution.

Everything offensive in ablution is offensive in ritual bath with the addition of supplication, as has been mentioned.

There is no estimation for the amount of water to be used for ritual bath and ablution because of the different states of people. However, a balance must be maintained without being wasteful or stingy.

Section 20 - Sunna Ritual Baths

Ritual bath is sunna in four instances.

1. Friday Prayer

This is sunna, according to the correct position, because it is more virtuous than the time. It is also said that it is sunna for the day. The difference manifests in the case of a person who nullifies ablution after performing ritual bath and then performs ablution. According to the correct position, that person does not attain the virtue of the ritual bath. However, according to the less favourable position, that person does attain the virtue. *M'iraj Diraya* mentions that if a person performs ritual bath on the Thursday or the Friday night the sunna has been attained because the purpose, being to rid of bad odours, has been attained.

The Messenger of Allah, upon him be peace and blessings, said, *"Whoever performs ablution on Friday then by it and how excellent. However, whoever performs ritual bath then that is more virtuous."*[128] This abrogates the apparent of his statement, upon him be peace and blessings, *"The ritual bath of Friday is necessary upon every adult."*[129]

2. Two 'Eid Prayers

---

[128] This is recorded by ibn Majah 1091. The rule is also highlighted in traditions contained in Muslim 1987 and 1988; Abu Dawud 1050 and Tirmidhi 498.

[129] This is recorded by Bukhari 858 and 895; Muslim 1957; Abu Dawud 341; Nasa'i 1378 and ibn Majah 1089. The word used in the tradition is *muhtalim* which means "one who has had a wet dream". However, the meaning intended, as pointed out by Imam 'Ayni, is an adult.

This is sunna because *the Messenger of Allah, upon him be peace and blessings, used to perform ritual bath on the Fitr Day, Adha Day and 'Arafa.*[130]

Ritual bath is sunna for the prayer in a statement of Abu Yusuf, as with Friday prayer.

3. Ihram

This is sunna for ihram of pilgrimage or lesser pilgrimage because of his action, upon him be peace and blessings. This ritual bath, however, is for cleanliness and not for purification. Hence, a woman menstruating or in postnatal bleeding also performs this ritual bath. As a consequence, in the absence of water dry ablution is not performed.

4. 'Arafa

Ritual bath is sunna for pilgrims at 'Arafa after zenith for the virtue of the time of standing.

Ritual bath is recommended in approximately sixteen instances.

1. Becoming Muslim whilst clean

This is recommended for a person clean of sexual impurity, menstruation or postnatal bleeding so that the traces of the past are washed away.

2. Coming of age

According to fatwa, the age is fifteen years for male and female.

3. Recovering from insanity

---

[130] This is recorded by ibn Majah 1316.

It is also recommended for a person recovering from intoxication or regaining consciousness.

4. After medicinal blood cupping

5. After washing a deceased body

This is recommended to remove oneself from disagreement between scholars over the necessity of ritual bath.

6. On the Night of Immunity

This is the middle night of Sh'aban. Ritual bath is recommended so as to spend the night in worship and because of its great status. In this night, provision and fixed life terms are apportioned.

7. On the Night of Influence

Ritual bath is recommended if a person knows with certainty of that night or knows by following the narrations indicating its time so as to spend the night in worship.

8. For entering the city of the Prophet, upon him be peace and blessings

This is recommended out of respect for its sanctity and because the person is coming into the presence of the Chosen One, upon him be peace and blessings.

9. For standing at Muzdelifa on the morning of Sacrifice Day

This is recommended because it is the second gathering place and is the place that the supplication of the Master of the two worlds for forgiveness of blood and oppression was answered for his community.

This is after dawn because that is the time when standing at Muzdelifa enters. The time when it leaves is just before sunrise.

10. On entering Mecca, Allah ennoble it, for the visiting circling

Furthermore, ritual bath is recommended for any circling so that the circling is performed with the better of the two purities. This also establishes the respect due to the Noble House.

11 and 12. For Solar and Lunar Eclipse Prayer

Ritual bath is recommended so that the sunna of these prayers is performed.

13. For Drought Prayer

Ritual bath is recommended for the seeking of rain as a mercy for creation through seeking forgiveness, humility and prayer with the better of the two purities.

14. From Fear

Ritual bath is recommended as a means by which one seeks refuge with Allah and His generosity so that the difficulty is removed.

15. Darkness during daylight hours

16. Violent wind

This ritual bath is recommended whether the wind is during day or night because Allah destroyed nations that had transgressed by this, such as 'Ad. Hence, the purified person seeks refuge with Allah.

Other instances include
- On repenting from sin.
- On returning from a journey.
- A woman with unnatural bleeding when the bleeding ceases.
- A person due to be killed.
- On stoning the sites.
- For a person who has been touched by an impurity but is not sure of its location. The entire body is then washed as is the entire garment, out of caution.

External purity does not benefit without internal purity through sincerity to Allah, ridding oneself of hatred, deceit, spite and envy and cleansing the heart of everything within the two worlds other than Allah. Therefore, he worships Him for His sake and not for any reason whilst being in need of Him. He is generous towards him by fulfilling his needs out of mercy to him by which he is desperate to Him. Thus,you are a lonely slave to the One,

Hasan Basri, Allah be merciful with him, said,
How many a concealed one his desire enslaved him   *was stripped of his covering and violated*

The person of desire is a slave who when   *he controls his desire becomes a king*

Thus, when he is sincere to Allah and performs all that He has required and is pleased with it, he rises and fulfils it divine providence surrounds him wherever he turns to and intends. He then teaches him that which he did not know.

Section 21 - Dry Ablution

Dry ablution is amongst the unique features of this community.

In Arabic language, it means any aspiration, as opposed to *hajj* which means aspiring to something venerated. In Sacred Law, dry ablution is wiping the face and hands with purifying dust. Aspiration is a condition because it is the intention.

It has a cause, condition, ruling, integral, description, and manner which will come.

The cause of dry ablution is the same as that of the original, i.e. to want that which is not lawful without it.

Its conditions have preceded.

Dry ablution is valid with eight conditions.

1. Intention

This is a condition because earth dirties and thus cannot purify without intention. Water, however, was created purifying.

The reality of intention, in Sacred Law, is attained by the heart focusing on generating an act, with certainty. The moment of intention is when the hands strike whatever the dry ablution is being performed on or when the limbs are wiped with earth that has touched them.

Intention itself has three conditions of validity.

1. Islam

This is so that the act leads to reward, which an unbeliever is deprived from.

2. Discernment

This is so that whatever is uttered is understood.

3. Knowledge of the intended act

This is so that the reality of the intended act is known. Intention, however, is a meaning other than the knowledge that precedes it.

The intention for dry ablution has one of three conditions that are specific to it, upon which dry ablution becomes a key to prayer.

1. Purity

This is to intend purity from ritual impurity. It is not a condition to specify sexual impurity. Thus, merely intending purity is sufficient because purity has been ordained for prayer and is a condition of validity and permissibility. Hence, intending purity is an intention that makes prayer permissible.

2. Making lawful the prayer

Prayer can only be made lawful by removing ritual impurity. Hence, it is valid by this intention. It is also valid with the intention of removing ritual impurity because dry ablution removes it, in the same manner as ablution.

3. Aspired worship that is not valid without purity

An aspired worship is that which is not required as a consequence of something else. Hence, an aspired worship is ordained as an approach to Allah.

The aspired worship referred to here must require purity, such as prayer or a part of prayer.

Examples of this intention include saying, "I intend dry ablution for prayer" or "funeral prayer" or "prostration of recitation" or "reading Koran" whilst sexually impure or a woman intending dry ablution for reading Koran after menstruation or postnatal bleeding has ceased. The last two examples both require purity.

Hence, any of the following people if they intend cannot pray.

- A person who intends dry ablution without bearing in mind any of the previous points.
- A person who intends dry ablution for reading Koran whilst in the state of minor ritual impurity because of the permissibility of the reading of a person in the state of minor ritual impurity, as opposed to a sexually impure person.
- A woman who intends to read Koran whilst not being ordered to do so due to menstruation or postnatal bleeding.

The dry ablution of a sexually impure person to touch the Koran, enter the mosque or teach someone does not permit prayer, according to the most correct position. Equally, dry ablution for visiting graves, azan, call to commence, saying salaam or responding to it does not permit prayer. Most scholars also include in this list dry ablution for Islam. However, Abu Yusuf said that the prayer is valid because entering Islam is the greatest of those acts by which one approaches Allah. Abu Hanifa and Muhammad both said that it is not valid, and this is the most correct position. If dry ablution is performed for prostration of thanks then the validity of the prayer is according to the difference of opinion on the prostration itself.

In the secondary narrations and according to Hasan it is permitted by intention alone.

2. Legitimising excuse for dry ablution

These are of various types.

- Being a distance of a mile from purifying water. The absence of water is determined by high probability, according to the chosen position, because of the difficulty involved in covering this distance whilst dry ablution was only legislated to remove difficulty. This is the case even if it be within a city, according to the correct position, because of the difficulty.
- Increasing the severity of a sickness, delaying the healing process or triggering it, such as fever or diarrhoea.
- Cold that it is feared, according to high probability, could result in some limbs being damaged.
- Sickness. This legitimises if the person is not in a city, i.e. a built-up area, even if it be a village which has heated water or the equipment to heat water, irrespective of whether the person is sexually impure or in a state of minor ritual impurity. However, if in a city there is no heated water or no equipment with which to heat water it is the same as a rural area, for He *"has not laid upon you in religion any hardship."*[131]

---

[131] al-Hajj 78.

- Fear of a human or other enemy. This legitimises whether the person fears for themselves, their wealth or something entrusted to them. The case is the same for a woman who fears from an immoral man at a watering hole or an insolvent borrower who fears being captured. There is no need for the above to repeat the prayer or for someone captured on a journey, as opposed to a person forced to leave ablution who then performs dry ablution.

- Thirst, irrespective of whether it is current or expected or whether it is affecting oneself, a companion on a journey or an animal, even if that animal be a dog, because whatever is set aside for a need is treated as being non-existent.

- Need for preparing dough that is required, but not for cooking sauce that is not required.

- Absence of equipment to extract water, e.g. rope or bucket, because without them the well is as if it is non-existent. Drinking water that it is set aside in fields or something similar does not prevent dry ablution unless it is in large quantities. The definition of large quantity is considered by general usage.

The person who has neither water nor earth due to imprisonment does not imitate, with them both. Abu Yusuf said that the person imitates by motions.

The person unable to perform ablution and cannot find assistance performs dry ablution, by agreement. However, if the person finds assistance he does not have ability through the ability of another, with the Imam, as opposed to them both.

- Fear of missing funeral or 'Eid prayer even if it involves building. This is also for a sexually impure person.

If the person can catch a takbir of the funeral prayer ablution is performed. The correct position is that there is no fear of missing for the responsible family member who therefore does not perform dry ablution. If a second funeral prayer begins before being able to perform ablution the person prays with the dry ablution from the first funeral prayer, with them both. Muhammad, however, said that he must repeat, as with the case of the one who was able and then became unable.

Dry ablution is performed if, due to performing ablution, Eid prayer is missed.

This is because of the narration from ibn 'Abbas where he said, *"If a funeral prayer unexpectedly occurs and you fear missing it then pray it with dry ablution."* Likewise, it is mentioned *from ibn 'Umar that a funeral was brought to him whilst he was not in ablution.* He performed dry ablution and prayed. The same has been transmitted from them both about the two 'Eid prayers.

The basis with both is missing them without a substitute.

If the person has to build in either prayer because of a ritual impurity escaping dry ablution is performed and the prayer is completed due to the person being unable to perform ablution with water before the funeral ends and the occurrence of an invalidator due to the congestion in 'Eid.

The fear of missing Friday prayer or a prayer time due to performing ablution is not an excuse because noon is prayed if Friday prayer is missed and missed prayers are made up. Hence, both have a replacement.

3. **Performing dry ablution with pure substance from the earth**

Pure clean substance is that which has not been touched by an impurity even if the impurity has disappeared by its trace having gone.

Examples of substances from the earth include cultivating and other earth, bare rock and sand, with them both, as opposed to Abu Yusuf. Furthermore, with them both, dry ablution is permitted with arsenic, lime, red earth, antimony, sulphur, turquoise, carnelian, other minerals and mountain salt, according to the correct position. Likewise, burnt earth or burnt clay that did not contain manure before being burnt can be used for dry ablution. Burnt earth can be used as long as ashes are not dominant. Equally, earth that is mixed with substances from other than the earth can be used as long as the earth is dominant. Substances other than from the earth are not permitted for dry ablution, such as firewood, silver, gold, copper and iron. The principle is that anything that becomes ashes or changes form after burning is not permitted for dry ablution, otherwise it is permitted, because of His statement, *"then take clean earth"*.[132] Earth is a name for the face of the earth, whether it be earth or not. The explanation that refers to it as earth is because it is the dominant substance, because of His statement, *"barren waste"*[133] i.e. bare rock.

4. Wiping the area

The area is the face and both hands to the elbows, according to the primary narration. This is the correct position and is the fatwa. Hence, any ring is removed, the fingers are saturated and all the skin and hair, according to the correct position, of the face and the clear space between the beard and the ear is wiped, as is the case with the original. It is also said that wiping most of the face and

---

[132] al-Nisa 43.
[133] al-Kahf 40.

both hands is sufficient – this position has been authenticated. Hasan has reported from Abu Hanifa that it is to the wrists.

The basis of the primary narration is his statement, upon him be peace and blessings, *"Dry ablution is two strikes, one strike is for the face and one strike is for the arms to the elbows."* He, upon him be peace and blessings, also did this when asked, *"How should I wipe?"* *He struck the ground with his palms and raised them to his face. He, then, struck again and wiped both sides of his arms until he touched his elbows.*

5. Wiping with all or most of the hand or anything taking its place

Therefore, wiping with two fingers is not permitted, as is mentioned in *Khulasa*. This is not permitted even if it is repeated until the whole area is covered, as opposed to wiping the head, as is mentioned in *Siraj Wahhaj* from *Idah*.

6. Dry ablution with two strikes of the palms

This is based on the narrations mentioned. If a person intends dry ablution and instructs someone to perform it on him it is valid. Dry ablution is valid even if the strikes are at one place, according to the most correct position, because the earth does not become used. The dry ablution is performed with the earth that is in the hand.

Earth touching the body replaces the two strikes if the person wipes the earth with the intention of dry ablution. Hence, if the person nullifies purity after striking the ground or after earth has struck and then wipes with the earth it is permitted, as has been stated by Isbijabi. This is like the case of a person who nullifies purity and has in his palms that with which purity is valid. According to the position chosen by *Shams Aimma* it is not valid because he held that the strike is an integral, as in the case of a person who nullifies purity after having washed a limb. The scholar ibn Humam has stated that research necessitates striking should not be considered as part of the phrase dry ablution in Sacred Law because the Koranic instruction only mentions wiping. Furthermore, his statement, upon him be peace and blessings, *"Dry ablution is two strikes"* has been mentioned because it is the dominant mode. And Allah knows best.

7. **Cessation of menstruation, postnatal bleeding or ritual impurity whilst performing ritual ablution**

This is a condition as is the case with its original.

8. **Removal of anything that prevents wiping on the skin, such as wax or fat**

The presence of these causes the wiping to take place on them and not on the skin.

There are eight conditions of obligation. These have been mentioned in ablution and hence do not need to be repeated.

The two integrals of dry ablution are wiping the hands and face. The two strikes have not been mentioned because of the difference over striking being part of the phrase dry ablution.

The manner has been described in his action, upon him be peace and blessings.

There are seven sunnas of dry ablution.

1. **Mentioning the name of Allah at the beginning**

This is the same as the original.

2. Maintaining the order

This is sunna as the Prophet, upon him be peace and blessings, did.

3. Continuity

This is sunna because it is related from the action of the Prophet, upon him be peace and blessings.

4, 5 and 6. Moving the hands forwards and backwards after placing them on the earth and then shaking them

The hands are shaken to protect from dirtying and disfiguring the face. Hence, dry ablution should not be performed with wet clay until it is dried unless there is fear of the prayer time elapsing.

The greatest Imam demonstrated this when Abu Yusuf asked him the manner of performing dry ablution. He bent down to the earth and moved his hands forwards and then backwards. He then lifted them up and shook them and then wiped his face. He then returned both his hands to the earth and moved them forwards and then backwards. He then lifted them up and shook them and then wiped with each hand the other arm to the elbows.

7. Spreading the fingers

This is sunna and is to be done at the moment of striking so as to be more thorough in purifying.

It is recommended to delay dry ablution for the person hopeful, through high probability, of finding water before the elapse of the recommended time – it is reported from Abu Hanifa that this is necessary. This is because there is no point in delaying unless it is to perform the better of the purities, as was done by the greatest Imam for sunset when he differed with his teacher Hammad. His teacher concurred with him. This was the first instance where he differed with his teacher. This incident took place when they went to the burial of A'amash, Allah be merciful to them.

It is necessary to delay if water is promised even if missing the prayer is feared, by agreement, if the water is present or near. There is no doubt in the permissibility of dry ablution and not delaying the prayer if the water is beyond a mile and the prayer time will elapse.

It is necessary to delay, with Abu Hanifa, if a naked person is promised clothes or if a person is promised equipment for extracting water, e.g. rope or bucket, as long as there is no fear of missing the prayer. However, if it is feared then dry ablution is performed because of the inability. They both said that delaying is necessary even if it is feared that the prayer will be missed, as with the promise of water, because ability exists by the fulfilment of the promise.

It is necessary for a person or their companion to seek water a distance of 300 to 400 footsteps in the assumed direction if it is thought that water is near by seeing a bird, greenery or through information, as long as it is safe to do so. If, however, it is unsafe or there is no indication of water then it is not necessary to seek it.

It is necessary to seek water from anyone present because it is normally something given. Hence, there is no disgrace in having to ask for it, as long as it is in a place where people are not known to be stingy. If water can only be acquired by being sold at its normal price or slightly over the normal price then it must be bought. However, if the price is excessive it does not have to be bought. Excessive price is that which is not within the price range set by valuators. It is also said that it is double the price. The water is only bought if money is available and is over and above travel expenses. These are the three conditions for the necessity of buying water. Hence, it is not necessary to buy water if the price is excessive, if the price is normal but no money is available or the money is needed for expenses. Money does not have to be borrowed for the water.

It is permitted to pray as many obligatory prayers with one dry ablution as a person wants, as with ablution, because of the order and because of his statement, upon him be peace and blessings, *"Earth is purification for the Muslim even for ten years as long as he does not find water."*[134] The best, however, is to repeat the dry ablution for every obligatory prayer so as to remove oneself from the disagreement with Shafi'. By consensus, as many optional prayers can be prayed with one dry ablution as a person wants.

It is valid to perform dry ablution before the prayer time because it is a condition which therefore precedes the act. Desire is the cause and that is present.

If most of the body is burnt then dry ablution is performed. Most, here, is determined by the number of limbs, according to the chosen position. Hence, if there is injury on the head, face and arms but not on the feet then dry ablution is performed, even if it is small. There are those who determine this by the individual limb. Thus, if most of any limb is injured dry ablution is performed. Likewise, if half of the body is injured dry ablution is performed, according to the most correct position, even if the person is sexually impure because no one has stated that the area between smallpox needs to be washed.

If most of the body is healthy then those areas are washed and the injured parts are wiped. If it is not possible to wipe the injured parts then a bandage should be wiped. However, if even this is harmful then wiping is left.

---

[134] This tradition is related with the wording, *"Pure earth is the ablution of the Muslim even if he does not find water for ten years"* in Nasa'i 323. Similar wordings are found in Abu Dawud 332 and Tirmidhi 124.

If there is a small injury on the stomach or back and water is harmful then, out of necessity, the rule of the body being predominantly injured holds.

It is not valid to combine between washing and dry ablution because there is no example of combining between the substitute and the original in Sacred Law. Combining between dry ablution and leftover water of donkey is in order to fulfil the obligation with one of the two and not with both. Equally, combining does not take place between, for example, amputation and compensating, capital punishment and dowry and bequest and inheritance.

In addition, ibn Shihna has composed the following line,
wiping the head drops from the one on whose head   *is an ailment which if wetted would be harmful*

Qari Hidaya has also passed this fatwa. Likewise, washing the head drops from sexual impurity, menstruation and postnatal bleeding because the excuse is the same.

Dry ablution is nullified by the nullifying agents of ablution because the nullifying agents of the original nullify the replacement. In addition, the disappearance of the legitimising excuse such as enemy, sickness or cold leaving or the appearance of extracting equipment nullifies. Therefore, more generally, the ability to use sufficient water once nullifies dry ablution. Hence, if the person was to wash thrice and then the water ran out before completing the ablution dry ablution is invalid, according to the chosen position, because earth is no longer purifying as stated in the tradition.

The one whose hands and feet have been severed and has an injury to the face prays without purity and does not repeat the prayer, according to the most correct position. Some have said that prayer is no longer required.

The one whose limbs have withered wipes the face and arms with earth and does not leave the prayer.

The amputee wipes whatever remains of the obligatory components, as is the case with washing. However, if the limbs have been severed beyond the area of the obligatory components nothing is required.

Section 22 - Wiping Footgear

Wiping footgear[135] has been established by the sunna, both orally and practically.

Its cause is wearing the footgear. Its condition is that the footgear covers the obligatory area and is suitable for wiping with the time period remaining. Its rule is that it legitimises the prayer in the time period. Its integral is wiping the obligatory amount. Its characteristic is that it has been legislated as an allowance. Its manner is to begin at the toes with the fingers working linearly to the shins.

It is permitted to wipe the footgear whilst purifying from minor ritual impurity because of the extensive number of narrations. Hence, unbelief is feared for the one who rejects it. However, if a person believes it is permitted and proceeds to remove them the reward is for the original because washing is more difficult.

If the traveler performs dry ablution whilst sexually impure and then nullifies ablution and sufficient water is found for the limbs of ablution the footgear must be removed and the feet washed. It is not valid to wipe the footgear for sexual impurity.

Wiping footgear is valid for men and women because the texts make no exception, which therefore includes women. It is also valid whether on journey or resident and whether there is a need or not.

Wiping is valid even if the footgear is of a thick material other than leather such as felt, broadcloth or cotton that remains on the feet without having to be tied and without water penetrating. Such a material performs the same function as leather. This is the stance of

---

[135] Footgear, or *khuff*, is a covering to the ankles. The word is derived from *khiffa*, or lightness, because the rule has been lightened from washing to wiping.

them both and is the legal position. This is also the position that the Imam reverted to.

The footgear can be socks that has leather bottoms – these are called *jawrab mun'al* – or the top and bottom being leather – these are called *mujallad.* Equally, they may have no leather at all, being thick.

Wiping footgear has seven conditions.

1. Wearing them after having washed the feet

This is permitted even if the feet have been washed legally, such as a splint being wiped that was on one or both feet after which the footgear is worn. In this case, it is permitted to wipe the footgear because wiping the splint is treated the same as washing the feet.

This is permitted even if the footgear was worn before ablution is completed as long as it is completed before being nullified because of the presence of the condition.

Footgear merely prevents the flow of ritual impurity. It does not raise the ritual impurity.

If the excused performs ablution and wears the footgear when the excuse has ceased the time period is the same as the non-excused. Otherwise, the excused is restricted by the time period and thus the footgear cannot be wiped after it.

2. The footgear covering to the ankles

This applies to the sides. Hence, being able to see the ankles from the top of the footgear of a person with thin legs does not affect. Footgear that does not cover the ankles is permitted to wipe upon if a thick material, such as broadcloth, is sewed on to it.

3. Ability to walk in the footgear

The allowance disappears because its condition, which is being able to walk, is no longer present. Hence, it is not permitted to wipe on footgear made from glass, wood or metal.

4. The footgear being free of any holes more than the size of three toes, each toe equivalent in size to the smallest toe

The measurement is based on the smallest toe because toes are the area of walking. There is a difference of opinion as to whether the toes are considered as being closed or spaced. However, if toes appear out of the footgear the individual toes are considered. Therefore, if the large toe along with the next toe appears, even if the two equal the size of three toes, it does not harm, according to the most correct position. If a rip appears that extends lengthwise and is more than three toes in length however nothing of the foot appears on walking because of the strength of the footgear it does not prevent wiping.

A hole less than three toes on one foot is not added to another hole on the other foot. The minimum hole that is included is one in which a needle can enter – anything less is not considered.

5. The footgear remaining without having to be tied

This indicates that the footgear is thick because thin footgear is not suited to covering a distance.

6. The footgear preventing water reaching the body

This means that they do not absorb water.

7. Amount of three small fingers remaining from the front of the foot on each foot

This means that the obligatory area of wiping is present. If one foot is amputated above the ankle it is permitted to wipe the other foot. However, if less than the amount of three fingers remains below the ankle it is not wiped because it is obligatory to wash the remainder and it is not permitted to combine this with wiping of the healthy foot.

If the front of the foot is not present it is not permitted to wipe the footgear even if the back of the foot is present because it is not the area that is wiped. However, it is obligatory that it be washed.

The resident wipes for a day and night and the traveller wipes for three days and nights. These time periods have been narrated from the Messenger of Allah, upon him be peace and blessings.

The time period for both resident and traveller begins from the moment the ritual impurity appears after having worn the footgear in a state of purity, according to the correct position. This is the moment that the footgear prevents the ritual impurity from flowing to the foot and before this the purity of washing was present. It is said that the moment is upon wearing the footgear. It is also said that it is from the moment of wiping.

If a resident wiped and then travelled before the time period is over the time period is completed as a traveller because the consideration is with the end of the time, as with prayer. If a traveller becomes resident after having wiped for a day and night the footgear is removed because the allowance of travelling no longer remains. However, if the traveller has wiped for less than a day and night the time period is completed as a day and night, being the time period of the resident.

The obligatory wiping is the equivalent size of three small fingers[136], according to the most correct position. The fingers are the tool by

---

[136] The word finger in Arabic is both masculine and feminine.

which wiping is performed as has come in the sunna, and three is the majority. If the amount is wetted, even if it be with a rag or by pouring, it is permitted.

The place of wiping is the surface of each foot once. Hence, it is not valid to wipe on the bottom, heel and sides of the foot or on the shin. It is not sunna to repeat the wiping.

The sunna of wiping is to pass spaced out fingers beginning from the tips of the toes to the shin. *The Messenger of Allah, upon him be peace and blessings, passed by a man performing ablution who was washing his footgear. He nudged him with his hand and said, "We have only been ordered to wipe as such." He then showed him from the front of the footgear to the bottom of the shin once and he spaced out his fingers.*

Thus, if a person begins from the shin or wipes across the foot it is valid but contradicts the sunna.

The nullifying agents of wiping are four.

1. Everything that nullifies ablution

This nullifies because wiping is a replacement. Therefore, the nullifying agents of the original nullify the wiping.

2. Removing most of the footgear

This nullifies because, on removing the footgear, the ritual impurity flows to the foot – in reality, this is the nullifying agent. Thus, mentioning removal as being the nullifying agent is figurative. Once one footgear has been removed the other must be removed because the ritual impurity has flown to the foot and the both feet are obligatory to wash.

The wiping is nullified even if the removal takes place by most of the foot coming out, according to the correct position, because the area of wiping has separated from its place and the majority has the rule of the whole.

3. Water touching most of one foot

This is according to the correct position and is the same as the whole foot being wet. It is then compulsory to remove the footgear and wash both feet so as to avoid combining between washing and wiping.

If a person washed both feet without removing the footgear it suffices for the washing. Hence, its purity does not become invalid by the time period passing.

4. Time period passing for resident and traveller

Mentioning passing of the time period as being the nullifying agent is figurative. The nullifying agent, in reality, is the previous ritual impurity that only now has appeared. Hence, if the time period completes whilst in prayer the prayer is invalid. In the absence of water dry ablution is performed.

If there is a fear that due to cold the person's foot or part of will be damaged it is permitted to wipe until the fear passes. The apparent statement of the texts is that the attribute of wiping remains. However, *M'iraj Diraya* states that the whole footgear is wiped, as with splints.

With the last three, i.e. removal of footgear, wetting most of the foot and passing of time period, only the feet need to be washed. If the person was in ablution, it is not necessary to repeat the rest of the ablution because the previous ritual impurity would have affected the feet.

It is not valid to wipe on a turban, hat, veil or a pair of gloves because wiping footgear has been established in contradiction to analogical deduction and hence nothing else can be added to it.

Section 23 - Wiping Splints

If a person bleeds, is injured or has damaged a limb and puts a plaster or splint on the area and is not able to wash the limb, with either cold or hot water - it is said that it is not necessary to use hot water - and is not able to wipe the limb it is necessary to wipe the plaster once, according to the correct position. It is also said that wiping the splint is repeated except on the head.

There is a narration that states that wiping is recommended. It is also said that it is obligatory because the Prophet, upon him be peace and blessings, used to wipe his bandage. Furthermore, when Ali, Allah be pleased with him, broke his forearm at Uhud or Khaybar the Prophet, upon him be peace and blessings, ordered him to wipe his splints.

The person wipes on most of the material tied on the limb so as to avoid harming the wound by wiping over all of the material – this is the correct position. It is sufficient to wipe over any part of the limb that is exposed between bandages if undoing the bandage is harmful because of the necessity. This would prevent water flowing to the wound thereby harming it. However, the bandage is opened if there is no harm in undoing it with the healthy part being washed and the injury wiped. If wiping the injury is harmful it is left.

Wiping splints and the likes of it is regarded as being the same as washing the skin beneath and not as a substitute, as opposed to wiping footgear which is a substitute. Hence,

- there is no time period stipulated for wiping splints because it is the original.
- it is not a condition that the splint be tied whilst in a state of purity, thereby removing hardship.
- it is permitted to wipe a splint on one foot whilst washing the other foot because it is the original.

- it does not invalidate by coming off before the injury has healed because the excuse remains.
- it is valid to wipe whether the person is sexually impure or in a state of minor ritual impurity.
- it is permitted to wipe the upper bandage after having wiped the lower bandage, if a person has more than one bandage tied. However, there is no need to wipe the lower bandage after undoing the upper bandage.
- wiping splints does not invalidate if the skin beneath becomes wet, as opposed to the footgear.
- it is permitted to change the bandage after having wiped. It does not then become necessary to wipe on the fresh bandage. However, it is better to wipe on the fresh bandage because of the semblance to being a substitute.

If a person suffers eye inflammation, has a broken nail or suffers an ailment on which ointment or cream has been used and is ordered by a skilled Muslim doctor, or high probability indicates, not to wash the eye and removing the ointment would equally be harmful it is permitted to wipe because of necessity. If wiping is harmful it is left because necessity is judged according to the situation.

Intention is not necessary for wiping footgear, according to the most apparent position. However, it is said that it is a condition as with dry ablution because it is a substitute. Likewise, it is not necessary for wiping splints and wiping the head. None of these are dependant upon intention because they are all forms of purity that are performed with water.

Section 24 - Female Bleeding

Menstruation, postnatal and irregular bleeding are the three different bleeding that emanate from the vagina. However, the source of menstrual and postnatal bleeding is the womb.

Menstruation is amongst the most important sections of law because many legal issues hinge on it. However, at the same time it is amongst the most obscure sections. Amongst those legal matters that are based upon it is divorce, freedom, confirmation of non-pregnancy, post-marital waiting period, parentage, permissibility of intercourse, prayer, fasting, reciting and touching Koran, spiritual retreat, entering the mosque, circling the Kaaba and coming of age.

Menstruation in Arabic language is *hayd*. The original meaning of the word is a flow. Hence, it is said *"hada al-wadi"* to mean the wadi flowed.

The legal meaning of menstruation is the blood that pours from the womb of an adult[137] who is not suffering an ailment that causes bleeding, nor pregnant – this is a pattern that Allah has set whereby the mouth of the womb of a pregnant woman closes due to pregnancy and hence nothing can come out until birth - nor has reached menopause[138].

The minimum time period for menstruation is three days and nights. These are the conditions of menstruation. The average time period is five days and nights and the maximum is ten days and nights. This is based on scriptural text. The integral of menstruation is the appearance of the specific blood described above. Its attribute is that it is close to being black and is pungent.

---

[137] This is from the age of nine years.

[138] The age of menopause is fifty five years, according to the legal position.

Postnatal bleeding in Arabic language is *nifas*, which is the verbal noun of "*nufisat al-mar'a*" or "*nafasat al-mar'a*" which means to give birth – such a woman is termed *nufasa*. In Sacred Law, postnatal bleeding is the blood that emerges after giving birth or after most of the child has emerged, even if it be stillborn whilst having some discernible features. If the child emerges normally postnatal bleeding begins from the emergence of the chest. However, if the child emerges feet first postnatal bleeding begins from the emergence of the navel. From this moment onwards, the post-marital waiting period ceases, the slave girl becomes *umm walad*[139] and an oath is broken.

However, unless most of the child emerges alive the child does not inherit nor is funeral prayer prayed.

If no blood is seen after childbirth the woman is not regarded as being in the state of postnatal bleeding, according to the correct position. She is then only required to perform ablution, with them both. We have previously mentioned that with the Imam, out of caution, ritual bath is obligatory.

The maximum time period for postnatal bleeding is forty days because the Prophet, upon him be peace and blessings, set the time period as forty days for women unless she sees purity before then.[140] There is no minimum because there is no need for an additional indicator over and above childbirth whereas, other than it extending for three days, there is no indicator for menstrual blood.

Irregular bleeding is bleeding that is less than three or more than ten days in the case of menstruation or bleeding that is more than forty days in the case of postnatal bleeding because of the narrations that have been mentioned. It is also bleeding that is more than the woman's

---

[139] *Umm walad* is the term for the slave girl who bears child to her master. She becomes free on her master's death.
[140] This is recorded by ibn Majah 649.

average which extends beyond the maximum time period in the case of both menstruation and postnatal bleeding.

The minimum interval between two menstruations is fifteen days because of his statement, upon him be peace and blessings, *"The minimum menstruation is three, its maximum is ten and the minimum between two menstruations is fifteen days."* There is no maximum interval because it could potentially extend for more than a year.

If a woman comes of age through irregular bleeding her menstruation is taken as ten days, her interval as fifteen days and her postnatal bleeding as forty days. However, if a woman has an average and her bleeding extends beyond her average such that it is more than the maximum menstruation or postnatal bleeding her average remains unaltered and the additional is considered as irregular bleeding.

If a woman forgets her average she is termed 'confused'.

There are eight prohibited actions due to menstruation and postnatal bleeding.

1. Prayer

2. Fasting

The above two are not valid because of the absence of the conditions of validity.

3. Reciting a Koranic verse

This is prohibited unless remembrance is intended if the verse contains it. It is not permitted if the verse contains rulings and narrations. However, Hunduwani stated, "I do not pass fatwa that it is permitted with the intention of remembrance even if it has been narrated from Abu Hanifa."

There is a difference in authentication of reciting less than a verse. Absolute prohibition is the chosen position because of his statement, upon him be peace and blessings, *"The menstruating woman and the sexually impure person should not read anything of the Koran."*[141] The woman in the state of postnatal bleeding is the same as the menstruating woman.

4. Touching a Koranic verse unless it has a cover

This is prohibited, whether the verse is written on a sheet of paper, coin or wall, because of His statement, *"Which none may touch except the purified."*[142]

It is not prohibited if the Koran has a cover separate to it or if there is a barrier such as a bag, according to the correct position.

It is severely offensive to touch the Koran with the sleeve because it carries the rule of the person.

There is an allowance for people who use books of Sacred Law to touch them with the sleeve or the hand with the exception of touching books of Koranic commentary for which ablution is necessary. However, ablution is recommended for touching books of Sacred Law.

It is permitted to turn over pages of the Koran with the likes of a pen for reciting. Children are instructed to carry and raise the Koran because of the necessity of teaching.

It is not permitted to wrap anything in paper that has legal matters, the name of Allah or the name of the Prophet, upon him be peace and blessings, written upon it.

---

[141] This is recorded by Tirmidhi 131 and ibn Majah 595 and 596.
[142] al-Waqi'ah 79.

It is prohibited to erase the name of Allah with saliva. The same applies to the name of the Prophet, upon him be peace and blessings, out of respect.

The Koran is covered when a man has sexual relations with his wife, out of modesty and respect.

Pencil sharpening and the grass of a mosque are not thrown in dirty places.

5. Entering the mosque

This is prohibited because of his statement, upon him be peace and blessings, *"I do not make lawful mosques for a sexually impure person or a menstruating woman."*[143] The woman in the state of postnatal bleeding is the same as the menstruating woman.

6. Circling the Kaaba

This is prohibited even though the act is valid because purity is a condition of perfection. Hence, if a menstruating woman circled the Kaaba she is released from ihram. However, she is required to sacrifice a camel for the obligatory circling. A person in the state of minor ritual impurity sacrifices a sheep. Sacrificing is not required if the circling is repeated in the state of purity. Circling is prohibited whilst impure because of the nobility of the House and because circling is like prayer, as is mentioned in the sunna.

7. Sexual intercourse

8. Sexual enjoyment from beneath the navel to beneath the knees.

---

[143] This is recorded by Abu Dawud 232 and ibn Majah 645.

These are prohibited because of His statement, *"and do not touch them until they are clean again"*[144], and because of his statement, upon him be peace and blessings, *"for you is that which is above the loincloth."*[145]

Thus, it is recommended to give in charity a dinar or half a dinar if sexual intercourse is performed, without legitimising it. He should then repent and not repeat the act. In *Mabsut* and other books it has been stated unequivocally that legitimising the act is unbelief. However, in *Khulasa*, the position stating that it is not unbelief has been authenticated because it is a non-intrinsic prohibition. The prohibition of sexual intercourse with a woman in the state of postnatal bleeding has been explicitly stated. However, I have not come across the rule of excommunication or otherwise.

If bleeding ceases at the maximum time period for menstruation and postnatal bleeding it is lawful to have sexual intercourse without ritual bath being taken because of His statement, *"and do not touch them until they are clean again"*[146] with a lightened *ta*. By this, Allah has made purity the limit of the prohibition. However, it is recommended not to have sexual intercourse until ritual bath has been taken because of the reading with emphasis, thereby removing oneself from disagreement. The woman in the state of postnatal bleeding is the same as the menstruating woman.

It is not lawful to have sexual intercourse with a Muslim woman whose menstruation or postnatal bleeding ceases at less than the maximum time period even if her average has been completed without one of the following three.

- Performing ritual bath

---

[144] al-Baqarah 222.

[145] This is recorded by Abu Dawud 212.

[146] al-Baqarah 222.

The time to take a ritual bath is considered as part of menstruation if the time period is not the maximum. Hence, by performing ritual bath she is free from menstruation.

However, if bleeding ceases at less than her average he does not approach her until her average has passed because the possibility of recurrent bleeding is high. Thus, ritual bath has no impact before the average is completed.

• Performing dry ablution due to an excuse and praying
The prayer must be performed, according to the most correct position, even if it be an optional prayer, to confirm the dry ablution. Ritual bath, however, does not need any confirmation.

• The prayer becoming a debt upon her
The prayer becomes a debt upon her if she finds after the bleeding has ceased, on completion of her average, enough time for a ritual bath and the prohibiting takbir and anything beyond it yet does not perform ritual bath or dry ablution until the time has elapsed. From that moment onwards, sexual intercourse is lawful with her because the prayer has become a debt upon her – this is amongst the rules of cleanliness for women.

If the time does not suffice for ritual bath and the prohibiting takbir she is not considered to have become pure without using water or performing dry ablution. Hence, nightfall is not upon her nor does she fast the following day being as if she arose whilst having menstruation.

The three conditions mentioned above have been discussed in relation to a Muslim woman because sexual intercourse is lawful with a Jewish or Christian woman on completion of her average before the ten days have passed the moment her bleeding ceases since she is not obliged to perform ritual bath.

We have mentioned a confirmer along with the cessation of blood if the time period is less than the maximum so as to marry the two readings.

The menstruating woman and the woman in the state of postnatal bleeding makes up fasts and not prayers because of the tradition of 'Aisha, Allah be pleased with her, *"That used to happen to us whereupon we were ordered to make up the fast and not the prayer."*[147] There is a consensus on this.

There are five prohibited actions due to sexual impurity.

1. **Prayer**

This is because of the order to purify in the verse.

2. **Reciting a Koranic verse**

This is because of his, upon him be peace and blessing, prohibition of it.

3. **Touching the Koran unless it has a cover**

This is because of the scriptural prohibition.

4. **Entering the mosque**

5. **Circling**

This is because of the aforementioned scriptural text.

---

[147] This is recorded by Bukhari 321; Muslim 761 to 763; Abu Dawud 262 and 263; Tirmidhi 130; Nasa'i 382 and ibn Majah 631. The wording in the text occurs in Muslim 763 where Mu'adha said, *"I asked 'Aisha and said, "How is it that the menstruating woman makes up the fast and does not make up the prayer?" She said, "Are you a Haruri?" She said, "I am not a Haruri but I am asking." She said, "That used to happen to us whereupon we were ordered to make up the fast and not the prayer.""*

There are three prohibited actions due to minor ritual impurity.

1. Prayer

2. Circling

3. **Touching the Koran unless it has a cover**

This is prohibited even for a verse because of the prohibition in the verse.

Irregular bleeding is blood that comes from a vein that has burst and not from the womb. Its attribute is that it has no smell. This blood, as with a constant nosebleed, does not prevent prayer. The injunction does not drop and the bleeding does not prevent the prayer being valid as long as it remains for a complete prayer time, as will be mentioned. Likewise, this bleeding does not prevent either an obligatory or an optional fast. Nor does it prohibit sexual intercourse because it is not harmful.

The purity of excused persons is a necessity. Hence, the woman with irregular bleeding or a person with an excuse - such as urine incontinence, bowel movement, flatulence, constant nosebleed or an injury that does not heal - that cannot be checked without difficulty by using a dressing, sitting or motioning in prayer, performs ablution for the time of every obligatory prayer, and not for every obligatory or optional prayer. This is because of his statement, upon him be peace and blessings, *"The woman with irregular bleeding performs ablution for the time of every prayer"*[148] – this has been narrated by Sibt ibn Jawzi from Abu Hanifa, Allah be pleased with him. The remaining types of excused persons carry the rule of the woman with irregular bleeding. Hence, the proof covers them. The excused person then prays any

---

[148] This tradition has been mentioned by Zayla'i in *Nasb Raya*, in the Section on Menstruation.

obligatory prayer with the ablution in the prayer time, whether it be current or missed prayer - whether the prayer was missed whilst the person was healthy or not - optional prayer, necessary prayer, such as witr and 'Eid, funeral prayer, circling and touching the Koran.

The ablution of the excused is invalid, if no other nullifying agent occurs, only by the prayer time leaving, such as sunrise at dawn, with Abu Hanifa and Muhammad. Zufar regards the ablution to be invalid only by the prayer time entering. However, Abu Yusuf held that it is invalid by them both. Hence, the excused prays noon with midmorning and 'Eid ablution, according to the correct position, as opposed to Abu Yusuf and Zufar. Also, 'Eid is not prayed with dawn ablution, as opposed to Zufar. Hence, the excused prays noon with midmorning and 'Eid ablution, according to the correct position, as opposed to Abu Yusuf and Zufar. Also, 'Eid is not prayed with dawn ablution, as opposed to Zufar. Attributing the nullifying to the prayer time leaving is figurative because the appearance of the previous nullifying agent is the true nullifying agent.

A person suffering from a nullifying agent does not become excused until the excuse remains with the person a complete prayer time without any interval equivalent to the time needed to perform an ablution and prayer. If this interval is present the person is not excused. The condition for the excuse to be established is that the excuse remains with the person. The excuse remaining can be total such that the excuse remains with the person throughout the prayer time and it may also be legal such that there are brief intervals. However, these intervals are not sufficient to allow the person to perform purity and prayer.

The condition for the excuse to persist is that the excuse is present in any prayer time, after the initial prayer time, even if it be present once. By this, it is known to be present.

The condition for the excuse to have ceased and for the excused to no longer be considered as such is for the person to be totally free of the excuse for a complete prayer time.

We ask Allah for His pardon and for health by His favour and generosity.

Section 25 - Cleansing Impurities

Ritual impurity has been discussed first because even if a small area, however small it may be, that needs cleansing is not cleansed worship remains impermissible. However, with intrinsic impurity, a small amount is exempted, as are large amounts in cases of necessity.

Najas, the plural of which is *anjas*, is the name for any filthy substance, in Sacred Law. Originally, the word was a verbal noun. However, it was then used as a noun in His statement, *"The polytheists are impure."*[149]

The word is used for both ritual and intrinsic impurity. However, the word *khubth* is used specifically for intrinsic impurity and the word *hadath* is used specifically for ritual impurity.

Hence, *najas*, with a *fatha*, is a noun which does not accept *ta*. However, *najis*, with a *kasra*, is an adjective which accepts *ta*.

Purification is either confirmation of purity at a place or removal of impurities from it. It is obligatory for any amount that is not exempted. It has been mentioned that the first thing that the slave will be asked about in his grave is purity and that most of the punishment in the grave is because of negligence towards it and towards impurity, in particular urine.

Intrinsic impurity is of two categories. The first category is severe impurity. The severity is in terms of the size of the exempted amount and not the manner of purifying it because this is irrespective of whether the impurity is severe or slight. The second category is slight impurity which, again, is slight in terms of the size of the exempted amount and not the manner of purifying. The manner of purifying does not vary for both impurities.

---

[149] at-Tawbah 28.

The following are examples of severe impurity. These are considered severe because of the absence of any contradicting scriptural text regarding it being impure, with the Imam, such as blood poured forth.

1. Alcohol.

2. Blood poured forth is severe because of the noble verse, *"or blood poured forth."*[150] However, the following types of blood are not impure.
    - that which remains in emaciated or healthy meat
    - that which remains in the veins of legally sacrificed meat
    - blood of the liver, spleen and heart
    - blood that does not nullify ablution, according to the correct position
    - blood of bedbugs, fleas and locust even if it is plentiful
    - fish blood, according to the correct position
    - blood of the martyr as long as it is on him

3. Flesh of carrion that has blood. Hence, the flesh of fish, locust and anything that does not have blood flowing in it is not impure.

4. Hide of carrion before being tanned.

5. Urine of an animal whose flesh cannot be eaten such as a human – including a suckling male child – or wolf. Rat urine makes water impure because it is possible to avoid it by covering the water container. However, a small amount is exempted, as with its faeces, in food or on clothes, out of necessity.

---

[150] al-An'am 145.

6. Dog and pig faeces or the faeces of predatory animals such as a cheetah.

7. Saliva of predatory animals because the saliva is the product of its impure flesh.

8. Chicken, duck and goose faeces because it is foul.

9. All that nullifies ablution by coming out of the human body such as flowing blood, sperm, pre-ejaculation fluid, urinary fluid, irregular bleeding, menstrual blood, postnatal blood and a mouthful of vomit. By agreement, the impurity is severe because, with him, there is nothing that contradicts the proof of its impurity and, with them both, there is no possibility for analogical deduction concerning it being pure.

Slight impurity is impurity in which a contradictory proof is established, such as his statement, upon him be peace and blessing, *"avoid urine"*, along with the report of 'Uraniyyin which indicates the purity of camel urine. The following are examples of slight impurity.

1. Horse urine, according to the legal position, because it is edible even if its flesh is offensive. However, with Muhammad horse urine is pure.

2. Urine of lawful animals such as grazing or wild livestock, e.g. sheep, goats and gazelles. Only urine is mentioned here because, with the Imam, horse, mule, donkey, cow, sheep and goat faeces are severe impurity due to the absence of any contradictory texts. However, with them both, they are slight impurity because of the difference between scholars concerning it – this is the most apparent position because of the general necessity. Muhammad did finally hold that it is pure by saying, "Faeces does not prevent even if it is abundant due to the general necessity for people because streets and districts are

filled with it." Camel cud is the same as its faeces as is the cud of cow and livestock. Fish blood and mule and donkey saliva are pure according to the primary narrations – this is the correct position.

3. Predatory bird droppings, such as a falcon and a kite, according to the most correct position because of general necessity. In a narration that has been authenticated by Sarkhasi it is pure.

The exempted amount for severe impurity is the weight of a dirham[151] for a solid and the area of the palm for a liquid, as has been reconciled by Hunduwani – this is the correct position. Hence, if the amount is more than a dirham it is not exempted, if it can be removed. The exempted amount for slight impurity is less than a quarter of a complete garment or the whole body, according to the correct position, because, in this instance, a quarter substitutes for the whole, as with wiping and cutting a quarter of the hair and the purity of a quarter of the garment. According to the Imam, this is a quarter of the least garment permitted to pray in, such as loincloth. Imam Baghdadi, who is better known as Aqt'a, said, "This is the most correct position related on this. However, it only deals with the garment." It is also said that it is a quarter of the soiled area, such as the hem and the sleeve. In *Tuhfa*, the author states, "It is the most correct position." *Haqaiq* states, "This is the fatwa." Other statements have also been made.

The spray of urine is exempted, even if it is severe, such as the size of a pinhead or the eye of the needle, out of necessity, even if the garment or body is covered in it. It is not *necessary* to be washed if a large amount of water touches it. However, according to Abu Yusuf, it is *necessary*.

If impurity is dropped in water and the water touches the person at the moment that the impurity hits it does not make impure as long as no trace of the impurity appears.

---

[151] The weight of one dirham is equal to twenty qirat.

Anything that cannot be avoided from the impurity of a deceased body is exempted whilst being treated because of the general necessity. However, after the impurity has gathered it makes impure anything it touches.

If impure fat expands more than the exempted amount it does not prevent, according to the choice of Marghaynani and a group of scholars, who take into consideration the moment that it touched. However, the chosen position of others is that it prevents. Thus, if the person prays before it spreads it is valid but not after – according to *Siraj Wahhaj*, the majority have taken this position.

If a person walks in the market and his feet become wet from water that splashes prayer is not valid because of the dominance of impurity in it. However, it is said that it suffices. Mud, that has impurity in it, is exempted, out of necessity, unless the impurity is known.

If an impure bed or ground is wetted due to the sweat of a sleeping person or wetness on a foot and the trace – being the taste, colour or smell – of the impurity appears on the body and foot they are impure because of its presence as indicated by the trace. However, if no trace appears they do not become impure. Likewise, a dry pure garment that is wrapped in a wet impure cloth that does not drip when squeezed does not become impure because the body of the impurity has not separated. The scholars have differed on the question of a dry pure garment such that if it was squeezed it does not drip. Halawani has mentioned that, according to the most correct position, it does not become impure. However, there is a problem with this view because many impurities are absorbed by dry garments that do not drip when squeezed, as is observed when washing commences. Thus, that which connects to it is not merely the wetness. This holds unless the impure garment does not drip by squeezing, whereupon the fatwa becomes other than that which Halawani has authenticated.

A wet garment does not become impure by being spread on impure dry ground, which is impure from urine or faeces, such that the ground becomes wet due to the wet garment as long as no trace appears on it.

A garment does not become impure by a wind that blows over impurity which then touches the garment unless the trace of impurity appears on the garment. However, it is said that the garment becomes impure if it is wet because the impurity becomes connected to the garment. If wind escapes and the rear orifice is wet *Shams Aimma* has judged that it makes it impure. However, others have stated that it does not. Mention has been made previously that the correct position is that escaping wind is pure. Therefore, wet garments do not become impure.

Anything that has a visible impurity, even if it the impurity is severe, such as blood, whether it is on a body, garment or container, becomes pure by removing its substance even if it is removed by one washing, according to the correct position. It is not a condition to repeat the washing because the impurity is present by the substance being present. Hence, the impurity is removed once the substance is removed. Faqih Abu J'afar holds that it is washed a further two times after the substance has been removed thereby attaching it to non-visible impurity that has been washed once. According to *Fakhr Islam*, it is washed thrice after it as with non-visible impurity that has not been washed. Wiping the point on the body where medicinal blood cupping has been performed with three wet clean rags suffices in place of washing because it performs the same function.

It does not harm if the trace remains when it is difficult to be removed. Difficulty is defined as needing other than water or liquid to remove the impurity, such as *hurd* and soap, because the tool set aside for purification is water. Hence, a garment dyed with an impure substance becomes pure when the water becomes clear even though the colour remains. It is also said that it is washed thrice afterwards.

Trace of impure oil does not harm, according to the most correct position, by removing the adjacent impurity through washing as opposed to the fat of a deceased animal which is intrinsically impure.

Impure fat and oil is purified by pouring water on it thrice and removing it thrice. Honey is purified by pouring water and boiling it until it reverts to its original state thrice. Fresh pottery is purified thrice by ensuring that with each wash the water has stopped dripping. It is also said that fresh pottery is burnt and old pottery is washed. Smooth containers are purified by wiping. Fresh wood is chiselled and old wood is washed. Well-cooked meat that is cooked in impurity can never be purified and its sauce is poured away because there is no good in it. It is also said that it is boiled thrice in pure water. The same is the case with boiled chicken that has not had its intestines removed. However, if it is left to the extent that the pores are opened so that the feathers can be plucked it is purified by washing. Coating metal after having watered it with impurity several times purifies – it is then burnt a further time. Before coating the outer surface is purified by being washed thrice. Coating purifies the inner surface according to Abu Yusuf, and this is the fatwa. Molecular change purifies impure substances, such as carrion becoming salt and faeces becoming earth or ashes. Further examples include wet impurity in a furnace by burning, the head of a sheep if the blood is removed from it, alcohol that is made into vinegar or becomes vinegar and impure oil that becomes soap.

It is necessary to purify any area that has a non-visible impurity by washing thrice and rinsing each time. It is recommended to wash the impurity of a dog seven times with earth used once, thereby removing oneself from disagreement. Estimation is made according to high probability that each rinse has removed the impurity, according to primary narrations. However, one narration mentions that one rinse is sufficient – this is the most appropriate. Placing it in flowing water removes the need to wash thrice and squeeze. If the impure area is forgotten and an area of the garment is washed without investigation it is judged to be pure, according to the chosen position. However, if the impurity appears in another area any prayers performed are repeated.

Intrinsic impurity that is on a garment or body, whether it is visible or non-visible, is purified by absolute water, by agreement, and by used water, according to the correct position, because of the strength of removal by it. Likewise, it is purified from a garment or body, according to the correct position, by any purifying removing liquid because the impurity has been removed by it. Hence, it is not purified by oil because it does not leave by itself. Likewise, it is not purified by milk, even if it is churned milk, according to the correct position. It is reported from Abu Yusuf that if blood on a garment is washed with grease, fat or oil such that its trace goes it is permitted. Removers include, for example vinegar, rosewater and liquid extracted from herbs because the strength of removal for the parts of the impurity is the same as water. This is as opposed to ritual impurity because it is legal. By scriptural text water has been specified and it is so widely available, hence there is no difficulty.

If a breastfeeding child vomits on the breast of the mother the breast is purified by the saliva of the child thrice. The mouth of a person who drinks alcohol is purified by the saliva circulating and being swallowed. If fingers have an impurity on them it is purified if they are licked thrice.

However, Muhammad has specified water for purification and this is one of two narrations from Abu Yusuf.

Footgear and the likes of it, such as sandals, are purified from an impurity that has density by water and liquid and by rubbing on the ground and earth. This is the case even if the impurity is acquired from something else, according to the correct position, such as earth and ash that was placed on the footgear before drying from a liquid impurity. The same is the case if the impurity is a wet solid, whether by itself or acquired, according to the chosen position for fatwa – this is the position of most scholars, because of his statement, upon him be peace and blessings, *"If one of you steps on impurity with his footgear their purity is earth"*[152] and his statement, upon him be peace and blessings, *"If one of you comes to the mosque he should look at his footgear. If he sees an impurity or dirt he should wipe them and then pray in them."*[153] This has been restricted to footgear to exclude garments and carpets and also to exclude the body with the exception of sperm.

Swords and the likes of it, such as mirrors, smooth containers, varnished wood, ebony and nails, are purified by wiping with earth or a rag because parts of the impurity does not enter into these. Likewise, the wool of a slaughtered sheep is purified by wiping because after wiping only a little impurity remains and this amount is not considered. Wiping, according to a narration, produces actual purification. Hence, if a watermelon is cut with it eating it is lawful – this has been chosen by Isbijabi. However, it is prohibited on the narration that it lessens – this has been chosen by Quduri. There is no difference between dry and moist impurity and urine and faeces, according to the chosen position for fatwa because the companions, Allah be pleased with them, used to kill the unbelievers with their swords and then wipe them and pray with them.

If the trace of impurity disappears from the ground and has dried, even if it be by other than the sun, according to the correct position, it is purified and prayer is permitted on it, because of his statement, upon him be peace and blessings, *"Any ground that has dried has purified."* However, dry ablution is not permitted with it, according to the most apparent position, because of the scriptural condition of cleanliness. It is also reported that it is permitted from it.
Anything that grows on the ground such as trees, herbage or grass is purified by drying from the impurity and by the trace of the impurity disappearing, following on from the ground, according to the chosen

---

[152] This is recorded by Abu Dawud 385 to 387.
[153] This is recorded by Abu Dawud 650.

position, and not by its moisture drying. It is also said that it must be washed.

An impurity that has undergone molecular change is purified, such as it becoming salt, earth or clay or by burning until it becomes pure ashes, according to the correct position. This is pure because the nature has altered. For example, juice becomes alcohol thereby being impure and then becomes vinegar thereby being pure.

The steam in public lavatories, stables and hot baths if it drops is not impure, by hidden analogical deduction. However, drops that fall from impurity is impure such as that which is known as *'araqi* and it is prohibited. It is said that the eggs of animals that are not eaten is impure, as with its meat. It is also said that it is pure.

Dry sperm is purified, even if it is female sperm, according to the correct position, by scraping it from the garment, even if it is a new lined garment, and by scraping from the body, according to the primary narration. This is the manner as long as the sperm has not been defiled by another impurity, such as urine. Wet sperm is purified by washing because of his statement, upon him be peace and blessings, *"Wash it if it is wet and scrape it if it is dry."* If water touches it after scraping it is the same as the ground drying, hide tanned by the sun or dried-up well. There is a difference in authentication – the best is to consider all of the above pure, as is indicated in the texts. Pure coming into contact with pure like it does not produce impurity.

Section 26 - Tanning

Dead animal hide is purified by tanning. This includes elephant hide because it is the same as other carnivores, according to the most correct position, and because he, upon him be peace and blessings, used to comb with an ivory comb and ivory is an elephant bone. Dog hide is purified because it is not intrinsically impure, according to the correct position. Tanning can be genuine tanning such as tanning carried out using *qarath*[154] leaves, sant fruits, horse chestnut, pomegranate peel or alum. It can also be legal tanning such as using earth, drying in the sun or leaving in the wind.

Prayer is permitted in it, on it and ablution from it because of his statement, upon him be peace and blessings, *"Any hide that has been tanned is pure."*[155] *The Prophet, upon him be peace and blessings, wanted to perform ablution from a water skin. It was said to him, "It is a dead animal." He said, "Its tanning is a remover of its filth or impurity or dirt."* He, upon him be peace and blessings, said, *"Use dead animal hide if it has been tanned, whether by earth, ashes or salt or whatever it is after it has become suitable."*[156]

The exception is pigskin because it is intrinsically impure. Tanning removes the impure moisture from skin which was originally pure whereas pigskin is intrinsically impure. Likewise, human skin is an exception because of its sanctity which is to preserve the nobility of humankind. Hence, even though it is judged that tanning purifies human skin it is not permitted to use it, as with all other human parts.

Legal sacrificing purifies hides of unlawful animals other than pig because the sacrificing performs the function of tanning in removing the moist impurities in a manner better than tanning itself. Legal

---

[154] *Qarath* is a variety of acacia from the sant tree.
[155] This is recorded in Tirmidhi 1728 and ibn Majah 3609.
[156] This is recorded by Daraqutni 123.

sacrificing does not purify the meat of unlawful animals according to the more correct of the two different authenticated fatwas concerning the meat and fat of unlawful animals sacrificed legally because of the need for the hide. The sacrifice of a Zoroastrian, the person who hunts whilst in ihram and the person who intentionally does not mention the name of Allah when sacrificing does not purify.

Any animal part, other than pig, through which blood does not flow, does not become impure by the animal dying because the impurity is caused by blood retention which cannot occur in those parts. Examples include hairs, cut feathers – plucked feathers are impure because the roots are impure, horns and hooves. Bones that do not have fat on them are pure because fat is an impurity from the dead animal. Hence, if it is removed from the bone it is no longer impure. The bone is intrinsically pure because of the narration with Daraqutni, *"The Messenger of Allah only prohibited the meat of the dead animal."*[157] As for the skin, hair and wool there is no problem. Nerve is impure, according to the correct position, because there is life in it which is indicated by pain being felt if it is cut. It is also said that it is pure because it is non-rigid bone.

Musk container is pure like musk, on which there is a consensus on its purity, without exception, even if it is spoilt by water touching it, as has been mentioned when discussing legal tanning. Eating musk is lawful. This has been scripturally mentioned because being pure does not necessitate that eating it is lawful, for example, earth is pure but not lawful to eat.

Civet[158] is pure and the prayer of a person scented with it is valid because of the molecular change that results in it becoming scent.

---

[157] This is recorded by Daraqutni 115. In Bukhari 1492, the wording is, *"only eating is prohibited"* and in Muslim 806 to 807, the wording is *"only eating has been prohibited."*

[158] Civet is a catlike mammal of Africa and South Asia, typically having spotted fur and secreting a powerfully smelling fluid from anal glands, or the yellowish fatty

Molecular change is purifying. Allah is the facilitator by His favour and generosity.

---

secretion of such an animal, used as a fixative in the manufacture of perfumes or the fur of such animals.

Salah

Section 1 - Prayer Times

It is essential to clarify its meaning in Arabic language and according to Sacred Law, the time it became obligatory, the number of its units, clarification of it and its units, the wisdom of it being obligatory, its cause, its conditions, its ruling, its integral, and its attribute. In Arabic language, prayer is an expression that refers to supplication. However, in Islamic terminology, it is an expression that signifies specific integrals and actions. It was made obligatory on Ascension Night. The number of its times is five because of the tradition[159] and consensus. Witr is necessary and is not part of it. Originally, it was made obligatory as sets of two units except sunset. This was continued on travel and was increased for the resident except for dawn. The wisdom of it being obligatory is to thank the One who gives favours. Its primary cause is the eternal statement of Allah whereas the times are apparent causes to facilitate. You will soon know its conditions. Its rule is that the obligation is dropped and reward is attained. You will soon know its integrals and its attribute is either obligatory, necessary or sunna which you will soon know detailed, God willing.

There are three things that are conditional for it to be obligatory, i.e. for a person to have legal responsibility of it.

1. Islam

---

[159] This is a reference to the tradition recorded by Bukhari 46; Muslim 100 and 101; and others in which a Bedouin asked the Prophet, upon him be peace and blessings, about Islam. *The Messenger of Allah, upon him be peace and blessings, said, "Five prayers during the day and night." He said, "Is there any other than them upon me?" He said, "No, unless you perform optional prayers."*…

This is a condition for divine injunction of the secondary points of Sacred Law.

2. Maturity

There is no divine injunction upon a minor.

3. Intellect

Without it legal responsibility is absent.

However, children are ordered on reaching seven years old. They are hit to do it at the age of ten years old with the hand and not with wood, i.e. a stick, such as a palm leaf stalk, being gentle but firm according to his ability. He does not do so more than three times with his hand. He, upon him be peace and blessings, said, *"Order your children to pray when they are seven years old, hit them to do it when they are ten years old, and separate them in their beds."*[160]

Its causes are the prayer times. It is necessary, i.e. doing them is obligatory, at the beginning of the time as an extended obligation. Hence, there is no difficulty until the time becomes restricted for the prayer to be performed. At that point, the prayer is a must and any further delay is sinful.

The prayer times[161] for the obligatory prayers are as follows.

1. Dawn Prayer

The time for dawn prayer is from the rise of true dawn because Gabriel led the prayer[162] when true dawn rose. True dawn is that

---

[160] This is recorded in Abu Dawud 494 to 495.

[161] Time is a period that is determined for any matter.

[162] This is a reference to the tradition recorded by Bukhari 521, 3221 and 4007; Muslim 1379 and 1380; Abu Dawud 393 and 394; Nasa'i 495; and ibn Majah 667.

which rises and spreads across. False dawn is that which appears lengthwise and then disappears. The community have agreed that the beginning of dawn prayer is true dawn.

The end of dawn prayer is just before sunrise because of his statement, upon him be peace and blessings, *"The time for dawn prayer is as long as the first horn of the sun has not risen."*[163]

2. Noon Prayer

The time for noon prayer, by agreement, is from the sun passing from the centre of the sky and extends until the time for midafternoon prayer. There are two narrations about this from the Imam. In one narration, this is until just before the shadow of everything is twice its size other than the zenith shadow[164] because of the contradictory statements. This is the correct position and most scholars and texts are on this. The second narration is when the shadow is its size other than the zenith shadow. The zenith shadow is exempted in both narrations.

Tahawi and the two Colleagues, Abu Yusuf and Muhammad, chose the second position because Gabriel led the midafternoon prayer at that time. However, as you are aware, most scholars have

The wording of Abu Dawud 393 mentions "… from ibn 'Abbas, Allah be pleased with them both, from the Prophet, upon him be peace and blessings, said, *"Gabriel led me in prayer at the House twice. He prayed with me noon when the sun passed and was the size of a lace. He prayed midafternoon with me when its shadow was its size. He prayed with me sunset when the person fasting breaks it. He prayed with me nightfall when dusk disappeared. He prayed dawn when food and drink is prohibited on the person fasting. Then, on the next day, he prayed noon when its shadow was its size. He prayed with me midafternoon when its shadow was twice its size. He prayed with me sunset when the person fasting breaks it. He prayed with me nightfall to a third of the night. He prayed dawn when it brightened. He then turned to me and said, "Muhammad, This is the time of the prophets before you. The time is between these two times.""*

[163] This is recorded by Muslim 1389.

[164] The zenith shadow is called *fay'* and has a hamza. *Fay'* is that which transcribes the sun of an evening. *Dhill* is that which the sun transcribes of a morning.

stipulated that the shadow reaches twice its size. Taking this position is the safest because it relieves the conscience with certainty since bringing the prayer before its time is not valid but prayer is valid if the time leaves. Thus, what if the time is still remaining, by agreement?

In the narration of Asad, if the time for noon prayer leaves by the shadow becoming its size midafternoon does not enter until the shadow of everything is twice its size. Thus, between them is a disregarded time. Hence, caution is to pray noon before the shadow becomes its size and midafternoon after twice its size thereby performing both by agreement, as is mentioned in *Mabsut*.

3. Midafternoon Prayer

The beginning of midafternoon prayer is from the moment that there is an increase on the size or twice the size, based on the difference we have mentioned, until sunset, according to the well-known position. This is because of his statement, upon him be peace and blessings, "*Whoever catches a unit of midafternoon before the sun sets has indeed caught midafternoon.*"[165] However, Hasan ibn Ziyad said that if the sun yellows midafternoon time leaves. This is interpreted as the chosen time.

4. Sunset Prayer

The beginning of sunset prayer is from sunset until just before the red dusk has disappeared, according to fatwa. This is a narration from the Imam and the fatwa is on it. This is also the position of them both because of the statement of ibn 'Umar, Allah be pleased with them both, "*Dusk is the redness.*"[166] Furthermore, this is the narration from the leading companions and there is a consensus of

---

[165] This is recorded by Bukhari 579; Abu Dawud 412; Tirmidhi 186; and ibn Majah 1122.

[166] This is recorded by Daraqutni 1045.

the linguists on this. It has been transmitted that the Imam reverted to this position.

5. Nightfall Prayer

The beginning of both nightfall and witr prayers is from the disappearance of the dusk, in accordance with the difference mentioned, until just before true dawn because of the consensus of the early Muslims. The tradition of Gabriel leading the prayer does not negate anything beyond the time in which he led the prayer. He, upon him be peace and blessings, said, *"Indeed, Allah has increased you with a prayer, which is witr. Therefore, pray it between the last nightfall to the rise of dawn."*[167]

Witr prayer is not prayed before nightfall prayer because of this tradition and because of the required order between the obligatory nightfall prayer and the necessary witr prayer with the Imam.

There is no prayer upon a person who does not find nightfall and witr prayer time, for example, at a land such as Bulgar and the Far East where, during the shortest nights of the year, daybreaks before dusk disappears. There is no prayer because of the absence of the cause which is the time. This, however, is not like the day which is like a year from the days of the Antichrist because of the order to estimate the times. Likewise, fixed time periods in trade, rent, fast, pilgrimage, and post marital waiting period are estimated as we have clarified in the original to this summary. Allah is the facilitator.

Two obligatory prayers are not combined in a prayer time because the prayer brought before its time is not valid and it is not lawful to delay the current prayer until another prayer time enters. This is not permitted even with an excuse such as travel or rain. The narrations that mention combining are interpreted as the first prayer being

---

[167] This is recorded by Bukhari 1418 and Tirmidhi 452.

delayed until just before the end of its time and on completing the first prayer the prayer of the second enters and so it is prayed in it.

The exception is 'Arafa for the pilgrim alone, on the condition that the pilgrim prays both the noon and midafternoon prayer with the Greatest Imam, i.e. the leader, or his representative, even if both prayers are performed as latecomer. Furthermore, the ihram must be for pilgrimage and not for lesser pilgrimage whilst praying both noon and midafternoon prayer, even if ihram is worn after noon, according to the correct position. Finally, the validity of noon prayer is a condition. Hence, if the invalidity of noon prayer becomes clear it is repeated and midafternoon prayer is repeated when its normal time enters. These are the four conditions for combining to be valid with the Imam. However, with them both, the pilgrim combines even if praying individually. In *Burhan*, it is stated that this is the most apparent position. Thus, the pilgrim prior combines noon and midafternoon prayer at the beginning of noon prayer time at Namira Mosque, as is the practice there, with one azan and two commencements, to highlight the combining. They are not separated by optional prayers or the sunnas of noon.

Likewise, the pilgrim delay combines sunset and nightfall prayer. Hence, they are both prayed at Muzdelifa with one azan and one commencement because of the lack of need to highlight the entrance of both times. The only conditions required here are the place and ihram. Sunset prayer is not permitted on the way to Muzdelifa because of his statement, upon him be peace and blessings, *to the one whom he saw praying sunset prayer on the road, "Prayer is ahead of you."*[168] If a person does pray on the way and does not repeat it by the time daybreaks or as it is feared that dawn is about to rise it is valid.

After having clarified the original time he now clarifies the recommended times.

---

[168] This is recorded by Bukhari 1672 and Muslim 3099 to 3103.

1. Dawn Prayer

It is recommended for men to delay dawn prayer until the brightening such that if it becomes clear that the prayer is invalid it is repeated with the sunna recitation before sunrise because of his statement, upon him be peace and blessings, *"Brighten with dawn prayer for it is greater for reward."*[169] He, upon him be peace and blessings, also said, *"Lighten with dawn prayer, it will be blessed for you."* Furthermore, brightening will increase the group whereas darkening will lessen the number and whatever results in an increase is better. It also makes easier to attain that which is mentioned from Anas, Allah be pleased with him, who said, *"The Messenger of Allah, upon him be peace and blessings, said, "Whoever prays dawn in group and then sits remembering the name of Allah until the sun rises and then prays two units has the like of the reward of a complete pilgrimage and a complete lesser pilgrimage.""*[170] – fair tradition. Also, he, upon him be peace and blessings, *"Whoever says after dawn prayer, whilst his legs are folded, before speaking, "There is no god but Allah, alone, without partner. His is the dominion, His the praise and He has power over all things" ten times, ten good deeds are written for him, ten bad deeds are wiped away from him, he is raised ten degrees, that day will be a refuge from everything disliked, he will be guarded from the Devil, and it is not befitting for any sin to overtake him on that day other than ascribing associates to Allah, Most High."*[171] – Tirmidhi said that this is a fair tradition. However, Nawawi has mentioned that in some manuscripts fair-sound has been mentioned. He, upon him be peace and blessings, said, *"Whoever remains in his place of prayer after dawn until sunrise is like the one who frees four of the offspring of Ishmael."* He, upon him be peace and blessings, also said, *"Whoever remains in his place of prayer after midafternoon until sunset is like the one who frees eight of*

---

[169] This is recorded by Tirmidhi 154 and Nasa'i 549.

[170] This is recorded by Tirmidhi 586. The narration mentions *"...has the like of the reward of a pilgrimage and lesser pilgrimage."* He said, *"The Messenger of Allah, upon him be peace and blessings, said, "complete, complete, complete."*

[171] This is recorded by Tirmidhi 3474.

the offspring of Ishmael." The increased reward is for waiting for the obligatory prayer. In the first one, it is for the optional prayer.

Brightening for dawn is recommended on travel and in residence for men. The exception is at Muzdelifa for the pilgrim where darkening is better because of the necessary standing after it at Muzdelifa. Likewise, darkening is always better for women because it is more concealing. However, with other than dawn, waiting until men have completed the group prayer is best.

2. Noon Prayer

Cooling is recommended for noon during the summer in all lands because of his statement, upon him be peace and blessings, *"Cool with noon because the heat intensity is from the violent raging of Hellfire."*[172] Friday prayer is like noon. However, in winter, spring and autumn it is recommended to pray noon early because he, upon him be peace and blessings, would pray noon early in the cold. The exception is on a cloudy day out of fear of praying before its time. Hence, it is recommended to delay noon on a cloudy day because there is no offence in its time and, therefore, there is no harm in delaying.

3. Midafternoon Prayer

It is recommended to delay midafternoon prayer during summer and winter as long as the sun has not changed because *he, upon him be peace and blessings, used to delay midafternoon as long as the sun was clear, white.*[173] This also allows performance of optional prayers before it. The sun changing is determined by its light weakening such that the sight of a person is not dazed – this is the correct

---

[172] This is recorded by Bukhari 533 to 534, 536, and 538; Muslim 1395 to 1400; Abu Dawud 402; Tirmidhi 157 to 158; Nasa'i 501 to 502; ibn Majah 677 to 681; and Malik, Book of Prayer Times, 28.
[173] This is recorded by Abu Dawud 408.

position. Delaying to the change is severely offensive. The Messenger of Allah, upon him be peace and blessings, said, *"That is the prayer of the hypocrites – thrice. One of them sits until the sun yellows and is between the two horns of the Devil. He pecks like the pecking of a rooster, remembering Allah only a little."*[174] It is not permitted to delay due to sickness or travelling. It is recommended to pray midafternoon prayer early on a cloudy day after having ensured that it has entered from fear of the offensive time.

4. Sunset Prayer

It is recommended to pray sunset prayer early in both summer and winter because Gabriel prayed with the Prophet, upon him be peace and blessings, at the beginning time on both days. There should be no more than the extent of three verses or a brief sitting between the azan and call to commence. He, upon him be peace and blessings, also said, *"My community is still fine as long as they do not delay sunset until the stars become numerous and intermixed, imitating the Jews."*[175] Thus, delaying it is offensive. The exception is on a cloudy day or due to the excuse of travel, sickness or food being present when delaying slightly is not offensive. Sunset is prayed first, followed by funeral prayer and then the sunna of sunset. It is not recommended to pray early on a cloudy day from fear of praying before sunset because of the high degree of uncertainty. Thus, it is delayed until sunset is certain.

5. Nightfall Prayer

It is recommended to delay nightfall prayer to the first third of the night, according to the narration of *Kanz*. However, Quduri states that it is delayed to before the third. The Prophet, upon him be peace and blessings, said, *"Were I not to cause difficulty on my community I would have delayed nightfall to a third of the night or*

---

[174] This is recorded by Muslim 1412; Tirmidhi 160; and Nasa'i 512.
[175] This is recorded by Abu Dawud 418 and ibn Majah 689.

half of it.[176] *Majma' Riwayat* mentions that delaying to half is allowed during winter because of the contradiction between the proof of recommendation, which is preventing the prohibited night conversation, and the proof of offence, which is lessening of the group because rarely do people stay up until half of the night. The two proofs contradict and thus permissibility is established. Delaying until after half the night is offensive because the proof of offence is, at this point, free of any contradictory proof. The offence is severe.

It is recommended to pray nightfall early on a cloudy night, according to the primary narration, because delaying would lessen the group due to the possibility of rain and darkness.

We have qualified night conversation by the prohibited type. This is anything that is futile, causes night vigil to be missed or results in dawn being missed. However, if the night conversation is for an important matter, reciting Koran, remembrance, relating stories of the righteous, revising legal matters, or conversing with a guest there is no problem. The prohibition is so that the scroll is sealed with worship in the same manner it began thereby causing all mistakes in between to be wiped away, *"for good deeds will annul evil ones."*[177]

It is recommended to delay witr[178] prayer to just before the end of the night for the person confident of waking at that time and not before sleeping because of his statement, upon him be peace and blessings, *"Whoever is afraid of not rising at the end of the night should pray witr at its beginning. Whoever hopes to rise at the end of the night should pray witr at its end because night prayer is witnessed,*

---

[176] This is recorded by Tirmidhi 167 and ibn Majah 691.

[177] Hud, 114.

[178] *Witr* is the opposite of *shaf'* and can also be said as *watr.*

and that is best.[179] We will mention the difference over the Ramadan witr.

---

[179] This is recorded by Muslim 1766 and 1767; Tirmidhi 455; and ibn Majah 1187.

Section 2 - Offensive Times

There are three times in which no obligatory or necessary prayers, that were required before the entrance of these times, are valid. These offensive times are as follows.

1. **From sunrise until it has ascended**

This is when the sun whitens and is a height of one or two spear lengths[180].

2. **From the sun settling at the centre of the sky until it passes by moving to the west**

3. **From the sun yellowing until it sets**

The sun yellowing is known by it weakening until the eye is able to face it.

This is because of the statement of 'Uqba ibn 'Amir, Allah be pleased with him, *"Three times that the Messenger of Allah, upon him be peace and blessings, forbade us from praying in and from burying our deceased in, from sunrise until it has ascended, at noon until it has inclined and from it inclining until it has set"* – Muslim narrated it.[181] The meaning of his statement *"from burying our deceased"* is funeral prayer because burying is not offensive. However, it has been used figuratively in place of the funeral prayer because the two are inseparable. This has been explained by sunna, *"The Messenger of Allah, upon him be peace and blessings, forbade us from praying on our deceased at three (times), at sunrise ...."*

---

[180] A spear length is a distance equal to the sun's diameter appearing between the sun and the horizon.

[181] This is recorded by Muslim 1929; Abu Dawud 3192; Tirmidhi 1030; Nasa'i 561; and ibn Majah 1519.

If the sun rises whilst the person is praying dawn, it is invalid. Thus, ablution is not nullified by loud laughter after it. However, on the basis that it becomes optional, it is invalid.

We do not forbid lazy people from dawn prayer at the time of rising because it is possible that they could completely leave the prayer and validity on the statement of a qualified legal scholar is preferred to leaving.

Performance of anything that became necessary during these three times is valid with offence, according to primary narration, such as a funeral that appears, prostration verse recited, optional prayer that he began in it, or a prayer that he vowed to pray in it. However, according to primary narration, the prayer should be cut short and made up in a complete time but if he continues it, it is valid. Equally, midafternoon of that day is valid if performed at sunset because the reason, which is the portion of time that performance is connected to. However, it is offensive because of the prohibited delay and not because of the time itself. This is not the case with a midafternoon prayer that has passed because, by its time leaving, it is required to be performed in a complete time and therefore cannot be performed in a deficient time.

It is severely offensive to perform optional prayers in the three times mentioned, even if it has a reason, such as the vowed prayer, two units of circling, two units of ablution, greeting the mosque, the regular sunnas, and in Mecca. Abu Yusuf said that optional prayer is not offensive at noon on Friday because it is exempted in the tradition of 'Uqba.[182]

---

[182] This is a reference to the tradition mentioned in footnote 181. In some variants of this tradition Friday is exempted from the prohibition. However, Abu Hanifa and Muhammad, Allah be pleased with them both, viewed this addition to be strange and hence is not considered, as mentioned by Tahtawi.

The following are times when it is offensive to pray optional prayers.

1. After dawn other than its sunnas before performing the obligatory prayer

This is because of his statement, upon him be peace and blessings, *"Those of you present should convey to those of you absent that there is no prayer after dawn other than two units."*[183] Furthermore, this allows all the time to be legally occupied by obligatory prayer. This is also the reason for the recitation of the dawn sunnas being lightened.

2. After the obligatory dawn prayer

3. After the obligatory midafternoon prayer

This is offensive even if the sun has not changed because of his statement, upon him be peace and blessings, *"There is no prayer after midafternoon prayer until the sun has set and there is no prayer after dawn prayer until the sun has risen"* – this is narrated by the two Shaykhs[184].[185] The prohibition is not connected to the time but is to allow the time to seem as if it is legally occupied by the obligatory prayer of the time alone. This is better than actual optional prayers. Thus, this does not affect obligatory prayers that are being made up. This is the meaning deduced from the understanding of the text.

4. Before sunset prayer

---

[183] This is recorded by Abu Dawud 1278.

[184] This is a reference to Bukhari and Muslim.

[185] This is recorded by Bukhari 586 and 588; Muslim 1920 to 1923; Abu Dawud 1276; Tirmidhi 183; Nasa'i 562 to 563; and ibn Majah 1248 to 1250.

This is because of his statement, upon him be peace and blessings, *"Between every two azans is a prayer, if he wants, other than sunset."* Khattabi said that this means azan and call to commence.

5. When the speaker emerges from his area

This remains offensive until the prayer is completed because of the prohibition, irrespective of whether it is a Friday, 'Eid, pilgrimage, marriage, completion of Koran recitation, solar eclipse, or drought sermon.

6. At the call to commencement for ever obligatory prayer other than dawn sunnas

This is only if the person feels safe of not missing the group prayer.

7. Before 'Eid prayer and after it in the mosque

It is offensive to perform optional prayers before 'Eid prayer even at home. It is offensive after 'Eid prayer at the mosque, i.e. at the 'Eid prayer area, but not at home, according to the choice of the majority because *he, upon him be peace and blessings, used to pray nothing before 'Eid. However, when he returned to his home he would pray two units.*[186]

8. Between the two combinings

This is the combining at 'Arafa, even the noon sunnas, and the combining at Muzdelifa, even the sunset sunnas, according to the correct position, because he, upon him be peace and blessings, did not perform optional prayer between them.[187]

9. When the time for the obligatory prayer is restricted

---

[186] This is recorded by ibn Majah 1293.
[187] This is recorded by Bukhari 1273 and Muslim 2950.

This is because praying optional prayers at such a time would result in the obligatory prayer passing out of its time.

10. Whilst holding back either of the two filths

The two filths are urine and faeces. The same is the case for wind. This is also offensive during obligatory prayer.

11. In the presence of food one would like to have

12. In the presence of anything that distracts and diminishes humility in prayer

This is anything that distracts from summoning the Divine greatness and establishing the right of His service. Anything of this nature is offensive if there is no necessity because of the introduction of deficiency into the prayer.

Section 3 - Azan

After having mentioned the times which are apparent reasons, and an announcement of the favour of Allah and His unseen order, he has mentioned azan, which is an announcement of the times entering. The cause has been mentioned before the sign because of its closeness, and because the times are an announcement for the select whereas azan is an announcement for the masses.

The discussion is in relation to its establishment, its naming, its preference, its explanation in Arabic language and in Sacred Law, the reason for its legislation, its reason, its condition, its ruling, its integral, its attribute, its manner, the location in which it is legislated, its time, the requirement from its listener, and the reward prepared for the person performing it.

Azan is established in the Koran and sunna. It is named azan because it is of the form *taf'il*. There is a difference with us over its preference – leading prayer is better than it[188]. Its linguistic meaning is an announcement and according to Sacred Law its meaning is a specific announcement. The reason for its legislation is the consultation that occurred with the companions over a sign by which prayer time with the Prophet, upon him be peace and blessings, could be known. It was legislated in the first year after migration, at Illuminated Medina. It is also said that it was legislated in the second year. Its cause, which is a condition for it, is the time entering. In addition, it is to be in Arabic, according to the correct position, from a sane person. Its conditions of

---

[188] Likewise the call to commencement is better than it as mentioned in Tanwir. That is because of the continuous practice of the Prophet, upon him be peace and blessings, in leading the prayer, as well as the rightly guided caliphs after him. The statement of 'Umar, Allah be pleased with him, "Had it not been for the caliphate I would have performed azan" does not necessitate its preference over leading the prayer. In fact, what he meant was that I would have performed azan along with leading the prayer not whilst leaving it. This also indicates that the best is that the Imam is the muezzin – this is our school and Abu Hanifa was on this. Tahtawi

perfection include that the muezzin be righteous, learned in the time, pure, review peoples' states, harsh with those who abandon group prayer, having a strong voice[189], performed at an elevated place and facing the direction of prayer. Its ruling is that responding to it is required physically and orally. Its integral is specific phrases. Its attribute is that it is an emphasised sunna. Its manner is a leisurely pace. Its time is the prayer times, even for a missed prayer. The listener is required to respond orally, as well as physically. Its phrases and their meanings will be mentioned, along with its reward.

Azan and call to commence is an emphasised sunna having the strength of necessary for obligatory prayers including Friday prayer. It is not necessary, according to the most correct position, because he, upon him be peace and blessings, did not teach it to the Bedouin. It is an emphasised sunna because of the statement of the Prophet, upon him be peace and blessings, *"When prayer arrives one of you should call azan for you and the eldest of you should lead you"*[190] and because of the continuous practice. There is no azan for 'Eid, drought, funeral, and witr. Nightfall azan does not fall upon witr, according to the correct position. If a person performs obligatory prayers individually at an open space an army of Allah prays behind him. Azan is an emphasised sunna for men whether the prayer is current or missed, and on a journey or as resident, as was done by the Prophet, upon him be peace and blessings. However, both azan and call to commence are offensive for women because of the narration of ibn 'Umar that mentions them both as being offensive for women.[191]

---

[189] The meaning of a strong voice is a good loud voice. It is narrated from 'Umar ibn 'Abdul 'Aziz that he said to a muezzin, "Call the azan in a good manner otherwise leave us." Tahtawi

[190] This is recorded by Bukhari 628, 631 and 685; Muslim 1535 to 1539; Abu Dawud 589; Nasa'i 635; and ibn Majah 979.

[191] The essential state of women is concealment and raising their voices is prohibited. The general state of call to commencement is with a raised voice except that it is lesser than the voice for the azan. Tahtawi

Takbir is repeated four times at the beginning of the azan, according to primary narration. Hasan has narrated that it is twice.[192] The *ra* is made quiescent in the *takbir*. The phrases of azan and call to commence are actually pronounced vowel less whereas with call to commence stopping is intended because of his statement, upon him be peace and blessing, *"Azan is quiescent, call to commence is quiescent and takbir is quiescent"* - i.e. for opening the prayer. The last takbir of azan is repeated twice, thereby repeating the glorification, as are the other phrases of the azan. The wisdom of repetition is to magnify the status of prayer in the minds of the listeners. There is no reiteration of the two testimonies because Bilal, Allah be pleased with him, did not reiterate[193] – this is to lower the voice with the two testimonies and then to reiterate them by raising the voice. The call to commence is like the azan because of the action of the descending angel. The muezzin adds after the dawn success "Prayer is better than sleep", repeating this twice because the Prophet, upon him be peace and blessings, ordered Bilal to do so. This is specific to dawn because it is a time of sleep and heedlessness. The muezzin adds, after the call to commence success, "Prayer is commencing", repeating this twice, as the angel did. The azan is performed at a leisurely pace with separation by pausing between phrases but the call to commence is performed rapidly because of the order to do so from the sunna.

Azan that is performed in Persian[194], i.e. not in Arabic, does not suffice even if it is known that it is azan, according to the most apparent position, because the azan of the descending angel came in Arabic.

It is recommended that the muezzin be

- righteous[195], i.e. pious, because he is a entrusted in religion

---

[192] This is a narration from Abu Yusuf and Malik has said this. Tahtawi

[193] He did not reiterate in all situations and likewise ibn Umm Maktum. Shafi' said that it is sunna because Abu Mahthura reiterated due to the order of the Prophet, upon him be peace and blessings. Tahtawi

[194] The apparent is that the call to commencement is the same as it because of the cause mentioned. Tahtawi

- learned in sunnas of azan
- learned in the prayer times for the correction of worship
- being in ablution because of his statement, upon him be peace and blessings, *"only a person in ablution should perform azan"*[196]
- facing towards the direction of prayer as was done be the descending angel unless he is riding because of the necessity of travel or mud. It is offensive to perform azan riding whilst a resident, according to primary narrations.

It is recommended for the muezzin to

- place his fingers in his ears because of his statement, upon him be peace and blessings, to Bilal, Allah be pleased with him, *"place your fingers in your ears because it is louder for your voice"*[197] and he, upon him be peace and blessings, *"no jinn, human or anything hears the extent of the voice of the muezzin except that it will testify for him on Judgement Day and every wet and dry thing that hears him asks forgiveness for him"*[198]
- turn his face right with prayer and left with success even if he is alone, according to the correct position, because it is a sunna of azan
- move about in the minaret if the announcement is incomplete by turning his face

---

[195] This is because of his statement, upon him be peace and blessings, *"The best of you should call azan for you and the best reciter amongst you should lead you in prayer"*. Tahtawi

[196] This is recorded by Tirmidhi 200.

[197] This is recorded by ibn Majah 710.

[198] This is recorded by Bukhari 609 and Nasa'i 645 to 647.

The azan and call to commence is separated, because of the offence in connecting them[199], to the extent that the prayer regulars can attend because of the order to do so[200] whilst taking into account the recommended time.[201] The separation in sunset is a pause the extent of reciting three short or one long verse or three or four steps.

Repeating the call is after azan at all prayer times because of the appearance of laxity in religious matters, according to the most correct position. Repeating the call of each country is in accordance to that which the people are acquainted with, such as the muezzin saying after the azan "Worshippers, prayer, prayer. Come to prayer."

Talhin, which is rhythms and grammatical mistakes, is offensive. Beautifying the voice through other than it is sought after.

The azan and call to commence of the ritually impure person is offensive because of the narration that we have mentioned and because it contains a call that he cannot respond to. I have followed this narration because it accords with the text of the tradition[202], even if the azan of the ritually impure person has been authenticated as not being offensive[203]. There is only one narration for the azan of the sexually impure person which is that it is offensive, as is his call to commence.

The azan of the following is offensive – in fact, they are not valid

---

[199] The offence is in all prayers by consensus. Tahtawi

[200] This is a reference to the tradition recorded by Tirmidhi 195 where the Messenger of Allah, upon him be peace and blessings, said to Bilal, Allah be pleased with him, *"and have between your azan and your call to commence the extent that a person eating would finish his food and a person drinking from his drink…"*

[201] Thus delaying to the offensive time is not permitted in all situations. Tahtawi

[202] This is a reference to the tradition mentioned in footnote 189, *"only a person in ablution should perform azan"* – Tahtawi.

[203] This position is the primary narration and the school as mentioned in Durar. Tahtawi

- undiscerning child – it is said that this also applies to the discerning child[204], because of that which we have narrated[205]
- insane and demented person
- intoxicated because of his immorality and his inability to differentiate reality
- woman[206] because if she lowers her voice she has diminished the announcement and if she raises it she has committed an act of disobedience as her voice is nakedness[207]
- immoral individual because his information is not accepted in religion

Azan performed for others sitting[208] is offensive because it opposes the description of the descending angel.

Speaking during the azan is offensive[209] even if it be to respond to salaam[210]. Likewise, it is offensive to speak during call to commence because the sunna of continuity is lost. It is recommended to repeat the azan, but not the call to commence, if speaking occurred during it because repetition of azan is legislated as in the Friday prayer.

---

[204] The primary narration is that it is valid without offence because he is from the people of group prayer as is mentioned in Siraj and Bahr. Tahtawi

[205] This is a reference to the tradition mentioned in footnote 195, "*the best of you should call azan for you*" – Tahtawi

[206] Siraj mentions that if they do not repeat the azan of a woman, it is as if they have prayed without an azan. Tahtawi

[207] Her voice being nakedness is weak. The relied upon position is that it is tribulation and thus it is not invalid by her raising her voice. Tahtawi

[208] Call to commencement without standing is offensive in all situations –Tahtawi.

[209] If he stops to clear his throat or to cough he does not repeat unless the pause is lengthy as is mentioned in Qunya. Tahtawi

[210] He does not respond at that moment, on completion, or to himself. Tahtawi

Azan and call to commence is offensive for Friday noon in an urban area as with their group prayer for whoever has missed Friday prayer, such as prisoners.

Azan and call to commence is performed for missed prayer[211] as the Prophet, upon him be peace and blessings, did for the dawn that he made up on the morning of stopover night. Likewise, azan and call to commence is performed for the first missed prayers. The most perfect is to do them both for each of them[212] as the Prophet, upon him be peace and blessings, did when the unbelievers kept him occupied from praying four prayers, being noon, midafternoon, sunset and nightfall, on Confederates Day. He made them up in order and continuously and ordered Bilal to perform azan and then call to commence for each one of them. It is offensive to leave call to commence, but not azan, in the remaining missed prayers if they are all performed at the same place[213] because this contradicts the action of the Prophet, upon him be peace and blessings,[214] due to there being an agreement in the narrations that call to commence was performed with all prayers that were made up whilst some narrations only mention call to commence after the first missed prayer. Thus, it is not offensive to leave azan for other than the first missed prayer.

If a person hears the sunna azan, which is the azan the does not contain grammatical mistakes or *talhin*, he should refrain from everything, including recitation, even if he is in the mosque – this is best. *Fawaid* [215]mentions that he continues his recitation if he is in the mosque and likewise if he is in his house but the azan is not the azan of his mosque.[216] If a person is speaking on legal points and legal theory it is

---

[211] This is because azan and call to commencement are sunnas of the prayer and not of the time – Tahtawi

[212] This is because taking the narration that has the addition is preferred particularly in worship as is mentioned in Bada'i – Tahtawi

[213] However, if it is different, he calls azan for the first prayer in the second place - Tahtawi

[214] Leaving the call to commencement is offensive – Tahtawi

[215] It is said that this was the first commentary on Hidaya.

[216] However, responding to it is recommended - Tahtawi

necessary for him to respond. If he hears it whilst walking it is best to stop and respond. If there are a number of azans he responds to the first. He does not respond whilst in prayer[217], even funeral prayer, sermon or listening to it, studying and teaching knowledge, eating, sexual intercourse, or relieving oneself. The sexually impure person responds but the menstruating woman and the woman in the state of postnatal bleeding does not respond because of their inability to physically respond.

The description of the response is to utter what the muezzin utters in response to him. Hence, the phrases uttered in response are the same as the phrases of the muezzin. However, on hearing the "two Comes"[218], which are "Come to prayer" and "Come to success" he utters, "There is no power or strength except through Allah",[219] i.e. there is no power for us to turn away from disobedience and there is no strength for us to be obedient other than through the favour of Allah, as has been mentioned. If he were to utter the same he would become like a person mocking because the one who relates the word of the instructor is mocking him. The remaining phrases, however, contain praise and supplication is answered after responding with the same as the muezzin uttered. In the dawn azan, the response to the muezzin saying "Prayer is better than sleep" is either "You have spoken the truth and piously" or "That which Allah wills will surely come to pass, and that which He

---

[217] If he does respond, it is invalid – Tahtawi

[218] Responding in the manner mentioned is the statement of Thawri, our three scholars, Ahmad, according to the most correct position from him, and Malik in a narration. Nakha'i, Shafi', Ahmad, in a narration, and Malik, in a narration said that he utters what the muezzin utters. In Fath, Kamal has chosen combining them thereby acting upon the traditions mentioning them. We have seen scholars of the spiritual path combining between them. Tahtawi

[219] The secret in these two particularly is that once he has sought from them by the first phrase to come to prayer and by saying, "come to success" and salvation which can only happen by movement of which the slave has no ability over, it is appropriate that he says "there is no power" i.e. no movement nor ability with me over anything that you have sought from me except with the strength of Allah, Exalted is He. This is better than the statement of the author, "he would become like a person mocking". Tahtawi

does not will will not come to pass." By this, he avoids appearing to mock. Our scholars have differed over the rule of responding. Some have explicitly stated that it is necessary whereas other have explicitly stated that it is recommended.

After responding to the azan, the person blesses the Prophet, upon him be peace and blessings, and then supplicates for *wasila*. He says, as has been narrated by Jabir, Allah be pleased with him, *"Whoever utters after having heard the call, "Allah, Lord of this comprehensive invitation and enduring prayer, grant Muhammad a place near to You and an excellence and bestow on him the praiseworthy station that You have promised him" my intercession will be due for him on Judgement Day."*[220] Also, from ibn 'Umar, Allah be pleased with them both, from the Prophet, upon him be peace and blessings, *"When you hear the muezzin say what he says and then bless me once for whoever blesses me once Allah blesses him because of it ten times. Then ask Allah for me wasila for it is a station in Heaven that is only befitting for a believing slave of Allah and I hope that I am him.*[221] *Therefore, whoever asks wasila for me intercession will be due him."*[222]

Know that from this station branches out all of the gardens of Heaven and it is the Garden of Eden, the mansion of eternity. It has a branch in every garden of Heaven from which our master Muhammad, upon him be peace and blessings, appears to the residents of that Heaven and it is the greatest place in every Heaven. Allah make us from the successful through his intercession and his proximity in his mansion of honour.

---

[220] This is recorded by Bukhari 615 and 4719; Abu Dawud 529; Tirmidhi 211; Nasa'i 681; and ibn Majah 722.

[221] This is etiquette with Allah and being distant from appearing to dominate over Him, or he said it before Allah made him aware that it was him - Tahtawi

[222] This is recorded by Muslim 850; Abu Dawud 523; and Nasa'i 679.

Section 4 - Conditions and Integrals of Prayer

Conditions[223] and integrals[224] are mentioned together to highlight for the worshipper that by which the prayer is valid. The validity of the prayer requires twenty seven things, although this number is not restrictive. Those who mention the six conditions external to the prayer and the six conditions internal to the prayer intend merely to approximate, otherwise the person praying requires all that we have mentioned and more. So, our intention is to highlight those conditions of validity needed for entering prayer and those by which the prayer remain valid. All of these are obligatory components. The word thing[225] is a reference to conditions and integrals.

Amongst the conditions are

1. **Purity from ritual impurity[226]**

This includes minor, major, menstruation and postnatal bleeding because of the ablution verse.

2. **Purity of the body, garment and prayer place from non-exempted impurity**

---

[223] *Shurut* is the plural of *shart* and *ashrat* is the plural of *sharat*, both of which mean signs. In Islamic terminology, condition is that which the presence of a thing is dependant on but is external to its nature. Maraqi Falah

[224] *Arkan* is the plural of *rukn* and, in Arabic language, means the strongest side. However, in Islamic terminology, it is the intrinsic part that the nature is constructed from and from other than it. Maraqi Falah

[225] Here the author is explaining usage of the word "thing" at the beginning of this paragraph in the sentence, "The validity of the prayer requires twenty seven things".

[226] In Arabic language, *hadath* means an occurring thing. However, in Islamic terminology, it is a legal preventative that occurs within the limbs until a remover reaches it. Maraqi Falah

Prayer is permitted if a person spreads something thin that suffices as covering for nakedness[227], which is that through which the body cannot be seen. If the impurity is moist and he places felt on it, folds double something that is not thick, or covers over it with earth and the odour of the impurity is not found, prayer is permitted.[228] If he holds a rope that is tied to an impurity or a clean end of his turban remains, the impure end of which does not move when he moves, prayer is permitted. If, however, it does move prayer is no longer permitted. This is the same as the case of a person whose head touches an impure tent. A sitting baby that clings to the laps of a person praying or an impure bird on his head does not invalidate the prayer if no preventative impurity separates from it because the condition is purity.

Purity of the prayer place includes the feet. Thus, prayer is invalid by the presence of a preventative impurity under either of them or by a combination of them estimated, according to the most correct position. Standing on one foot is correct with offence. Moving from a pure place to an impure one without remaining there an integral length does not invalidate.[229] However, remaining there an integral length does invalidate, according to the chosen position.

This includes purity of the place of hands and knees, according to the correct position, because prostration is obligatory on seven bones – Faqih Abu Layth has chosen this and rejected the position that this is not obligatory – and because the narration that prayer is permitted with the place of hands and knees being impure is strange.

---

[227] The prayer is valid if the impurity cannot be smelt through it - Tahtawi

[228] If however the odour is smelt, it is not permitted as mentioned in Khaniya – Tahtawi

[229] This is because remaining briefly on a small amount of impurity is like remaining a while with a small exempted amount of impurity – Tahtawi

This also includes the place of the forehead, according to the most correct position of the two narrations from Abu Hanifa – this is also the statement of them both, Allah have mercy on them all – so that the prostration is confirmed, because, even though the obligatory component is fulfilled by the size of the tip of the nose according to the outweighed statement, the placing of the nose becomes legally nonexistent by it being on impurity, even if it was repeated on purity, according to primary narration. Impurity at the area of the nose does not prevent if the remaining area is pure, by agreement, because the nose is less than a dirham thereby becoming as if the person praying restricted to the forehead with offence.[230] Purity of place is more necessary than purity of garment, which is a condition by scriptural text,[231] through inference because there is no prayer without place but prayer does exist without a garment. There is no harm in the garment touching an impurity that does not stick to it whilst in prostration.

3. Covering the nakedness[232]

This is a condition because of the consensus that it is obligatory, even in darkness. The condition is covering from all sides, according to the correct narration. Hence, there is no harm if the nakedness can be seen from the neck, according to the statement of most scholars. Likewise, there is no harm if someone looks at the nakedness from the bottom of the garment because there is difficulty in preventing this. Prayer is permitted with offence in silk[233], stolen garment and on the property of another.

---

[230] The offence is severe because placing the nose is necessary and if he places it on impurity it is as if he has not placed it - Tahtawi

[231] This is mentioned in His statement, Exalted is He, "*Cleanse your garments*", al-Muddaththtir, 74 - Tahtawi

[232] The shape of the nakedness being formed by a tight covering sticking does not harm as is mentioned in Hilabi - Tahtawi

[233] Here the discussion is about praying in it. As for praying on it, Qahastani has mentioned that prayer is permitted on a silk prayer mat because the prohibition is in wearing but benefiting in all other manners in not prohibited – Tahtawi

It is recommended to pray in three of a person's best garments: shirt, loincloth, and turban. It is offensive in loincloth with the ability to do otherwise.

4. Facing[234] the direction of prayer

This is a condition by the Book[235], sunna and consensus.

The meaning is facing the area and not the building such that if a person intends the building Kaaba it is not permitted unless the direction of Kaaba is intended. If the prayer niche is intended it is not permitted.

It is obligatory for the Meccan who sees the Kaaba to face it exactly, by agreement, because of the ability to do so with certainty.

It is obligatory for the person who cannot see the Kaaba to face its direction – this is the correct position. The intention of direction of prayer is not a condition and turning towards it removes the need for intention – this is the most correct position. The direction is that which a person, when turning towards it, is either facing the Kaaba or its space, precisely or approximately. Precisely means that if a line were to be drawn from the person's face at a right angle to the horizon it would pass through the Kaaba or its space. Approximately means that the line swerves from the Kaaba or its space such that facing is not totally lost by a part of the face still facing it or its space. This applies equally if the person is near or far, even at Mecca whereby a building or a mountain is between

---

[234] *Istiqbal,* i.e. facing, is from *qabalatu al-mashiya al-wadi,* i.e. the livestock came to the wadi, meaning that they faced it. The *sin* is not for seeking because the condition is facing and not seeking it. Maraqi Falah

[235] This is His statement, Exalted is He, *"turn towards the Sacred Mosque",* al-Baqara, 144.

him and the Kaaba, according to the correct position, as mentioned in *Diraya* and *Tajnis*.

5. Time

The condition is the time for the five obligatory prayers by the Book, sunna, and consensus. Many of the authoritative books have stated this as a condition. However, other authoritative books, such as *Quduri*, *Mukhtar*, *Hidaya*, and *Kanz*, despite mentioning the times, have left mentioning time in the section on Conditions of Prayer. I am not aware of the secret in their not mentioning it, even if it is described as being the reason of performance, container for that which is being fulfilled, and condition of necessity, as is discussed in its place.

6. Belief that the time has entered

This is a condition so that the worship is with a definitive intention because the doubtful person is not definitive. Therefore, if a person prayed and, according to him, the time has not entered and then it became apparent that it had entered the prayer does not suffice because once he had judged that his prayer was invalid based upon legal proof, i.e. his investigation, it does not become permitted if the opposite to it becomes apparent.[236] Consequently, it is feared for him in his religion.

7. Intention

This is definitive desire so that worship is distinct from normal practice. Sincerity for Allah, Glorified and Exalted is He, must be realised in the intention.

---

[236] This is similar to the case of a person who prays in a garment believing it to be impure but it turns out to be pure, his prayer is invalid - Tahtawi

8. Prohibiting[237]

This is not an integral, according to the correct position – most of
the learned scholars are on this. It is a condition by the Book,
sunna and consensus.

There are twelve conditions for the prohibiting being valid.

9. Prohibiting and the intention to be synchronised

They can be either actually or legally synchronised with no alien
separator, such as eating, drinking, or speech, between them that
prevents them being connected because of the consensus on it.
However, walking to prayer and ablution do not prevent.

10. Uttering the prohibiting standing

Likewise, it can be uttered whilst inclining slightly but before the
incline is closer to bowing. *Burhan* mentions that if a person
catches the imam bowing and inclines his back and then utters the
takbir, if he is closer to standing the entry is valid even if he
intended the bowing takbir. His intention is void because the
person who catches the imam in bowing does not need takbir
twice, as opposed to some of them. However, if he is closer to
bowing the entry is not valid.

11. Not to delay the intention from the prohibiting

Prayer is worship and does not fragment. Thus, any part that does
not have an intention is not worship and there is no difficulty in
not delaying it as opposed to fasting. It is true by being
simultaneous and before. The best is that it be actually

---

[237] *Tahrim* is to make things prohibited. The *ha* in *tahrima* is to confirm it as a noun.
The opening takbir or anything that takes its place is called *tahrima* because it
prohibits things permitted outside of prayer. Maraqi Falah

simultaneous, out of caution, thereby removing oneself from disagreement, and producing it after the time has entered, thereby making allowance for it being an integral.

12. Uttering the prohibiting such that he can hear himself

This is on the basis that the person is not deaf. An unspeaking person does not need to move his tongue, according to the correct position, otherwise it is a condition that the person hears that which he utters – this is the most correct position, as Shams Aimma Halawani and most scholars have stated. This is on the basis that the true nature of audible is to make others hear and silent is to make oneself hear. Hunduwani said that it does not suffice if his ears and anyone close to him cannot hear. Hearing is a condition for anything that is linked to uttering with the tongue, including prohibiting, silent reciting, testification, remembrances, mentioning the name of Allah when sacrificing, prostration of recitation being necessary, freedom, divorce, exemption, oath, vow, Islam, and faith. Thus, if a person divorces on his heart and moves his tongue without pronouncing that can be heard it is not effected, even if letters are correct. Karkhi said that reciting is correcting letters even if there is no sound such that it can be heard. The correct position, however, is other than this, as the learned scholar Kamal ibn Humam, Allah have mercy on him, said, "Know that reciting, despite being the action of the tongue, is speech and speech is by letters. Letters is a condition that happens to the voice and is more specific than breath which occurs by striking. Thus, letter is a product of voice and not of breath. Hence, the mere correcting of letters without any sound indicating the letters with the phonetic muscles is not letters. Hence, there is no speech."

Amongst those matters connected to the heart is intention for sincerity. This is not conditional upon uttering, as with unbelief by intention. The traditions master ibn Qayyim Jawziyya, Allah have mercy with him, said, "It is not established from the Messenger of Allah, upon him be peace and blessings, by a sound or weak path that he used to say when beginning, "I pray such and such", nor from any companion or followers.[238] In fact, the transmission is that he, upon him be peace and blessings, when he used to rise for prayer would pronounce takbir. Hence, this is an innovation." *Majma' Riwayat* mentions that pronouncing the intention is deemed offensive by some because 'Umar, Allah be pleased with him, reprimanded the one who did so. Others have permitted it because it assists the action of the heart and removes whisperings. 'Umar, Allah be pleased with him, only reprimanded those who were audible in pronouncing. As for being silent there is no problem. Thus, those amongst our scholars who said that pronouncing is sunna did not intend the Prophetic sunna, upon him be peace and blessings. Rather, they intended the sunna of some scholars because of the difference in the age and the multitude of distractions for the heart after the time of the Followers.

13. Intention of following for the follower

This intention is along with the original prayer intention. The common intention[239] is because of that which has preceded. However, the specific intention, which is the intention of following, is because invalidity of the imam's prayer extends to him due to the commitment. Hence, he intends the obligatory prayer of the time and following the imam in it or he intends to enter the prayer of the imam. It is said that if he intends following him and no one else it does not suffice. However, the most correct position is that it is permitted because he has made himself subordinate to the imam without exception and being subordinate is only realised when he prays that which the imam prays. It is also said that

---

[238] ibn Amir Hajj has added, nor from the four Imams - Tahtawi

[239] This is a reference to the intention common to the follower, Imam, and individual - Tahtawi

whenever he waits for the takbir of the imam, it suffices him from the intention of following. However, the correct position is that he does not become a follower by merely waiting because he is in limbo between being a follower and normal practice. It is befitting not to specify the imam out of fear of the prayer becoming invalid by the appearance of other than him. If he imagines it to be Zayd and it turns out to be 'Amr it does not harm, in the same way as if it did not occur to him that it is Zayd or 'Amr. We have specified the follower because it is not a condition to intend leading for men as opposed to women.

14. Specifying the obligatory prayer

This is specified at the beginning of entry. Thus, if he intends an obligatory prayer and enters into it then forgets and imagines it to be an optional prayer and completes it as such it is a dropped obligatory prayer. Likewise, with the opposite situation it is an optional prayer.

Intending the number of units is not a condition.[240]

It is a condition to specify that which is being prayed because of the various congested obligatory prayers, such as noon, for example. If he intends the obligatory prayer of the time it is valid except for Friday prayer.[241] If he combines between the intention of obligatory and optional prayers it is valid for the obligatory prayer because of its strength, with Abu Yusuf. However, Muhammad said that it does not hold for either of them because of the contradiction. If he intends an optional and funeral prayer it is an

---

[240] This is because the obligatory and necessary prayers are set and the intention of specifying removes the need. Thus if he intends four units for dawn, the intention of four is void and he prays only two units. Tahtawi

[241] Thus, intention of the obligatory prayer of the time is not valid because the time is noon according to the school - Tahtawi

optional prayer. If he intends an obligatory and funeral prayer it is an obligatory prayer.

15. Specifying the necessary prayer

This has been mentioned without exception which therefore includes making up an optional prayer that was invalidated, vow, witr, two units of circling, and the two 'Eids because of the difference in reasons. However, they have said that with the two 'Eids and witr he intends 'Eid and witr prayer without restricting it to necessary because of the difference over it. It is not necessary to specify the prostrations for the prostrations of forgetfulness. However, in recitation he specifies to remove the congestion from the thanks and forgetfulness prostrations.

Additional conditions for the validity of the prohibition are as follows

- To be in Arabic for the one able to do so[242], according to the correct position.
- Not to stretch a *hamza* in it[243] nor the *ba* in *akbar*. Likewise, stretching the *ha* from the Divine Name is a linguistic mistake but it does not invalidate the prayer. The same is the case with placing a *sukun* on it.
- To be a complete sentence comprising of a subject and predicate.
- To be a remembrance solely for Allah, Exalted is He.[244]
- Not to be with the *basmala*.
- Not to omit the *ha* from the Divine Name.

---

[242] As for a person unable to do so, there is no difference over the validity of his entering prayer with whatever language he is able - Tahtawi

[243] Thus, by it he has not entered the prayer and his prayer is invalid during it if it was valid initially - Tahtawi

[244] Thus, if he begins with the likes of "Allah, forgive me" it is not valid because it is not sole remembrance - Tahtawi

- To mention the *hawiy* – this is the *alif* in the second *lam*. Thus, if it is omitted it is not valid.
- Not to connect the takbir with anything that would invalidate it. Thus, it is not invalid by saying, "Allah is the greatest, the knower of the non-existent and the existent" or "the knower of the states of creation" because it resembles human speech – this last point is mentioned in *Bazaziyya*.

This is from that which Allah, Glorified is He, has favoured to the awakening of gathering it. I have not found it collected before this. Thus, to Him is praise because His favouring and bounty is not restricted, forbidden or prohibited.

16. Specifying is not a condition for optional prayer

This is not a condition even for dawn sunna, according to the most correct position. The same is the case with tarawih, according to most scholars – this is the correct position. However, the most cautious is to specify. Thus, he intends bearing in mind its attribute as being tarawih or the sunna of the time.

17. Standing in other than optional prayers

This is an agreed upon integral in obligatory and necessary prayers.

The definition of standing is such that when he stretches his hands he cannot reach his knees.

However, it is not required in optional prayers.

18. Reciting

This is obligatory and only occurs by it being heard, as has been mentioned, because of His statement, Exalted is He, *"Recite from the Koran as much as is easy.*[245][246] According to the majority, it is an additional integral because it drops without necessity from the follower with us and from the person who catches the bowing, by consensus. By scriptural text, recitation is obligatory even if it be a small verse comprising two words, such as His statement, Exalted is He, *"Then he looked round,"*[247] according to primary narration. However, the scholars have differed over verses that are one word, such as, *"Dark green with foliage"*[248] or one letter such as, *"Sad"*[249], *"Nun"*[250] and *"Qaf"*[251], two letters such as, *"Ha. Mim."*[252] and *"Ta. Sin."*[253] or letters such as, *"'Ayn. Sin. Qaf."*[254] and *"Kaf. Ha. Ya. 'Ayn. Sad."*[255] The most correct position is that prayer is not valid with them. Quduri has said that the correct position is permissibility. Abu Yusuf and Muhammad said that the obligatory component is reciting a long verse or three short verses.[256]

Memorising that by which prayer is valid of the Koran is an individual obligation. Memorising al-Fatiha and a chapter is necessary on every Muslim. Memorising the whole Koran is a communal obligation.

Reciting is obligatory in any two units of an obligatory prayer. It is not valid by reciting in one unit alone as opposed to Zufar and

---

[245] al-Muzzammil, 20.

[246] The basis of the proof is that the instruction to recite necessitates compulsion and reciting is not compulsory outside of the prayer by consensus. Hence the instruction is applicable to prayer. - Tahtawi

[247] al-Muddaththir, 21.

[248] ar-Rahman, 64.

[249] Sad, 1.

[250] al-Qalam, 1.

[251] Qaf, 1.

[252] al-Mumin, 1; Fussilat, 1; ash-Shura, 1; az-Zukhruf, 1; ad-Dukhan, 1; al-Jathiya, 1; and al-Ahqaf, 1.

[253] an-Naml, 1.

[254] ash-Shura, 2.

[255] Maryam, 1.

[256] Caution is in their statement and this is sought after particularly in worship – Tahtawi

Hasan Basri because the order does not necessitate recitation. We concur with this but say that it is required in the second because of their resemblance from all angles. Therefore, the first is by the explicit meaning of the text and the second is by its inferred meaning.

Reciting is obligatory in every unit of an optional prayer because each set of units of it is an individual prayer. Reciting is also obligatory in every unit of witr prayer – this is apparent on the basis that it is sunna but, on the basis that it is necessary, out of caution.

Nothing of the Koran is specified for the validity of prayer because of the unrestricted nature of the verse. However, we do specify al-Fatiha as being necessary, as we will mention.

The follower does not recite but listens whilst the imam is audible and whilst he is silent because of His statement, *"And when the Koran is recited, listen to it and pay heed"*[257] and because he, upon him be peace and blessings, said, *"The recitation of the imam suffices you whether he is audible or silent."*[258] The Greatest Imam, his colleagues, Imam Malik, and Imam Ahmad ibn Hanbal agreed on the validity of the prayer of the follower without reciting anything, and I have elaborated on this in the original. We say that if the follower recited al-Fatiha or something else it is severely offensive because of the prohibition.

19. Bowing

This is obligatory because of His statement, Exalted is He, *"Bow."*[259] Bowing is to incline both the back and head. The perfect bow is for the head and posterior to be level. Abu Yusuf and Shafi'

---

[257] al-A'raf, 204.
[258] This is recorded by Daraqutni 1238.
[259] al-Hajj, 77.

said that remaining motionless is obligatory. Abu Muti' Balkhi, the student of Abu Hanifa, said that if a person reads less than three bowing and prostrating glorifications his prayer is not valid. The hunchback whose curve reaches the level of bowing indicates bowing with his head because he is unable to do anything else.

20. Prostrating

This is obligatory because of His statement, Exalted is He, *"and prostrate yourselves"*[260], by sunna, and consensus. Prostrating only occurs by placing the forehead alone – not the nose – with one hand, one knee, and the tip of any toe of either foot on pure ground. If this does not occur there is no prostration. This prostration is valid, according to the chosen position, with offence. The complete prostration occurs by the necessary components being present. This is by placing all of both hands, both knees, both feet, the forehead, and the nose, as Kamal and others have mentioned. The conditions for the validity of the prostration include

- Prostrating on something whose bulk is present such that if he placed pressure, the point of his head would not sink below the point where he prostrated. Hence, prostrating is not valid on cotton, snow, straw, rice, sorghum, and linen seed. However, the forehead[261] does settle on wheat and barley because their seeds settle on top of each other due to their coarseness and thus prostrating is valid. Prostration is valid even if it is on the palm of the person prostrating, according to the correct position, or on the fringe of his garment as long as the area that the palm or fringe is placed on is pure, according to the most correct position, because they

---

[260] al-Hajj, 77.

[261] The forehead is the noun for that which touches the ground from the area above the eyebrows to the point where hair growth ends.

are connected. However, it is offensive without an excuse, such as prostrating on the coil of his turban.

- It is necessary to prostrate on the hard part of the nose because the tip of the nose is not the place of prostration, being a condition of perfection and not a condition of validity. Prostration is with the forehead as it is not valid to restrict to the nose, according to the most correct position, unless there is an excuse with the forehead. The most correct position is that the Imam reverted to agreeing with his two colleagues on the impermissibility of entering prayer in Persian for a person able to do so in Arabic and the impermissibility of restricting to the nose in prostration without any excuse with the forehead because of the tradition, *"I was ordered to prostrate on seven bones: on the forehead"*[262]

- The place of prostration should not be elevated more than half an arm length from the point of the feet so that the description of prostrating is accomplished. A slight elevation does not harm. However, if the elevation is more than half an arm length the prostration is not valid. If he performs another prostration it is valid. If, however, he completes the prayer without repeating it the prayer is invalid. The exception is if there is congestion such that he prays on the back of a person praying his prayer, out of necessity. Hence, if the person being prostrated on is not praying or is praying a different prayer the prostration is not valid.

- Placing one hand and one knee, according to the correct position, as has been mentioned.

- Placing a part of the toes with the interiors facing the direction of prayer whilst prostrating on the ground. Placing the surface of the foot does not

---

[262] This is recorded by Bukhari 812 and Muslim 1098.

suffice for the validity of prostration because it is not its place due to his statement, upon him be peace and blessings, *"I was ordered to prostrate on seven bones: on the forehead, the two hands, two knees and the tips of the feet"*[263] – agreed upon. This is the choice of Faqih[264]. There is a difference over the permissibility of placing one foot.

- Bowing to be before prostration, as with reciting being before a bowing after which no standing remains in which the obligatory reciting is valid.

- Rising from prostration to being close to sitting, according to the most correct position, from the Imam, because a person is considered sitting by being close to sitting, otherwise the prostration is not valid. Hence, prostration is confirmed by returning after it to it, otherwise it is not. Some scholars have mentioned that if he separates his forehead from the ground and then returns his forehead it is valid – no authentication is known for this position. Quduri has mentioned that it is the extent to which the noun rising can be applied to it – Shaykh Islam has made this the most correct position – or that which the observer would call rising.

21. Returning to the second prostration

This is obligatory because the second prostration is obligatory, like the first, by consensus of the community and it cannot occur, like the first, without placing the seven limbs. Repetition does not exist until after separation from the place of the first prostration. Hence, it requires raising and then placing so that repetition can exist. This is also how it has been mentioned in sunna, *"He, upon him be peace*

---

[263] This is recorded by Bukhari 812 and Muslim 1098.
[264] This is a reference to Abu Layth Samarqandi.

and blessings, when he prostrated and raised his head from the first prostration would raise his hands from the ground and place them on his thighs" and he also said, upon him be peace and blessings, *"Pray as you see me pray."*[265] He, upon him be peace and blessings, further said, *"Indeed, the two hands prostrate as the face prostrates. Hence, when one of you places his face he should place them and when he raises it he should raise them."*[266]

It is said that the wisdom of repetition is devotional. It is also said that it is to spite the Devil who did not prostrate once. Another explanation states that when Allah ordered the humankind to prostrate when making the pact the Muslims raised their heads and on seeing that the unbelievers had not prostrated fell down in prostration a second time as thanks to the favour of facilitation and fulfilment of the order.

22. Final sitting

This is obligatory by the consensus of scholars even if they differed over its extent. With us, the obligation is sitting the extent of reciting the testification, according to the most correct position, because of the tradition of ibn Mas'ud, Allah be pleased with him, when he taught him the testification, *"When you have said this – or done this – you have completed your prayer. If you want to stand then stand and if you want to sit then sit."*[267] He linked completing the prayer to it and anything that completes an obligation is an obligation. One of our scholars believed that the obligation in the sitting is that in which the two testimonies can be brought, being therefore, an active obligation. It is a condition for the final sitting to be after the integrals because it was legislated to conclude them. Hence, it is repeated for a core prostration that he remembered.

---

[265] This is recorded by Bukhari 631.

[266] This is recorded by Abu Dawud 892 and Nasa'i 1093.

[267] This is recorded by Abu Dawud 970; Darimi 1341; and Daraqutni 1319 to 1322.

It is a condition for the validity of the integrals and other than them that they be performed waking. Hence, if a person bows, stands, or prostrates sleeping it is not considered. If sleep overpowers him whilst praying everything before it is valid. However, there is a difference over the final sitting. *Munya Musalli* states that if he does not repeat it the prayer is invalid. *Jami' Fatawa* states that it is considered sleeping because it is not an integral and its basis is on rest. Hence, sleep is harmonious with it. I say that this is the manifestation of the difference over it being a condition or integral.

It is a condition for the validity of performing the obligation knowledge of the manner of prayer. This is by knowing the reality of the traits of the prayers, i.e. its obligatory characteristics, meaning that it is obligatory. Therefore, he must believe that the two units of dawn, the four of noon, etc. are obligatory. This should be in a manner that differentiates the sunna characteristics, such as the regular and other sunnas, by believing that those before and after noon are sunna, etc. This does not mean, nor is it a condition, to differentiate between the obligatory components and sunnas contained within the dawn prayer, such as believing that the standing is obligatory and the praise and glorification is sunna. The person praying may instead believe that all the prayers being prayed are obligatory, for example, believing that the four of dawn are obligatory whilst praying each two individually or praying three followed by two for sunset believing the five to be obligatory, such that an obligatory prayer is not prayed as an optional one because an optional prayer is fulfilled with the intention of obligatory prayer. However, obligatory prayer cannot be fulfilled with the intention of optional prayer, as is mentioned in *Tajnis wa Mazid* and *Khulasa*.

There are four agreed upon integrals from amongst the twenty seven or more integrals that have been mentioned. These are standing, reciting, bowing, and prostrating. It is also said that the final sitting the extent of the testification is also an integral. However, it is also said that it is a condition. We have mentioned the difference manifesting in it. It is said that the prohibiting is also an integral.

The remaining obligatory components are conditions. Some of these are conditions, which are those outside of the prayer, for validity of entering the prayer. These are purity from ritual impurity, filth, covering the nakedness, facing the direction of prayer, time, intention and prohibiting. The other conditions are conditions for the validity to remain.

Section 5 – Further Conditions and Integrals of Prayer

Prayer is permitted, i.e. valid, on felt whose surface is pure and bottom has a preventative impurity. It is considered as two garments due to its thickness or like a thick slab that can be split into two slabs whose bottom is impure. Prayer is permitted on the pure side of it according to them both as opposed to Abu Yusuf, being like two things on top of each other.

Prayer is valid on a pure garment whose lining is impure if it is not lined because it is like two garments on top of each other.

It is valid on the pure part of a carpet, mat, or garment even if the impure part moves with his motion because he is not wearing it, according to the correct position. If a part of his turban or wrap becomes impure and he lowers it leaving the pure part on his head and the impure part does not move with his motion his prayer is permitted because he is not wearing it. However, if the impure part moves with his motion his prayer is not permitted because he is legally carrying it unless he cannot find anything else, out of necessity.

The person who does not have anything to remove the preventative impurity prays with it without repeating the prayer because legal responsibility is in accordance to ability.

There is no repeating on the person who cannot find anything to cover his nakedness, even silk. If he finds silk he must pray in it because the obligation of covering is stronger than the prohibition of wearing it in this state. Likewise, if there is grass, mud, or murky water, he prays inside it with motions because it is a covering generally.

If he finds a covering, even by permission, with a quarter of it being pure, his prayer is not valid naked, according to the most correct position, as with water that is permitted to be used for the one who has performed dry ablution because no indebtedness is connected to it. Quarter of a thing takes the place of the whole in instances including this. The impure three quarters does not take the place of the whole because of the requirement of covering and dropping the rule of impurity by the purity of the quarter.

He is given an option if less than a quarter is pure. However, prayer in it is better because of the covering and performance of bowing and prostrating. If he prays naked with motions sitting, it is valid but lesser than the previous. If he prays standing it is permitted but this is the least preferred option. The person affected by two problems should choose the lesser of them. However, if they are equal he chooses.

Praying in a completely impure garment is better than praying naked because of what we have mentioned.

Diraya states that if he covers his nakedness with non-tanned hide and prays in it, his prayer is not permitted as opposed to an impure garment because the impurity of the hide is severer on the basis that it is not removed by washing thrice as opposed to the impurity of the garment. I say that there is a problem with this because it is purified with something less than washing, such as in the sun or drying by the wind.

If he finds something that will cover part of his nakedness, it is necessary for him to use it to cover himself with. He covers the front and rear orifice if he is only able to cover that extent. It is said that if he is only able to cover one of them he covers the rear orifice because it is more obscene whilst bowing and prostrating. It is also said that he covers the front genitalia because he faces the direction of prayer with it and it is not covered by anything as opposed to the rear orifice which is covered by the buttocks. However, this is flawed because it is covered by the thighs and by placing the hands over them.

The prayer of the naked person is recommended sitting with motions stretching his feet towards the direction of prayer because of the covering it contains. If the naked person prays standing with motions or standing with bowing and prostration it is valid because he has performed the integrals. Hence, he chooses whichever of them he wants, with the better being the first option. If he prays naked forgetting a covering, there is a difference over its validity.

The nakedness[268] of a man, whether free or a slave, is the area between the navel and the limits of the knee, according to primary narrations. The lawgiver, upon him be peace and blessings, defined it by his statement, *"The nakedness of the man is that which is between his navel to his knee"*[269] and his statement, upon him be peace and blessings, *"The knee is from the nakedness."*[270]

The female slave, whether a complete, child bearing, *mudabbara*[271], contract, and *mustas'a*[272] with Abu Hanifa because of the presence of slavery, has in addition to the man the stomach and the back because they have a specific facet. Her chest and breasts are not nakedness due to difficulty.

The whole body of a freewoman is nakedness except her face and her hands, the surface and the palms of them, according to the most correct position, which is the chosen position. The forearm of a freewoman is nakedness, according to primary narrations which is the most correct position. However, it is also narrated from Abu Hanifa that it is not nakedness. Her feet are not nakedness, according to the

---

[268] It is called nakedness, in Arabic language, because of its foul appearance and because gazes are lowered from it. In Sacred Law, it is that whose covering is obligatory. Maraqi Falah

[269] This is recorded by Daraqutni 876 and 877.

[270] This is recorded by Daraqutni 878.

[271] *Mudabarra* is a slave whose freedom has been linked to the death of the master by a statement such as, "If I die, you are free"

[272] *Mustas'a* is a slave who has been freed partially and is working to have the rest freed - Tahtawi

most correct of the two narrations, whether the surface or sole, because of the general nature of the necessity. Thus, the hair of the freewoman including the hair that extends beyond the head is nakedness, according to the most correct position and this is the legal position. Hence, uncovering quarter of it prevents the validity of prayer and it is not permitted to look at it clipped, according to the most correct position, as with his pubic hairs and his severed penis. It has been mentioned in Azan that her voice is nakedness. This does not mean her speech alone. Rather it is not permitted to listen to whatever comes from softening.

Uncovering quarter of a limb of the severe or slight nakedness from the man or woman prevents validity of prayer in the presence of covering. Less than quarter does not prevent.

The following are individual limbs
1. knee and thigh, according to the most correct position
2. woman's ankle with her shin
3. her ear independent of her head
4. her limp breast – if her breast is firm then it is with her chest
5. penis independently
6. testicles without including them with the penis, according to the correct position
7. the area between the navel and pubic hairs with the sides of the body
8. each buttock
9. the rear orifice as the third of them, according to the correct position

If the uncovering is dispersed over the limbs of the nakedness but the total area is equal to quarter of the smallest uncovered limb, it prevents the validity of prayer if the time it was uncovered was the time to perform an integral. If the amount is not a quarter of the smallest limb or it is a quarter but the time of uncovering is not lengthy, it does not prevent validity, out of necessity, whether rich or poor.

Whoever is incapable of finding the direction of prayer by himself due to sickness, fear of drowning whilst on wood, inability to dismount by himself from his animal whilst moving or if wild, an elderly person who cannot ride without a helper, fears a human enemy or predatory animal for himself, his animal, his wealth or his trust, fear intensifies due to fighting, or fleeing from an enemy riding, his direction of prayer is the direction that he is able, out of necessity. The direction of prayer for the person in fear is the direction of his safety. If he fears that the enemy will see him if he prays sitting, he prays reclining with motions to the direction of his safety. The person able with the ability of another is not able with the Imam as opposed to them both. If he does not find anyone, there is no difference in validity.

If a person is unclear about the direction of prayer and he does not have a person to inform him from the area, nor anyone who has knowledge, or he asked him and did not inform him, nor is there a prayer niche at the place, he investigates, i.e. endeavours[273] even if it is recitation prostration. It is not permitted to investigate with the presence of prayer niches because they were originally placed correctly. Whoever is not from the area or does not have knowledge, his opinion should not be consulted even if two fellow travellers inform him because they are informing based on personal deduction. He should not leave his own personal deduction for the personal deduction of another. He is not required to knock doors asking for the direction of prayer, or touch walls out of fear of creatures or confusion due to arches other than the prayer niche.

If a blind man prays a unit to other than the direction of prayer and then a man comes to him and aligns him towards it and follows him, the blind man's prayer is valid as long as there was no one to inform when he began because he is not required to touch walls, and otherwise it is invalid. It is not valid for the man to follow him in both cases

---

[273] *Ijtihad* is expending effort to attain the aspiration.

because of his ability in the first case and because of his awareness of his mistake in the second case.

There is no repeating for the person who has investigated if he knew after completion that he was mistaken with the direction because of the statement of 'Amir ibn 'Uqba, Allah be pleased with him, *"We were with the Messenger of Allah, upon him be peace and blessings, on a dark night not knowing where the direction of prayer was. Each man prayed by himself. When we arose we mentioned that to the Messenger of Allah, upon him be peace and blessings, upon which "Whichever way you turn, there is the Face of Allah"[274] was revealed."[275]* Investigating direction of prayer is not like investigating ablution or covering because if the impurity of the water or garment becomes apparent, he repeats as it is a matter that does not accept change whereas direction of prayer does seeing as it was changed from Jerusalem to Mecca.

If he knows his mistake or his personal judgement changes whilst in prayer he turns from the right and not the left and builds on that which he performed with investigation because change in personal deduction is like abrogation. The people of Quba turned in their prayer to the Kaaba when the abrogation reached them and the Prophet, upon him be peace and blessings, commended it. If he remembers a core prostration, his prayer is invalid.

If a person begins without investigating and the direction is unclear, his action is suspended. If he completes it and after his prayer knows that he was correct, it is valid because by the correct direction becoming clear the rule by presumption of continuity is invalid and the validity of the prayer is established. If he knows that he is correct in it, even with high probability, it is invalid because, by it, his state has become strong. Hence, he does not build strong upon weak as opposed to Abu Yusuf. Likewise, it is invalid if he does not know that he is correct at all

---

[274] al-Baqara, 115.

[275] This is recorded by Tirmidhi 345 and 2957; ibn Majah 1020; and Daraqutni 1052. However, all the narrations mention the companion as 'Amir ibn Rabi'a.

because invalidity is established by presumption of continuity of the state which has not be removed by any proof thereby the invalidity being confirmed. The conditional act has not been attained actually or legally.

If his investigation results in a certain direction and he prays towards another direction, it does not suffice for him because he has legally left the Kaaba for himself, being the direction that he investigated, even if he is correct as opposed to Abu Yusuf who likened it to the person who investigates containers and leaves his investigation whereupon the purity of that which he purified with becomes apparent his prayer is valid. Based upon this, if he prays in a garment believing it to be impure, is ritually impure, or the prayer not having entered and the opposite becomes apparent, it does not suffice him even if the condition is found because of the absence of another condition which is the invalidity of his action from the offset because of the absence of certitude. However, with water purity is present actually and intention.

If a group of people investigate directions in darkness and are unaware of the direction of their imam, their prayer suffices them other than the person who steps ahead of his imam as with praying inside the Kaaba.

Section 6 – Necessary Components of Prayer

In Arabic language, necessary has the meaning of must, dropping, and conflicting. In Sacred Law, it is the noun of that which is required of from us based on a proof that has doubt. Fakhr Islam says that it is called that either because it drops from us as knowledge, it drops upon us as action, or that it oscillates between being obligatory and sunna or between it being necessary or not because it is required from us as action and not knowledge.

Necessary components were legislated to complete obligatory components, sunnas to complete necessary components, and etiquettes to complete sunna so that each acts as a fort for that which it was legislated to complete.

The rule of the necessary component is

- punishment is deserving for leaving it intentionally
- the person who rejects it is not excommunicated
- reward for its performance
- necessity of forgetfulness prostration for leaving it forgetfully because of the deficiency in the prayer
- repetition of it for leaving it intentionally
- dropping of the obligatory prayer with deficiency if he does not prostrate and does not repeat it

There are eighteen necessary components

1. Reciting al-Fatiha

This is necessary because of his statement, upon him be peace and blessings, *"There is no prayer for the one who does not recite al-*

Fatiha."[276] This negates perfection because it is a solitary report which does not abrogate His statement, Exalted is He, *"Recite from the Koran as much as is easy."*[277] Hence, acting upon it is necessary.

2. **Attaching a short chapter or three short verses in any two units of an obligatory prayer and in all units of witr and optional prayers**

This is because of his statement, upon him be peace and blessings, *"There is no prayer for the one who does not recite Praise is to Allah and a chapter in an obligatory or other prayer."*[278] This is necessary in any two units of a non-two unit obligatory prayer and in all of a two unit prayer.

This is necessary in all units of witr because of the resemblance to sunna and in all units of optional prayers because of that which we have narrated, and that every pair in an optional prayer is an independent prayer.

3. **Specifying the necessary reciting in the first two units of the obligatory prayer**

This is necessary because the Prophet, upon him be peace and blessings, persisted in reciting in them.

4. **Reciting al-Fatiha before the chapter**

This is necessary because of persistence. Thus, if he recites a chapter first and then remembers, he should recite al-Fatiha and then the chapter after which he prostrates for forgetfulness, just as if he repeats al-Fatiha and then recites the chapter.

---

[276] This is recorded by Bukhari 756; Muslim 874 to 876; Abu Dawud 822; Tirmidhi 247; Nasa'i 911; and ibn Majah 837.
[277] al-Muzzammil, 20.
[278] This is recorded by ibn Majah 839.

5. Prostrating the hard part of the nose with the forehead

This is necessary because of persistence upon it. Prayer is not permitted by restricting to the nose whilst prostrating, according to the correct position.

6. Performing the second prostration in every unit before proceeding to other than it

Hence, it is necessary to maintain the order between the two prostrations in all prayers before proceeding to the remaining parts of the prayer because of persistence. If he misses the prostration, he prostrates it even if it be after the final sitting, after which he repeats the sitting.

7. Motionless in the integrals

Motionless is to straighten out by making the limbs stationary in bowing and prostration until the joints are motionless, according to the correct position, because it is for completion of the integral. It is not sunna, as Jurjani has said, nor is it obligatory as Abu Yusuf has said. The proof necessitates that being motionless is also necessary in the minor sitting, sitting, and rising from bowing because of the order in the tradition of the person who prayed badly and because of persistence on all of this. The learned scholar Kamal ibn Humam and his pupil ibn Amir Haj held this. He said that this is correct.

8. First sitting

This is necessary, according to the correct position, even if it is performed legally which is the sitting of the latecomer when making it up even if he sat the first following the imam because the Prophet, upon him be blessings and peace, persisted upon it.

He prostrates for forgetfulness because of what he has left and he stood forgetfully.

9. Reciting testification in the first sitting, according to the correct position[279]

This is to preclude the statement that they are both sunna or that the testification alone is sunna. This is necessary because of persistence.

10. Reciting testification in the final sitting

This is also because of persistence.

11. Rising to the third unit without delay after reciting the testification

Hence, if he adds the amount of performing an integral forgetfully he prostrates for forgetfulness because he has delayed the necessary rising to the third unit.

12. The phrase "salaam" and not "upon you"

This is twice to the right and left because of persistence. It is not obligatory because of the tradition of ibn Mas'ud. "Upon you" is not required because the aim is attained by the phrase "salaam" without its connected parts. It is also necessary because of persistence upon it.

13. Reciting witr supplication

This is necessary with Abu Hanifa, as is the supplication takbir, as mentioned in *Jawhara*. With them both, it is, like witr, sunna.

---

[279] This is connected to both the sitting and its testification – Maraqi Falah

14. 'Eid takbirs

Each takbir is necessary requiring forgetfulness prostration if left.

15. Specifying the takbir phrase for opening every prayer and not just the two 'Eids

This is necessary because of persistence upon it. *Dhakhira* says that it is offensive to begin with other than it, according to the most correct position. Sarkhasi has said that the most correct position is that it is not offensive, as in *Tabyin*. Thus, beginning the prayer with takbir is not just for the two 'Eid prayers as opposed to those who specify it for them alone. The basis for the general nature is that the Prophet, upon him be peace and blessings, persisted upon takbir when beginning every prayer.

16. Bowing takbir of the second unit of the two 'Eids

This is necessary in following the extra takbirs in it because it is connected to them as opposed to the bowing takbir in the first.

17. Audible[280] reciting of the imam

This is necessary in the following

- Two units of dawn
- First two units of the two nightfalls[281]

This is necessary even if they are being made up because of his action, upon him be peace and blessings.

It is also necessary in the following

- Friday

---

[280] Audible means to cause another to hear.

[281] The two nightfall prayers are sunset and nightfall with the second of the two prayers dominating in the wording.

- Two 'Eids
- Tarawih
- Witr in Ramadan

It is necessary on the imam because of persistence.

18. Silent[282] reciting

This is necessary in the following
- All units of noon and midafternoon, including the combining at 'Arafa
- The units after the first two of the two nightfalls, i.e. third of sunset and the third and fourth of nightfall
- Daytime optional prayers

This is because of persistence.

The individual praying an obligatory prayer has a choice in that which the imam recites audibly and in that which he makes up of the units missed in Friday and the two 'Eids. He is like the person praying optional prayers at night who has a choice whilst sufficing with reciting audibly at a minimum level, thereby not harming a sleeping person because he, upon him be peace and blessings, recited audibly in night vigil[283] and he would elate those awake without awakening those asleep.

If he left the chapter from a unit of the first two units of sunset or from both of the first two units of nightfall, it is necessary that he recites it,

---

[282] Silent means to cause oneself to hear – Maraqi Falah.

[283] This is mentioned in Tirmidhi 449 where it is stated, "Qutayba informed us that Layth informed us from Mu'awiya ibn Salih from 'Abdullah ibn Abu Qays who said, *"I asked 'Aisha, "How was the recitation of the Prophet, upon him be blessings and peace, at night? Did he used to recite silently or audibly?" She said, "He used to do all of that. Sometimes he would recite silently and sometimes he would recite audibly." I said, "Praise is to Allah who placed ease in the matter.""* Abu 'Isa said, "This is a fair-sound strange tradition.""

according to the most correct position, in the last two units of nightfall and the third of sunset with al-Fatiha audibly, according to the most correct position. Al-Fatiha is recited before the chapter – this is the most comparable. However, some have said that the chapter precedes whilst others have said that al-Fatiha is left because it is not necessary.

If he remembers al-Fatiha after reciting the chapter but before bowing he recites it and repeats the chapter, according to the apparent of the school. Likewise, if he remembers the chapter in the bowing he recites it and repeats it.
If he left al-Fatiha in the first two units, he does not repeat it in the last two units with them and he prostrates for forgetfulness. Reciting al-Fatiha in the second set is legislated as optional and hence by it being recited once it occurs for the performance because of its strength by its place. If he were to repeat it he would be opposing legislation in other than optional prayer as opposed to the chapter which is legislated as optional in the last two units without being repeated.

Section 7 – Sunnas of Prayer

There are approximately fifty one sunnas of the prayer.

1. **Raising the hands for the prohibiting parallel to the ears for men**

This is sunna because *the Messenger of Allah, upon him be peace and blessings, would, on beginning prayer, utter takbir and then raise his hands parallel, with his thumbs, to his ears. He would then say, "Glory be to You, Allah, and with Your praise ... "*[284]

The female slave raises parallel to her ears because her forearms are not nakedness. She is like the man in raising but like the freewoman in bowing and prostrating.

The freewoman raises her hands parallel to the shoulders, according to the correct position, because her forearms are nakedness and its basis is concealment. Hasan narrated that she raises parallel to her ears.

2. **Spacing the fingers**

The manner is neither to completely bring them together nor to completely spread them out. They should be left as they are spaced out because *he, upon him be peace and blessings, would, on uttering takbir, raise his hands with his fingers spaced out.*[285]

3. **Prohibiting of the follower to be simultaneous with that of his imam**

---

[284] This is recorded by Daraqutni 1135.
[285] This is recorded by Tirmidhi 239.

This is with the Imam because of his statement, upon him be peace and blessings, *"When he utters takbir, utter takbir."*[286] The particle when is actually for time. However, with them both, it is after the prohibiting of the Imam because with them the *fa* is for succession. There is no difference in permissibility, according to the correct position. The difference is in preference after certainty of the state of the Imam.

4. Placing the right hand on the left beneath his navel for men

This is sunna because of the tradition of 'Ali, Allah be pleased with him, *"From the sunna is placing the right on the left beneath the navel."*[287]

The manner of placing is to have the inside of the right palm on the back of the left circling with the little finger and thumb on the wrist because as it is mentioned that he placed palm on palm and grasping is mentioned, many scholars have approved of this form, thereby acting upon both traditions. However, it is said that this contradicts the sunna and the schools and therefore it is appropriate to act by the description of one of the traditions on occasions and by the other at other times thereby actually doing both.

---

[286] This is recorded by Bukhari 733 and 734; Abu Dawud 603; Nasa'i 922 and 923; and ibn Majah 846.

[287] This is recorded by Abu Dawud 756 and Daraqutni 1089 and 1090. Tirmidhi 252 records from Qabisa ibn Hulb from his father who said, *"The Messenger of Allah, upon him be peace and blessings, would lead us and would grasp his left with his right."*

He said, "In the section is from Wa'il ibn Hujr, Ghutayf ibn Harith, ibn 'Abbas, ibn Mas'ud and Sahl ibn S'ad." Abu 'Isa said, "The tradition of Hulb is a fair tradition and action is on this with people of knowledge amongst the companions of the Prophet, upon him be peace and blessings, the followers and those after them. They believe that the man places his right on his left in prayer. Some of them believe that he places them both above the navel and some of them believe that he places them both beneath the navel. All of that is easy with them."

The freewoman places her hands on her chest without circling because it is more concealing for her.

5. Praising

This is sunna because of that which we have narrated and because of his statement, upon him be peace and blessings, *"When you stand for prayer, raise your hands without diverging from your ears and say, "Glory be to You, Allah, and with Your praise, blessed is Your name, exalted is Your majesty and there is no god other than You." If you do not add to the takbir, it suffices you."* We will mention its meaning, God willing.

6. Taking refuge for the recitation

Hence, he says, "I take refuge with Allah from the accursed Devil" – this is the apparent of the school – or, "I seek refuge ..." – Hunduwani has chosen this.

The latecomer says it as does the Imam and the individual but not the follower because it follows the recitation, with them both. However, Abu Yusuf said that it follows the praising and is a sunna of the prayer to remove Satan's whisperings. *Khulasa* and *Dhakhira* state that the statement of Abu Yusuf is correct.

7. Mentioning the name of Allah at the beginning of each unit

This is sunna before al-Fatiha because *he, upon him be peace and blessings, used to begin his prayer with "In the name of Allah, All-Merciful, Most Merciful"*.[288] The statement that it is necessary is weak even if it has been authenticated because of the absence of persistence.

8. Amen

---

[288] This is recorded by Tirmidhi 245 and Daraqutni 1149 and 1152.

This is sunna for the imam, follower, individual, and reciter outside the prayer because of the order to do so in the prayer. He, upon him be peace and blessings, said *"Gabriel, on him be peace, instructed me amen on completing al-Fatiha. He said, "It is like a seal on a book.""*[289]

It is not from the Koran. The most eloquent language is elongation and lightening and means "answer our supplication".

9. Exalting

This is sunna for the follower and individual, by agreement, and also for the imam, with them both.

10. Reciting them[290] silently

This is sunna for the praising onwards because of the traditions mentioning that.

11. Being upright at the prohibiting without lowering the head

This is sunna from the beginning to the end as has been narrated.

12. Imam reciting audibly the takbir and hearing

This is sunna because of the need to announce entry and moving. The individual, like the follower, has no need to do so.

13. Separating the feet a distance of four fingers

---

[289] This has textual evidence in Abu Dawud 938.

[290] This is a reference to the opening supplication, taking refuge, mentioning the name of Allah, amen, and the exalting.

This is sunna because it is closer to humility. Swaying is better than planting the feet because it makes standing long easier and more lasting. Swaying is to put weight on one foot for a while and the other for a while.

14. If resident, the attached chapter to be from

- long[291] *mufassal*[292] in dawn
- median *mufassal* in midafternoon and noon
- short *mufassal* in sunset

The individual and Imam are alike in this. This is sunna if reciting it does not cause difficulty to the followers.

Mufassal is the seventh of the seven. It is said that, with most, it begins with al-Hujurat. It is also said that it is from Muhammad, al-Fath, or Qaf. Thus, long is from its beginning to al-Buruj, median is from it to al-Bayyinah, and short is from it to its end. It is also said that long is from al-Hujurat to 'Abasa, median is from at-Takwir to Ad-Duha, and the remainder is short.

It is narrated from ibn 'Umar, Allah be pleased with them both, that he used to recite from the short *mufassal* in sunset, median *mufassal* in nightfall and long *mufassal* in sunrise. Noon is like dawn because of their similarity in length of time. However, it has also been mentioned that it is like midafternoon because people are preoccupied with their important matters.

It is narrated from Abu Hurayra, Allah be pleased with him, that *the Prophet, upon him be peace and blessings, used to recite "Alif.*

---

[291] *Tiwal* and *qisar* are the plurals of *tawila* and *qasira* respectively. *Tuwal* is a tall man. Maraqi Falah

[292] *Mufassal* is known as such because of its many parts. It is also said that it is because of the small number of abrogated verses in it. Maraqi Falah

Lam. Mim. The sending down of the Book[293] and *"Has there come over man"*[294] *in dawn on Friday.*[295] The Hanafis, except for a few, have left this sunna whilst the Shaf'is, except for a few, have persisted in it. As a result, the ignorant followers of both schools believe the prayer to be invalid by doing or leaving. Therefore, it is not appropriate to leave or to constantly persist.

In necessity, he recites whatever chapter he wants because *the Prophet, upon him be peace and blessings, recited the two protectors in dawn. When he finished they said, "You have shortened?" He said, "I heard the crying of a baby and was afraid that his mother would face difficulty."*[296] Equally, if he is travelling he recites whatever chapter he wants because he, upon him be peace and blessings, *"recited the two protectors in dawn prayer on a journey."*[297] If it results in dropping of half of the prayer, it is more appropriate in lightening the recitation.

15. Lengthening the first in dawn alone

This is agreed upon because of inherited practice from the time of the Messenger of Allah, upon him be peace and blessings, until today. The recommended lengthening is two thirds in the first and one third in the second. If the variance is large it is not a problem. The phrase "alone" is a reference to Muhammad's statement, "The most beloved to me is that he lengthens the first in all prayers." By agreement, it is offensive to lengthen the second over the first by more than two verses. However, in optional prayers it is easier.

16. Bowing takbir

---

[293] as-Sajdah.

[294] al-Insan.

[295] This is recorded in Bukhari 891; Muslim 2031 to 2035; Nasa'i 956 and 957; and ibn Majah 821 to 824.

[296] This is recorded with slightly different wording by Bukhari 706 to 710 and 868; Abu Dawud 789; Nasa'i 826; and ibn Majah 989 to 991.

[297] This is recorded by Abu Dawud 1462 and Nasa'i 5438.

This is sunna because he, upon him be peace and blessings, used to utter takbir with every descending and rising except the rising from bowing because he would utter the hearing at it.[298]

17. Bowing glorification thrice

This is sunna because of the statement of the Prophet, upon him be peace and blessings, *"When one of you bows, he should say "My Lord Most Great is exalted above all limitation" thrice and that is the least of it. When he prostrates, he should say "My Lord Most High is exalted above all limitation" thrice and that is the least of it."*[299] The least of it refers to the least figurative perfection and not semantic – this is the combining by which the sunna is attained. The order is for recommended. Hence, it is offensive to recite less than it.

If the Imam rises before the follower has completed three, the correct position, is that he follows him. The Imam should not increase to an extent that would tire the people. Every time the individual increases it is better after having concluded on an odd number. It is said that the bowing and prostrating glorifications and their takbirs are necessary.

Nothing other than glorification should be recited in bowing and prostrating. Shaf'i said that in bowing he adds, "Allah, to You I have bowed, before You I have humbled, to You I have submitted and in You I place my trust" and in prostrating he adds, "My face has prostrated to the One who created and formed it and extracted its hearing and sight. So blessed be Allah, the Best of Creators!" as

---

[298] This is recorded by Tirmidhi 253 from ibn Mas'ud who said, *"The Messenger of Allah, upon him be peace and blessings, would utter takbir with every descending and rising and Abu Bakr and 'Umar."*
[299] This is recorded by Abu Dawud 886; Tirmidhi 261 and ibn Majah 890. Both Abu Dawud and Tirmidhi have mentioned that 'Awn ibn 'Abdullah did not meet 'Abdullah ibn Mas'ud.

has been narrated from 'Ali. We say that this is interpreted as during night vigil.

18. Grasping the knees with the hands whilst bowing

19. Spreading the fingers

This is sunna because of his statement, upon him be peace and blessings, to Anas, Allah be pleased with him, *"When you bow, place your palms on your knees, spread your fingers, and lift your arms from your sides."* Here alone spreading the fingers is sought to facilitate in levelling the back.

The woman does not spread her fingers because her state is based on concealment.

20. Firming the legs

This is sunna because it is the inherited practice. Curving them like a bow is offensive.

21. Levelling the back

This is sunna during bowing because *he, upon him be peace and blessings, would, when bowing, straighten his back such that if water was poured on it, it would settle.*[300] It is narrated that when he used to bow if a goblet of water was on his back, it would not move because of the evenness of his back.

22. Levelling the head with the posterior[301]

---

[300] This is recorded by ibn Majah 872.

[301] *'Ajuz* is on the form *rajul* and is the endpoint of anything. It is masculine and feminine. *'Ajiza* is specifically for women but it can be used for men. However, *'ajuz* is general and is that which is between the man and woman's hips. Maraqi Falah

This is sunna because the Prophet, upon him be peace and blessings, when bowing would not raise his head or lower it but between that.[302]

23. Rising from bowing

This is sunna, according to the correct position. It is narrated from Abu Hanifa that rising from it is obligatory – this has preceded.

24. Standing after it stationary

This is sunna because of inherited practice.

25. Placing the knees, then the hands, and then the face for prostrating and the opposite for getting up

The knees are placed first on the ground followed by the hands and face when going down. He prostrates between them. When getting up, the sunna is the opposite by raising the face, then hands, and then knees if he has no excuse. However, if he is weak or wearing footgear, he does whatever he can. It is recommended to descend with the right and get up with the left. *The Messenger of Allah, upon him be peace and blessings, would, when prostrating, place his knees before his hands and, when getting up, raise his hands before his knees.*[303]

26. Prostrating takbir

This is sunna because of what we have narrated.

27. Takbir for rising from it

---

[302] This is recorded by Muslim 1110; Abu Dawud 783 and ibn Majah 869.

[303] This is recorded by Abu Dawud 838; Tirmidhi 268; Nasa'i 1090; and ibn Majah 882.

This is sunna because of the narration.

28. Prostrating between the hands

This is sunna because *he, upon him be peace and blessings, would, when prostrating, place his face between his hands* – Muslim narrated it.[304] Bukhari mentions, *"When he prostrated he placed his hands parallel to his shoulders."*[305] Shaf'i has said this. Some learned scholars have combined by doing one manner once and the other another time even if between the hands is better – this is good.

29. Prostrating glorification thrice

This is sunna because of what we have narrated and is to say "My Lord Most High is exalted above all limitation."

30. Keeping the stomach apart from the thighs, elbows from the sides, and forearms from the ground for men

This is sunna if there is no congestion thereby avoiding the prohibited harming. *He, upon him be peace and blessings, would, when prostrating, keep apart such that if a small animal wanted to pass between his hands, it would do so.*[306] *He, upon him be peace and blessings, would space out such that the whiteness of his armpits could be seen.*[307] He, upon him be peace and blessings, said, *"Do not spread out like a predatory animal, lean on your palms and expose your upper arms. If you do that every one of your limbs prostrates."*[308]

---

[304] This is recorded by Muslim 896 and Tirmidhi 271.
[305] This is recorded by Abu Dawud 734.
[306] This is recorded by Muslim 1107; Abu Dawud 898; Nasa'i 1110; and ibn Majah 880.
[307] This is recorded by Muslim 1106. It is also recorded with slightly different wording by Bukhari 807; Muslim 1105, 1108 and 1109; and Nasa'i 1107.
[308] This is recorded by ibn Khuzayma 646.

31. Being compact and keeping the stomach and thighs together for women

This is sunna because he, upon him be peace and blessings, passed by two women praying and said, *"When you prostrate, bring together flesh to flesh."* The woman in that is not like the man because she is a concealed nakedness.

32. Rising from prostration

The sunna is to complete the rising because rising from prostration to close to sitting is obligatory. Hence, completing it is sunna.

33. Sitting between the two prostrations

34. Placing the hands on the thighs whilst sitting between the two prostrations as with the testification

This is sunna as was done by the Prophet, upon him be peace and blessings. He does not grasp his knees, according to the most correct position.

35. Spreading out the left and keeping the right foot upright for men

The toes are curled facing the direction of prayer as mentioned from ibn 'Umar, Allah be pleased with them both.

36. Inclining for women

This is by sitting on her posterior, placing thigh upon thigh whilst bringing out her leg from beneath her right hip. This is more concealing for her.

37. **Pointing, according to the correct position, with the index finger at the testifying raising it at the negation and lowering it at the affirmation**

This is sunna because *he, upon him be peace and blessings, raised his index finger curving it slightly.*[309] Whoever says that raising should not be done at all has gone against narration and understanding.

Pointing is only with the index finger of the right hand and occurs when finishing at the testifying in the testification because of the statement of Abu Hurayra, Allah be pleased with him, *"A man used to supplicate with two fingers. The Messenger of Allah, upon him be peace and blessings, said to him, "One. One. ""*[310]

The index finger is raised at the negation. This negates divinity from anything other than Allah, Exalted is He, by saying, "There is no god". It is then lowered at the affirmation. This affirms divinity to Allah alone by saying, "except Allah". Thus, raising is an indication of negation and lowering is of affirmation.

We have referred to the fact that he does not clenchl any of his fingers. It is, however, said that he only clenches when pointing with the index finger, as is narrated from them both.

It is sunna to recite testification silently.

38. Reciting al-Fatiha after the first two

This is according to the correct position. It is also narrated from the Imam that it is necessary. It is also narrated from him the choice between reciting al-Fatiha, glorifying, and remaining silent.

---

[309] This is recorded by Abu Dawud 987 to 991; Nasa'i 1264 to 1272 and 1275 to 1276; and ibn Majah 911 to 913.
[310] This is recorded by Tirmidhi 3557 and Nasa'i 1273 to 1274.

39. Blessings on the Prophet, upon him be peace and blessings, in the final sitting

Hence, he says as Muhammad, Allah be pleased with him, said when asked about its manner. He said, "He says, "O Allah, bless Muhammad and the folk of Muhammad as You blessed Abraham and the folk of Abraham. Show grace to Muhammad and the folk of Muhammad as You did to Abraham and the folk of Abraham in the worlds, for You are truly the Most Praiseworthy and Noble."" The addition "in the worlds" is established in the narration of Muslim and others. [311] Hence, prohibiting it is weak.

Blessings on the Prophet, upon him be peace and blessings, is obligatory once a lifetime. It is obligatory whenever his name is mentioned because of the presence of its reason.

40. Supplicating with phrases that resemble Koranic phrases and not human speech

This is sunna after blessings on the Prophet, upon him be peace and blessings, because of his statement, upon him be peace and blessings, *"When one of you prays, he should begin by exalting Allah, Mighty and Majestic is He, and praising Him. He should then bless the Prophet and then supplicate after with whatever he wants."* [312] However, because it has been narrated from him, upon him be peace and blessings, *"This prayer of ours, no human speech is suited to be in it"* [313] this prohibition takes precedent over the permissibility of supplication with whatever pleases him in prayer. Hence, he should only supplicate with phrases resembling Koranic phrases, such as, "Our Lord, do not cause our hearts to swerve" [314]

---

[311] This is recorded by Muslim 907; Abu Dawud 980; and Malik, Book of Shortening the Prayer on Travel, 67.
[312] This is recorded by Tirmidhi 3477.
[313] This is recorded by Muslim 1199; Abu Dawud 930; and Nasa'i 1219.
[314] Al-'Imran 8.

or phrases that resemble Prophetic phrases, such as the narration from Abu Bakr, Allah be pleased with him, that *he said to the Messenger of Allah, upon him be peace and blessings, "Teach me, Messenger of Allah, a supplication by which I may supplicate in my prayer." He said, "Say, "Allah, I have constantly wronged myself and none forgives sins except You. Forgive me with forgiveness from Yourself for You are the Ever-Forgiving, Most Merciful."*[315] Ibn Mas'ud used to supplicate with phrases including, "Allah, I ask You all good, that which I am aware of and that which I am unaware of. I take refuge with You from all evil, that which I am aware of and that which I am unaware of."

It is not permitted to supplicate in his prayer with anything resembling human speech because it invalidates it if it is before the sitting and the extent of the testification and causes the necessary component to be lost if it is present after it before the salaam by leaving it with it and not the salaam. It is, for example, saying, "Allah, marry me to such a woman" or "Give me such and such gold, silver, and position" because these are not impossible to obtain from humans. Those things that are impossible include pardon and well being.

41. Turning right then left with the two salaams

He, upon him be peace and blessings, used to utter salaam on his right saying "Peace be upon you, and the mercy of Allah" such that the whiteness of his right cheek was seen and on his left saying "Peace be upon you, and the mercy of Allah" such that the whiteness of his left cheek was seen.[316] If he utters less than this by saying "Peace be upon you", he has done bad by leaving sunna. However, his obligatory component is valid. He should not add "and His

---

[315] This is recorded by Bukhari 834; Tirmidhi 3531; Nasa'i 1303; and ibn Majah 3835.

[316] This is recorded by Abu Dawud 996; Tirmidhi 295; Nasa'i 1320 to 1326; and ibn Majah 914 to 917.

blessings" because it is an innovation and there is nothing established about it.

If he starts on his left forgetfully or intentionally he utters salaam on his right and does not repeat it on his left. If he forgets his left and stands up he returns as long as he has not left the mosque or spoken. He sits and utters salaam.

42. Imam intending the men, guardian[317] angels and righteous jinn with both salaams, according to the most correct position

The imam intends the men, women, children, and hermaphrodites. Likewise, he intends the righteous follower jinn. He intends all of them because he is addressing them. It is said that he intends them with the first salaam. It is also said that that indicating towards them suffices.

Guardian angels are referred to as such because they preserve every word and deed that emanates from the human being or because they guard him from jinn and causes of ruination.

Their number should not be specified because of the difference over it. Ibn 'Abbas, Allah be pleased with them both, mentioned that with every believer is five guardian angels, one on his right recording good deeds, one on his left recording bad deeds, one in front of him instructing goodness, one behind him repelling bad from him, and one at his forelock recording blessings on the Prophet, upon him be peace and blessings, and conveying it to the Messenger, upon him be peace and blessings. It is said that there are sixty angels with him. It is also said that there are one hundred and sixty that repel devils from him.

---

[317] *Hafadha* is the plural of *hafidh* – Maraqi Falah

Belief in them is like belief in the prophets, upon them be blessings and peace, without specifying their number.

43. Follower intending his imam in his direction

Hence, if he is on his right he intends him with the right salaam and if he is on his left he intends him with the left salaam. If he is directly in front of him he intends him with both salaams because he has a share in each direction and he is the most worthy of those present since he excelled towards the follower by taking liability of his prayer.

44. Individual intending the angels alone

This is sunna because there is no one else with him.

It is important to take note of these because only a few people of knowledge, let alone others, take note of this.

45. Lowering his voice for the second salaam over the first

46. Follower synchronising his salaam with that of the imam

This is sunna with the Imam thereby being in accord with him. With them both, it is after his salaam so that he does not hasten to worldly matters.

47. Beginning with the right

We have already highlighted this.

48. Follower waiting for the Imam to finish

This is sunna because following is necessary so that he knows that there is no forgetfulness on him.

Section 8 – Etiquettes of Prayer

Etiquette is that which is done by the Messenger, upon him be peace and blessings, once or twice without persisting upon it. Examples include additional glorifications in the bowing and prostration and adding to the sunna recitation. It has been legislated to complete the sunna.

The following are etiquettes of prayer.

1. **Bringing out his hands from his sleeves at the takbir for men**

This is etiquette for the prohibiting takbir because it is close to humility except for necessity such as cold.

Women do not expose their hands out of caution from exposing her forearms – likewise, hermaphrodites.

2. **Looking at the point of prostration whilst standing, surface of the foot whilst bowing, tip of the nose whilst prostrating, lap whilst sitting, and shoulders whilst uttering salaam for the worshipper**

This is etiquette for men and women and prevents the worshipper looking at anything that can distract from humility. Whilst doing this, he bears in mind his statement, upon him be peace and blessings, *"Worship Allah as if you see Him. However, even though you cannot see Him, He sees you."*[318] Hence, he does not occupy himself with anything else.

If he is blind or in the dark he bears in mind the Divine greatness.

3. **Holding back coughing as much as possible**

---

[318] This is recorded by Muslim 93; Tirmidhi 2610; and ibn Majah 63 to 64.

This is to be wary of invalidating because if it is without an excuse it invalidates. The same is the case with burping.

4. Covering the mouth when yawning

If he is unable to do so, he covers it with his hand or his sleeve because of his statement, upon him be peace and blessings, *"Yawning in prayer is from the Devil. Hence, if one of you yawns he should cover as much as possible."*[319]

5. Standing when "Come to success" is said

It is etiquette for the people and the imam to stand at this point if he is present near the prayer niche because it is an order which is answered. If he is not present each row stands when the imam reaches it, according to the most apparent position.

6. Imam beginning when "Prayer is commencing" is said

This is etiquette with them both. However, Abu Yusuf said that he begins when the call to commencement finishes. Thus, if he delays until the call to commencement finishes there is no problem, according to all of them.

---

[319] This is recorded by Abu Dawud 5026 to 5028 and Tirmidhi 2746 to 2748.

Section 9 – Manner of the Prayer[320]

When a person wishes to enter prayer, whatever prayer it may be, he brings out his hands from his sleeves, as opposed to a woman and a state of necessity, as we have pointed out. He raises them to his ears such that his thumbs are parallel to his ear lobes. He places the palms of his hands towards the direction of prayer, without completely spreading his fingers out or completely bringing them together. If he has an excuse he raises however much he is able. The freewoman raises parallel to her shoulders. The female slave is like the man, as has preceded.

He then utters takbir – this is the most correct position – without stretching, whilst intending. If he has not raised his hands until he has finished uttering takbir he does not do it because it is out of its place. However, if he remembers whilst uttering, he raises. If he stretches its *hamza*, he has not entered in the prayer and it is invalidated by it during the prayer. Intending is a condition for the validity of the takbir.

Entering is valid by every remembrance that is only for Allah, Exalted is He, free of any need of the seeker, even if it is offensive because the necessary component, being the takbir phrase, has been omitted. In this is an indication that there must be a complete sentence for the entering to be valid – this is the primary narration – e.g. "Glory be to Allah", "There is no god except Allah", or "Praise be to Allah".

Entering is also valid in Persian and other languages if he is incapable of Arabic. However, if he is able, entering and reciting is not permitted in Persian, according to the most correct position, from the statement of the Greatest Imam in agreement to them both because Koran is the name for both the words and the meaning. However, chanting talbiya

---

[320] This is a discussion on the manner of the prayer from beginning to end without clarifying their descriptions because they have preceded – Maraqi Falah.

at pilgrimage, salaam from the prayer, mentioning the name of Allah on the sacrificial animal, and belief is permitted in other than Arabic whilst being able to do so, by consensus.

He places his right on his left – its manner has preceded – beneath his navel without any pause reciting the opening supplication because it is a sunna of standing, according to the apparent position of the school. However, with Muhammad, he lowers whilst praising because it is a sunna of reciting. With them both, he folds in every standing containing a sunna remembrance such as praising, supplication, and funeral prayer. He lowers between the 'Eid takbirs because it contains no sunna remembrance.

The opening supplication is to say, "Glory be to You, Allah, and with Your praise, blessed is Your name, exalted is Your majesty and there is no god other than You." If he says, "sublime is Your praise", he is not prevented and if he is silent, he is not instructed. He does not recite the attention supplication before or after entering. However, it can be added to the opening supplication in night vigil.

The meaning of "Glory be to You, Allah, and with Your praise" is "I absolve You of defective attributes by glorification and affirm perfect attributes to Your essence by exalting." The meaning of "blessed is Your name" is "May Your name perpetuate, abide, and be unblemished." The meaning of "exalted is Your majesty" is "Your authority, greatness, and independence is raised by Your status." The meaning of "there is no god other than You" is "in existence worshipped in reality."

He began by absolving that goes back to unity. He concluded with unity, whilst rising in praising Allah, Exalted is He, in mentioning positive and affirmative attributes to the peak of perfection in majesty, beauty, and the all other actions, which is to be alone in divinity and that oneness and absoluteness which is specifically His.

Every worshipper recites the opening supplication, whether he is a follower or otherwise, as long as the Imam has not begun reciting.

He takes refuge with Allah from the accursed Devil because he is repelled from the presence of Allah, Exalted is He, and he wants to make you a partner with him in punishment. You do not see him. Therefore, you take security with the One who sees him so that He protects you from him by taking protection. Taking refuge is uttered silently for the reciting preceding it. Thus, the latecomer brings it at the beginning of that which he makes up after praising because he praises whilst following even in the pauses of the imam, according to what is said. However, he does not bring it in the bowing although he does bring the 'Eid takbirs in it because of their being necessary. The follower does not take refuge because it is for reciting and the follower does not recite. Abu Yusuf said that it follows the praising so he brings it. In the two 'Eids taking refuge is delayed after the extra takbirs because it is for reciting which is after the takbirs in the first unit.

He mentions the name of Allah silently, as has preceded, before al-Fatiha alone. Every one who recites in prayer mentions the name of Allah in every unit whether he prays an obligatory or optional prayer. He says, "In the name of Allah, All-Merciful, Most Merciful." However, ablution and sacrificing is not restricted to the specific mention of the name of Allah. In fact, any mention of Him suffices. Mentioning the name of Allah is not sunna between al-Fatiha and the chapter. However, there is no offence in it if it is done for the chapter, by agreement, whether the chapter is audible or silent. The person who said that mentioning the name of Allah is only in the first unit is mistaken.
He recites al-Fatiha.

The imam and follower utter amen silently, which is to cause oneself to hear, as has been mentioned.

He necessarily recites a chapter from the *mufassal,* as has preceded, three short verses, or one long verse.

Every worshipper utters takbir whilst bowing. He begins with takbir when he begins inclining and concludes it with its conclusion so that he can begin glorification. As a result, no state in the prayer is free of remembrance. He bows motionless, levelling his head with his posterior, grasping his knees with his hands, firming his legs – to curve them like a bow is offensive. The man spreads his fingers whereas the woman does not do so. Every worshipper glorifies in the bowing saying, "My Lord Most Great is exalted above all limitation" thrice. This number is its minimum perfection of sunna combining. It is offensive to recite Koran in bowing, prostration, and testification by consensus of the Community because of his statement, upon him be peace and blessings, *"I was prohibited from reciting whilst bowing or prostrating."*[321]

He raises his head and remains motionless standing saying, "Allah hears the one who praises" i.e. Allah accepts the praise of the one who praises. Hearing is mentioned but acceptance is intended figuratively as it is said, "The leader heard the words of the person" and as comes in the tradition, *"I take refuge from a supplication that is not heard"*[322] i.e. not answered. The *ha* is for pause and rest and not as a pronoun. He says, "Our Lord, Yours is the praise". Thus, if he is imam, he combines between hearing and exalting – this is the statement of them both and is a narration from the Imam that he chose in *Hawiy Qudsi.* Fadhli, Tahawi, and a group of the later scholars used to incline to combining and is the position of the people of Medina. If he is an individual he combines, which is agreed upon according to the most correct position from the Imam in agreement with them both. However, it is also narrated from him that he suffices with exalting and it is further narrated from him that he suffices with hearing. The follower suffices

---

[321] This is recorded by Muslim 1074 to 1080; Abu Dawud 876; and Nasa'i 1119 to 1120.

[322] This is recorded by Abu Dawud 1548 and Nasa'i 5472.

with praising by agreement because of the order in the tradition, *"When the imam says "Allah hears the one who praises Him", say "Our Lord, Yours is the praise""* – the two shaykhs narrated it.[323] The best is "Allah, Our Lord, and Yours is the praise" followed by "Allah, Our Lord, Yours is the praise" followed by "Our Lord, Yours is the praise".

Every worshipper utters takbir whilst descending for prostration and concludes it on placing his forehead for prostration. He places his knees, then his hands – if he has no excuse preventing him from this manner – and then places his hands between his palms, because of that which we have narrated. He prostrates with his nose and his forehead – the ruling has preceded. He prostrates, motionless, glorifying, by saying, "My Lord Most High is exalted above all limitation" thrice and that is its minimum, because of that which has preceded. The man keeps his stomach apart from his thighs and his upper arms from his armpits because it is more complete in prostrating with the limbs when it is not congested. If it is congested he makes himself compact thereby avoiding harming the adjacent person. He prostrates with his fingers facing the direction of prayer and completely brought together, which is only recommended here, because mercy descends upon him in prostration and with compactness he gains more. He directs his toes towards the direction of prayer. The woman lowers herself by bringing her upper arms to her sides and her stomach to her thighs because it is more concealing for her.

He then raises his head whilst uttering takbir. Every worshipper sits between the two prostrations placing his hands on his thighs, motionless. There is no sunna remembrance in it. The narration with it is interpreted as being in night vigil.

He utters takbir for prostration and prostrates after it, motionless, glorifying in it thrice. He keeps his stomach apart from his thighs and distances his upper arms.

---

323 This is recorded by Muslim 913 to 914; Abu Dawud 848; Tirmidhi 267; and Nasa'i 1064 to 1065.

He raises his head uttering takbir for rising, i.e. standing for the second unit, without support on the ground with his hands if he has no excuse and without sitting before the standing – this is termed the brief sitting and is sunna with Shafi'.

In the second unit he does the same as the first – and you now know what that contains – except that the worshipper does not praise because it is for the opening alone and he does not take refuge because the sitting has not changed. He does not raise his hands because raising the hands is not sunna in the states of bowing and its standing. However, it does not invalidate the prayer, according to the correct position. Thus, it is not sunna except on beginning every prayer, on uttering takbir for the witr supplication, and the extra takbirs for the two 'Eids because of the agreement of the reports. The description of raising in these is parallel to the ears. It is sunna to raise them stretched towards the sky on seeing the Honoured Kaaba, i.e. the moment of sighting it. Thus, the *'ayn* in *faq'as* is for the two 'Eids and sighting the House for supplication, which is accepted. It is sunna to raise them on touching the black stone directing the palms towards the stone. It is sunna to raise them stretched supplicating on standing on Safa and Marwa, standing at 'Arafa, standing at Muzdelifa, and after stoning the first and second site as has been mentioned in the honourable sunna. They are also raised in the drought supplication and its likes because raising the hands in supplication is sunna and likewise when supplicating after completing glorification, exalting and takbir, which we shall mention, after prayers as Muslims in all lands are upon.

When the man has completed the two prostrations of the second unit, he places his left foot on its side and sits on it and keeps his right foot up directing his toes towards the direction of prayer. He places his hands on his thighs stretching his fingers having them ending at the top of his knees. The woman sits inclined, whose description we have mentioned.

The worshipper recites, even if he is a follower, the testification of ibn Mas'ud, Allah be pleased with him, intending its meanings for himself, composing them as a greeting and salaam from himself. He points with the index finger of his right hand in the testimony, according to the correct position, raising it on negation and lowering it on affirmation. He does not add to the testification in the first sitting because of the necessity of standing for the third. It is, as he said, *"The Messenger of Allah, upon him be peace and blessings, taught me the testification. He took my hand between his hands in the same way he would teach me a chapter of the Koran, and said, "When one of you sits in prayer say, "Greetings to Allah, prayers and purity. Peace be upon you O Prophet, and the mercy of Allah, and His blessings. Peace be upon us and upon Allah's righteous slaves. I testify that there is no god except Allah, and that Muhammad is His slave and His Messenger."""*[324]

Tahiyyat (greetings) is the plural of *tahiyya* which comes from a person greeted another person when he supplicates for him on meeting him, as in their saying, *"Hayyak Allah"*, i.e. "May Allah preserve you." The meaning here is the greatest phrase that indicates kingdom and greatness. All verbal worship is for Allah. The meaning of prayers here is physical worship and the meaning of purity is financial worship is for Allah, Exalted is He. These phrases emanated from him on the Night Journey.

When the Prophet, upon him be peace and blessings, said that, by inspiration from Allah, Exalted is He, Allah responded to him and greeted him by saying, "Peace be upon you O Prophet, and the mercy of Allah, and His blessings." He countered the greetings with salaam which is the Islamic greeting. He countered the worship with mercy which is its meaning. He countered the purity with appropriate blessings for wealth, which is growth and abundance.

---

[324] This is recorded by Muslim 901 and Abu Dawud 970. Imam Tirmidhi, after mentioning the testification of ibn Mas'ud, relates that Khusayf said, "I saw the Prophet, upon him be peace and blessings, in a dream and said, "Messenger of Allah, people have differed over the testification?" He said, "Take the testification of ibn Mas'ud.""

After Allah, Glorified and Exalted is He, had poured upon the Prophet, upon him be peace and blessings, with His favours by responding to the three with three, the Prophet being the most noble and generous of the creation of Allah felt compassion, through his excellence, from that outpouring, for his brethren, the prophets, and the angels, and the righteous believers from humans and jinn by saying, "Peace be upon us and upon Allah's righteous slaves." He, thereby, covered them all, as he, upon him be peace and blessings, said, *"When you say it, it touches every righteous slave in heaven and earth."*[325] There is nothing amongst the attributes of creation nobler than servitude which is to be content with what the Lord does whereas worship is that which pleases Him. Servitude is stronger than worship because it remains in the Hereafter as opposed to worship. The righteous one is the person who fulfils the rights of Allah, Exalted is He, and the rights of creation.

After he, upon him be peace and blessings, had said that, from his excellence, the inhabitants of the celestial realm and the heavens, and Gabriel through inspiration testified, "I testify that there is no god except Allah, and that Muhammad is His slave and His Messenger", i.e. I know and I announce. He combines between the noblest of his names, the noblest attribute of creation, and the loftiest description that is a prerequisite for prophethood.

Thus, the worshipper intends composition of these phrases for himself, intending its meaning that has been placed for it from him. It is as if he is greeting Allah, Glorified and Exalted is He, sending salaams on the Prophet, upon him be peace and blessings, and on himself, and the saints of Allah, Exalted is He, as opposed to those who say that it is a narrative of Allah's greetings and not greetings emanating from the worshipper.

---

[325] This is recorded by Abu Dawud 967.

He recites al-Fatiha after the first two units of obligatory prayers, which includes sunset.

He then sits placing his left foot on his side keeping the right foot upright whilst the woman sits on an incline. He recites the mentioned testification.

He blesses the Prophet, upon him, be peace and blessings and then supplicates with phrases that resemble Koran and sunna so that it will be accepted after blessings on the Prophet, upon him be peace and blessings.

He utters salaams beginning on the right and ending on the left saying, "Peace be upon you, and the mercy of Allah" intending whoever is with him and the guardian angels, as has preceded, by the praise and favour of Allah, Glorified is He.

Section 10 – Leading the Prayer

We have previously mentioned certain statements that indicate the virtue of azan. With us, leading the prayer is better than azan because of his, upon him be peace and blessings, continuous practice, and that of the guided caliphs. The best is for the imam to be the muezzin – this is our school, which Abu Hanifa, Allah be pleased with him, was on.

Group prayer is an emphasised sunna, according to the most correct position, that resembles necessary in strength for freemen because of continuous practice and his statement, upon him be peace and blessings, *"Group prayer is better than the prayer of one of you alone by twenty five portions"*[326] – in one narration, *"degrees"*[327]. Thus, it is not possible to leave it without an excuse. If the people of an area leave it, they are ordered to do it. If they accept that, they are left but if they fail to do so they are fought because it is amongst the symbols of Islam and the unique features of the religion.

The reward of group prayer is attained with one person, even if it be a discerning child or a woman and even if it be at home with the imam. However, Friday prayer requires three or two people, as we shall mention.

The slave is not required to pray group prayer because he is engaged in serving his master.

Group prayer is only required of freepersons without an excuse because it drops with it.

The conditions of validity for leading the prayer for healthy men are six.

---

[326] This is recorded by Muslim 1472; Tirmidhi 216; and Nasa'i 839.
[327] This is recorded by Bukhari 645 to 646.

1. Islam

This is a general condition. Thus, leading the prayer of a person is not valid if he rejects resurrection, the caliphate of Abu Bakr, his companionship, insults the two shaykhs, rejects the intercession, or similar matters from people who manifest Islam with the appearance of an excommunicating trait.

2. Maturity

The prayer of a child is optional and his optional prayer is not required of him.

3. Intellect

His prayer is not valid without it, such as an intoxicated person.

4. Male

This excludes women because of the order to have them behind. The hermaphrodite is a woman and so none other than her can follow her.

5. Reciting

This requires memorising one verse by which prayer is valid, based on the difference.

6. Being free of excuses

The prayer of the excused is necessity. Thus, it is not valid for other than him to follow. Examples include constant nosebleed or flatulence. It is not valid for a person with flatulence to follow a person with urine incontinence because he has two excuses.

Likewise, a person who stammers the letter *fa* or *ta* and only speaks with them or a person who pronounces the letter *sin* as *tha* or the letter *ra* as *ghayn* or similar problems cannot be imam for another person. If such a person cannot find any part of the Koran free of his problem and he is unable to rectify his tongue day and night, his prayer is valid for himself. However, if he leaves correction and effort, his prayer is invalid.

This includes being free of the absence of a condition such as purity. If it is absent, for example by having filth that is not excused, it is not valid for him to lead the prayer for a pure person and, likewise, covering the nakedness because the naked person cannot be imam for a covered person.

The conditions of validity for following are approximately fourteen.

1. **The follower making intention of following synchronised with his prohibiting**

This can either be actually or legally synchronised, as has preceded. Thus, he intends prayer and following together.

2. **Intention of the man to lead the prayer for women**

This is a condition for the validity of the following for women because of the invalidity that is involved in being parallel – this issue is well known – even in Friday prayer and the two ʿEid prayers, according to what the majority say.

3. **The imam being ahead of the follower by his heel**

Thus, if his toes are ahead because of the length of his feet it does not harm.

4. **The imam not being a lesser state than the follower**

This, for example, is if the imam is praying an optional prayer and the follower an obligatory prayer, or the imam being an excused person and the follower free of it.

5. The imam not praying an obligatory prayer different to the obligatory prayer of the follower

This, for example, is noon and midafternoon or two noons of two days because of partnership. Thus, there must be unity. Hence, the following of a person who makes a vow with a person who makes a different vow to that of the imam is not valid because of the absence of responsibility over other than him in that which he has imposed upon himself. Likewise, it is not valid for a person who makes a vow with a person who swears an oath because the vowed prayer is stronger.

6. The imam not being resident for a traveller after the time in a four unit prayer

This is because of what we have mentioned thereby being the following of a person praying an obligatory prayer with a person praying an optional prayer in terms of the sitting or the reciting.

7. The imam not to be a latecomer

This is because of the doubt in his following.

8. Not to have a row of women between the imam and the follower

This is because of his statement, upon him be peace and blessings, *"Whoever has between him and the imam a stream, path or a row of women has no prayer."*

Thus, if there are three, the prayer of the three in every row directly behind them is invalid – the fatwa is on this. The following of the remainder is valid. It is also said that the three are a row preventing the validity of following for all those behind their row. If there are only two the prayer of the two behind them is invalid. If she is one and is parallel in the row, the prayer of the person parallel to her on her right and left and the one behind her is invalid.

9. Not to have a stream through which a rowboat can pass between the imam and the follower

This is according to the correct position.

10. Not to have a path through which a chariot can pass

This is if there are no connected rows. The preventor for prayer is a space of two rows, according to fatwa.

11. Not to have a large wall between them which leaves doubt about the movements of the imam

If there is no doubt by hearing or seeing and there is no way of getting to him following is valid, according to the correct position. This is the choice of Shams Aimma Halawani because it is narrated that *the Prophet, upon him be peace and blessings, used to pray in 'Aisha's room, Allah be pleased with her, whilst the people in the mosque would pray with him.* Based on this, following in houses connected to Masjid Haram or outside of its doors is valid if there is no doubt about the state of the imam by hearing or seeing and there is nothing between the wall and the person. Likewise, Shams Aimma mentioned about the person who prayed on his roof with his house connected to the mosque or in his house next to the mosque, and between him and the mosque is a wall, following the imam in the mosque whilst hearing the takbir of the imam or from the person relaying, his prayer is valid, as is mentioned in *Tajnis wa*

Mazid. The following of a person standing on the roof with a person in the house is valid as long as he is aware of his state.

12. The imam not riding whilst the follower is walking or vice versa or riding an animal other than the imam's animal

This is because of the difference in place. If, however, he is on his imam's animal, his following is valid because of the unity in place.

13. The follower not to be in a boat whilst the imam is in a different unattached boat

This is because they are like two animals. If they are attached it is valid because of the legal unity.

14. The follower not being aware from his imam, who is of a different school, an invalidator in the opinion of the follower's school such as the emission of flowing blood or a mouthful of vomit whilst knowing that he has not repeated his ablution after that

Thus, if he was absent for the extent of repeating ablution after he had seen that from him and he is not aware of his state the correct position is the validity of the following with offence. Equally, if he is unaware of his state once it is valid with offence. If he knows of him that he is not cautious in the issues of difference it is not valid to follow him whether he knows his state in the specific of that which he is following in or not. If he knows that he is cautious in the issues of difference following him is valid, according to the most correct position, but it is offensive, as is mentioned in *Mujtaba*. In his commentary, Dayri said that it is not offensive if he knows that he is cautious according to the Hanafi school. If the follower is aware from the imam of something that invalidates the prayer according to the opinion of the imam, such as touching a woman, the penis, or having an impurity the size of a dirham, whilst the imam is not aware of that, it is valid to follow him according to the position of the majority. Some, including Hunduwani, said that it is not valid because the imam regards this prayer as being invalid and so the prayer of the follower is invalid, following on from him. The basis of the first, which is the most correct position, is that the follower regards the validity of his imam's prayer and the consideration for himself is his own opinion. Thus, the position that it is valid is necessary, as is mentioned in *Tabyin* and *Fath Qadir*. The statement "and the imam is not aware of that" is mentioned so that he has certainty in intention and it is possible to interpret the validity of his prayer based on the belief of his imam. However, if he knows and he is on the belief of his school he has become like a mocker having no intention. Thus, there is no basis for interpreting the validity of his prayer.

Praying behind following is valid.

1. Person in ablution with a person in dry ablution

This is valid with them both. Muhammad said that it is not valid. The difference is based on whether the substitution is between the two tools, earth and water, or the two purities, ablution and dry ablution. With them both, it is between the two tools which is indicated by the apparent of the scriptural text and so the two purities are equal. With Muhammad, it is between the two purities, dry ablution and ablution and thus becomes building strong upon weak. There is no difference in the validity of following a person in dry ablution in funeral prayer.

2. Person who has washed with a person who has wiped

This is whether the wiping is on footgear, bandage, or plaster of an injury that does not seep through.

3. Standing person with a sitting person

This is valid because the Prophet, upon him be peace and blessings, prayed noon on Saturday or Sunday in his dyingl sickness sitting whilst the people behind him were standing. This was the last prayer that he prayed as imam. He prayed the second unit of sunrise on the Monday behind Abu Bakr as a follower and then completed it for himself – Bayhaqi mentioned this in *M'arifa*.

4. With a hunchback

If his curve has not reached the extent of bowing it is valid by agreement, according to the correct position. If, however, it has reached and he lowers slightly for bowing it is valid with them both. Most scholars have taken this and it is the most correct because it is of the degree of following a sitting person due to his lower half being level. With Muhammad it is not valid – Zayla'i said that *Thahiriyya* mentioned that it is the most correct position. Thus, there is a difference in authentication of it.

5. Person motioning with someone similar

This, for example, is if they are both sitting, reclining or the follower reclining and the imam sitting because of the strength of his state.

6. Person praying an optional prayer with a person praying an obligatory prayer

This is valid because it is building weak on strong and he has become a follower of his imam in reciting.

If the invalidity of the imam's prayer becomes apparent by the absence of a condition or integral, it is obligatory that he repeats the obligatory prayer because of his statement, upon him be peace and blessings,

"When the prayer of the imam invalidates the prayer of those behind him invalidates." This does not mean repeating to repair a fault in that which has been performed. However, if an invalidator arises there is no repeating upon the follower such as the imam apostatising, leaving for Friday prayer after his noon without them, or returning for a recitation prostration after they have left.

The imam whose prayer is invalid is required to inform the worshippers to repeat their prayer as much as he is able, even if it be through a letter or messenger, according to the chosen position. This is because *he, upon him be peace and blessings, prayed with them, then came with his head dripping, and repeated with them.*[328] Also, *'Ali, Allah be pleased with him, prayed with the people after which it became clear to him that he was ritually impure. He repeated and ordered them to repeat.*[329] *Diraya* states that the imam does not have to inform if they are unspecified. *Khizana Akmal* states that it is because he remained silent over an excused mistake. *Wabari* mentions that he informs them even if it is disagreed upon. A similar case is if a person sees someone performing ablution with impure water or with an impurity on his garment.

---

[328] This is recorded by Abu Dawud 233 to 235 and Daraqutni 1346 to 1348.
[329] This is recorded by Daraqutni 1355.

Section 11 – Leaving Group Prayer

Group prayer is left for one of eighteen reasons.

1. Heavy rain

2. Heavy hailstone

3. Fear of an oppressor

4. Intense darkness

This is according to the correct position.

5. Imprisonment

This is imprisonment of a poor or oppressed person.

6. Blindness

7. Paralysis

8. Amputated hand or foot

9. Sickness

10. Disability

11. Heavy mud

This is after the rain has stopped. He, upon him be peace and blessings, said, *"If sandals are soaked, prayer is at home."*

12. Chronic illness

13. Old age

14. Revising legal studies

This does not apply to Arabic grammar and language and is if he does not regularly leave the group prayer.

15. Being in the presence of food or drink that one wants to have

This is because his mind will be preoccupied as is the case with holding back one of the two filths or wind.

16. Leaving for a journey

This for a journey he has prepared for.

17. Taking care of a sick person

This is if the sick person would be harmed by his absence.

18. Severe winds at night but not during the day

This is because of the difficulty.

If he leaves the group prayer due to any legitimising excuse whilst he intended to be present had it not been for the excuse, he attains its reward because of his statement, upon him be peace and blessings, *"Actions are only by intentions and each person only has that which he intended."*[330]

---

[330] This is recorded by Bukhari 1, 54, 3898, 5070 and 6953; Muslim 4967 and 4968; Abu Dawud 2201; Tirmidhi 1647; Nasa'i 75, 3467 and 3825; and ibn Majah 4227.

Section 12 – The Best to Lead the Prayer and the Order of the Rows

If worshippers gather and the resident of the house in which they have gathered, the local imam, or a person in authority, e.g. a leader, governor, or judge are not present, the following order is maintained to determine the best person to lead the prayer is as follows.

1. The most learned in the rules of prayer who has memorised the sunnas of reciting and avoids open indecency even if he is not deeply learned in other sciences

However, if they gather the authority is preferred, followed by the leader, the judge, and finally the resident of the house. The resident is preferred to the landlord and the judge is preferred to the mosque imam because of the tradition, *"The man is not lead in prayer in his authority nor is his bed sat on in his house without his permission."*[331]

2. The best reciter

This is the one who is most learned in the rules of reciting and not merely memorising the most without it.

3. The most godly

Godliness is to avoid doubtful matters and is higher than piety which is to avoid prohibited matters.

4. The eldest

---

[331] This is recorded by Muslim 1532 to 1535; Abu Dawud 582 to 584; Tirmidhi 235; Nasa'i 781 and 784; and ibn Majah 980.

This is because of his statement, upon him be peace and blessings, *"The eldest of you should lead you."*[332]

5. The best character

Character is having friendship and love towards people.

6. The best looking

This is the most radiant because a radiant form indicates a radiant inner. This increases the desire of people for the group prayer.

7. The noblest lineage

This is because of the respect and honour due.

8. The best voice

This is so that people desire listening to it for humility.

9. The cleanest garment

This is because he is distant from impurities making desirous for it.

After these, the following are considered.

- the person with the best wife because of his stronger modesty
- the largest head
- the smallest limb
- the most wealth
- the best stature

---

[332] This is recorded by Bukhari 628, 631 and 685; Muslim 1535 to 1539; Abu Dawud 589; Nasa'i 635; and ibn Majah 979.

If they are equal, lots are drawn between them and whoever's lot is drawn leads, or the choice is with the worshippers. If they differ consideration is for the one who the majority choose.

If other than the preferred person leads they have done bad but have not sinned, as mentioned in *Tajnis*. It also mentions that if a person leads a group who dislike him there are three possibilities. If they dislike because of faults in him or because another person is more worthy of leading than him, it is offensive. However, if he is more worthy and there is no fault in him yet they still dislike him, it is not offensive for him to lead because the ignorant person and the immoral person dislike the righteous person and the scholar. The Prophet, upon him be peace and blessings, said, *"If it pleases you that your prayer be accepted, your scholars should lead you because they are your delegates between you and your Lord"*[333] – in one narration, *"the best of you should lead you."*

The leading of the following is offensive.

1. **Slave**

This is offensive if he is not a pious scholar.

2. **Blind**

This is offensive because he is unable to direct himself towards the direction of prayer and is unable to safeguard his garment from impurities. However, if none better than him is available there is no offence.

3. **Bedouin**

It is offensive for an ignorant Bedouin and for an ignorant city dweller.

---

[333] This is mentioned in *I'la Sunan* who mentions that Tabarani narrated it.

4. Ignorant illegitimate person

This is offensive if he has no knowledge or piety. This is why this, and the previous categories, has been qualified by the phrase "ignorant". Thus, if he is a learned pious person his leading is not offensive because the offence is due to deficiencies. Therefore, if the Bedouin is better than the city dweller, the slave better than the freeman, the illegitimate person better than the legitimate person, and the blind person better than the sighted person, the rule is reversed, as is mentioned in *Ikhtiyar*.

5. Immoral person

This is offensive if he is a scholar because of his lack of concern for the religion. Hence, it is necessary that he be humiliated in Sacred Law and should not be honoured by him leading the prayer. If it is not possible to prevent him, he should move from him to other than his mosque for Friday prayer and other than it. If he is the only one who performs Friday prayer, it is prayed with him.

6. Innovator

The innovator is the one who practices that which he has introduced against the truth that has been received from the Prophet, upon him be peace and blessings, whether knowledge, action, or state by a type of doubt or hidden analogy. Muhammad has narrated from Abu Hanifa, Allah be pleased with him, and Abu Yusuf that prayer behind people of desires is not permitted. However, the correct position is that it is valid with offence behind a person whose innovation does not excommunicate him because of his statement, upon him be peace and blessings, *"Pray behind every righteous person and sinner, pray on every righteous person and sinner, and fight with every righteous person and sinner"*[334], as

---

[334] This is recorded by Daraqutni 1750.

mentioned in *Burhan*. *Majm'a Riwayat* mentions that when a person prays behind an immoral person or an innovator, he attains the reward of the group prayer but he does not attain the reward of the person who prays behind a pious person.

Lengthening the prayer is offensive because it repels from the group prayer and because of his statement, upon him be peace and blessings, *"Whoever leads should lighten."*[335]

The group prayer of naked people is offensive because it can reveal some of their nakedness. Group prayer of women is offensive with one of them. They do not attend group prayer because of the tribulation and disobedience in it. However, if they do, it is necessary that the imam[336] stands at their centre[337] with her heel protruding. If she stands ahead like men, she is sinful and her prayer is valid. Likewise, the naked imam is at the centre of the naked group but sits. The best is for each one of them to stretch his legs so that he is concealed as much as possible, whilst praying by motions.

A single person, whether a man or a discerning child, stands on the right of the imam, whilst parallel to him and behind him with his heels. It is offensive to stand on his left or behind him, according to the correct position, because of the tradition of ibn Abbas *that he stood on the left of the Prophet, upon him be peace and blessings, who then positioned him on his right.*[338] If there is more than one person, they stand behind him because *he, upon him be peace and blessings, stood ahead of Anas and the orphan when he prayed with them.*[339] This is a

---

[335] This is recorded by Bukhari 90 and Muslim 1044 to 1051.

[336] Imam is anyone who is followed whether male or female – Maraqi Falah.

[337] *Wasat* is between the two sides of a thing, as here. *Wast* is a part of something being clear from the rest of it, such as, "I sat at the centre of the house". Maraqi Falah

[338] This is recorded by Abu Dawud 610 and 611.

[339] This is recorded by Bukhari 380; Muslim 1499; Abu Dawud 612; Tirmidhi 234; and Nasa'i 802

proof of the best whereas the narration of standing between them[340] is a proof of permissibility.

Men form a row because of his statement, upon him be peace and blessings, *"The intelligent adults from you should be next to me."*[341] Thus, the imam should instruct them to do so. The Prophet, upon him be peace and blessings, also said, *"Be straight so that your hearts be together, and touch each other so that you will be merciful to each other."* He, upon him be peace and blessings, also said, *"Straighten the rows, align the shoulders, fill the gaps, and soften with the hands of your brethren. Do not leave gaps for the Devil. Whoever connects a row, Allah connects him and whoever disrupts a row, Allah disrupts him."*[342]

By this the ignorance of the one who remains firm when a person enters at his side in the row believing it to be showing off is known. In fact, it is assistance in that which the Prophet, upon him be peace and blessings, instructed. If he finds a gap in the first row and not in the second, he should cut across it because they have not filled the first. If the row is orderly, he waits for another person to come. If, however, he fears missing a unit, he draws back a person learned in the rule who will not be harmed by it, otherwise he stands by himself. This refutes the statement that the one who makes space for a person entering by his side is invalid.

The best row is the first, then the nearest and those after it because it is narrated that Allah sends down His mercy first on the imam which then passes from him to those parallel to him in the first row, and then to the right, then to the left, and then to the second row. It is also narrated from him, upon him be peace and blessings, that he said, *"One hundred prayers are recorded for the one who prays behind the imam parallel to him, seventy five prayers for those on the right side, fifty prayers*

---

[340] This is reference to Abu Dawud 613 who records *that Abdullah ibn Mas'ud prayed between 'Alqama and Aswad and then said, "I saw the Prophet, upon him be peace and blessings, do the same."*
[341] This is recorded by Muslim 972 to 974; Abu Dawud 674; and Tirmidhi 228.
[342] This is recorded by Abu Dawud 666.

for those on the left, and twenty five prayers for those in the remaining rows."

Children then form a row because of the statement of Abu Malik Ash'ari that *the Prophet, upon him be peace and blessings, prayed positioning the men behind him, the children behind them, and the women behind them.*[343] If there is not a group of children, the child stands with the men.

Problematic hermaphrodites then form a row, out of caution, because if he is a man his standing behind the children does not harm him and if he is a woman he is behind. It is necessary to have hermaphrodites as one split up row thereby avoiding standing behind someone similar and from being parallel because of the possibility of masculinity and femininity – this is acting by the most harmful in his states.

Women then form a row if they attend, otherwise they are prohibited from attending group prayer, as has preceded.

---

[343] This is mentioned in *Nasb Raya* who mentions that Imam Ahmad, ibn Abi Shayba, and Tabarani have recorded it.

Section 13 – Latecomer Prayer

If the imam utters salaams or speaks before the follower completes reciting the testification, he completes it because it is from the necessary components. He then utters salaam because the sanctity of the prayer remains and it is possible for him to combine by doing them both. If, however, the blessings and supplications remain, he leaves them and utters salaams with the imam because leaving a sunna component is lesser than leaving a necessary component.

However, if the imam breaks ablution intentionally even by his loud laughter at uttering salaams, the follower does not recite the testification nor does he utter salaams because he has left prayer by the part that was affected by the ritual impurity of the imam being invalid. Thus, he does not build on invalidity. It does not harm the validity of the prayer but repeating it is necessary to repair its shortcoming of leaving the salaams. If he does not sit the extent of the testification, it is invalid by intentional ritual impurity.

If the imam stands to the third and the follower has not completed the testification, he completes it. If he does not complete it, it is permitted. *Fatawa Fadhli* and *Tajnis* mention that he completes it and does not follow the imam even if he fears missing the bowing because reciting part of the testification is not known as a devotional act and he will not actually miss the bowing because it is caught – thus he is behind the imam. Furthermore, clash of another necessary component does not prevent doing the one he is in from another necessary component because he will do it after it. Thus, delaying one of two necessary components whilst doing both of them is better than leaving one of them completely as opposed to a sunna component opposing it because leaving a sunna component is better than delaying a necessary component.

If the imam raises his head before the follower glorifies thrice in bowing and prostration, he follows him, according to the correct position. There are those who say that he completes it thrice because one of the people of knowledge said that prayer is not permitted by having it less than three.

If the imam adds a prostration or stands after the final sitting forgetfully, the follower does not follow him in that which is not from his prayer but waits. If the imam returns before adding a prostration on to the additional unit, he utters salaams with him. If he sits from his standing, he utters salaams with him. If the imam adds a prostration on to the additional unit, the follower utters salaams alone and does not wait for him because he has gone into other than his prayer. If the imam stands before the final sitting forgetfully, the follower waits for him and glorifies so that his imam is notified. If the follower utters salaams before his imam has added a prostration on to the additional unit, his obligatory prayer is invalid because the integral of sitting was performed alone whilst in the state of following. Likewise, it is invalid by the imam adding a prostration on to the additional unit because he has left the final sitting from its place.

The salaam of the follower is offensive after the testification of the imam, because of the presence of the sitting, before his salaam, because of leaving his following. His prayer, however, is valid such that it is not invalid by the sun rising at sunrise or the presence of water for the person who has performed dry ablution. The prayer of the imam is invalid, according to the less favourable position, but, according to the correct position it is valid, as we shall mention.

Section 14 – Remembrances after the Obligatory Prayer

It is sunna to stand to perform the sunnas that follow and are connected to the obligatory prayer. However, it is recommended to separate between them as *he, upon him be peace and blessings, when uttering salaam would remain for the extent of saying, "Allah, You are peace, from You is peace, and to You returns peace. You are exalted through Yourself above all else, O You of Majesty and Beneficence."*[344] He then stands for the sunna. Kamal said that this is the remembrance from which the sunnas are delayed that has been established from him, upon him be peace and blessings, and with it he separates between them and the obligatory prayer. I say that perhaps what is meant is other than that which has also been established after sunset whilst his legs were folded "There is no god except Allah … " and after Friday reciting al-Fatiha and the protectors seven times each.

Kamal mentions from Shams Aimma Halawani who said that there is no problem in reciting litanies between the obligatory prayer and sunna. Therefore, it is better to delay the litanies after the sunna by which offence is negated. This opposes that which is mentioned in *Ikhtiyar* that it is offensive to sit after it and supplicate for every prayer that is followed by a sunna. In fact, he should perform the sunna so that he does not separate between the sunna and the prescribed prayer. It is narrated from 'Aisha *that the Prophet, upon him be peace and blessings, used to sit for the extent of saying, "Allah, You are peace …"*, as has preceded. Thus, he does not increase on it or on its amount. Kamal then said that separating with the remembrances that are regularly practised in mosques in our time by reciting the chair verse, glorifications and its sisters thirty three times, and other than these is not established from him, upon him be peace and blessings. His statement, upon him be peace and blessings, to the poor migrants

---

[344] This is recorded by Muslim 1334 to 1337; Abu Dawud 1512; Tirmidhi 298 to 299; Nasa'i 1338 to 1339; and ibn Majah 924 and 928.

"*glorify, utter takbir, and praise after each prayer ...* "[345] does not necessitate that they be connected to the obligatory prayer but that they be after the sunna without doing anything that is unconnected to the prayer. By this, it is valid to be considered after it. We have indicated that if he talks excessively, eats, or drinks between the obligatory prayer and the sunna, it is not invalid but its reward decreases – this is the most correct position.

It is best to perform sunnas in any manner that is most distant from showing off and focuses sincerity the most, whether at home or elsewhere.

It is recommended that the imam, after his salaam, turn to the right of the direction of prayer for the optional prayer that follows the obligatory prayer. This is the direction opposite to his right, i.e. the right of the person facing the direction of prayer, because the right of the opposing direction is the left of the person facing the direction of prayer. This is because the right has virtue, so that it will remove any confusion by imagining that he is in the obligatory prayer – likewise for the worshippers[346] – and thus following him, and to increase his witnesses because it is narrated that the place of the worshipper testifies for him on Judgement Day.

It is recommended that he turns around and faces the people if he wishes after the optional prayer and after the obligatory prayer that has no optional prayer after it as long as there is no worshipper in facing him. This is because of that which is in the two authentic collections that *"the Prophet, upon him be peace and blessings, when he prayed would turn towards us with his face."*[347] If the imam wishes he turns from his left and has the direction of prayer on his right and if he wishes he turns from his right and has the direction of prayer on his left. This is

---

[345] This is recorded by Bukhari 843; Muslim 1347 to 1348; Abu Dawud 1504; and ibn Majah 927.
[346] This links to his statement, "it is recommended that the imam ..." Tahtawi
[347] This is recorded by Bukhari 845 and Muslim 5937.

better because of that which is in Muslim, *"When we prayed behind the Messenger of Allah, upon him be peace and blessings, we would love to be on his right so that he would turn towards us with his face."*[348] If he wishes he leaves for his needs. He, Exalted is He, says, *"And when the prayer is ended, then disperse in the land and seek of Allah's favour"*[349] – the order is for permissibility. *Majm'a Riwayat* mentions that when he finishes his prayer, if he wishes, he reads his litany sitting and if he wishes, he reads it standing.

They ask forgiveness of Allah who is exalted above all limitations thrice because of the statement of Thawban, *"The Messenger of Allah, upon him be peace and blessings, would on completing his prayer ask forgiveness of Allah, Exalted is He, thrice and say, "Allah, You are peace and from You is peace. You are exalted through Yourself above all else, O You of Majesty and Beneficence.""* – Muslim narrated it.[350] He, upon him be peace and blessings, said, *"Whoever asks forgiveness of Allah, Exalted is He, after each prayer thrice by saying, "I ask forgiveness of Allah besides whom there is no god, the Living, the Sustainer, and I turn to Him", his sins are forgiven even if he is fleeing from battle."*[351]

They then recite the chair verse because of the statement of the Prophet, upon him be blessings peace and blessings, *"Whoever recites the chair verse after every prayer only death prevents him from entering Heaven. Whoever recites it on laying down Allah will secure his home, his neighbour's home, and the people of the surrounding homes."*
They then recite the protectors because of the statement of 'Uqba ibn 'Amir, Allah be pleased with him, *"The Messenger of Allah, upon him be peace and blessings, instructed me to recite the protectors after each prayer."*[352]

---

[348] This is recorded by Muslim 1642.
[349] al-Jumu'ah, verse 10.
[350] This is recorded by Muslim 1334.
[351] This is recorded by Abu Dawud 1517.
[352] This is recorded by Abu Dawud 1523; Tirmidhi 2903; and Nasa'i 1337.

They then glorify Allah thirty three times, praise Him likewise thirty three times, and utter takbir likewise thirty three times. They then utter, to complete the hundred, "There is no god but Allah, alone, without partner. His is the dominion, His is the praise and He has power over all things." This is because of his statement, upon him be peace and blessings, *"Whoever glorifies Allah after each prayer thirty three times, praises Allah, Exalted is He, thirty three times, and utters takbir thirty three times that is ninety nine – he then said – the complete hundred is, "There is no god but Allah, alone, without partner. His is the dominion, His is the praise and He has power over all things." his sins will be forgiven even if they are like sea foam."* – Muslim narrated it.[353] The tradition of the poor migrants that we have previously mentioned is an indication the same.

They then supplicate for themselves and the Muslims with the transmitted comprehensive supplications because of the statement of Abu Umama, *"It was said, "Messenger of Allah, which supplication is most heard?" He said, "The middle of the night end and after the prescribed prayers.""*[354] The Prophet, upon him be peace and blessings, also said, *"Mu'adh, by Allah, I love you. I advise you, Mu'adh, not to leave after every prayer to say, "Allah, assist me in your remembrance, your thanks, and worshipping you well.""*[355] Whilst supplicating they raise their hands parallel to their chests with their palms next to their faces with humility and tranquillity. They then conclude with His statement, Exalted is He, *"Transcendent is your Lord, the Lord of Might beyond that they describe"*[356] because of the statement of 'Ali, Allah be pleased with him, *"Whoever loves to take the most complete allocation of reward on Judgement Day should have his final words on leaving his gathering, "Transcendent is your Lord"."* The Messenger of Allah, upon him be peace and blessings, also said, *"Whoever says after every prayer, "Transcendent is your Lord" thrice has taken the most complete allocation*

---

[353] This is recorded by Muslim 1352 to 1353.
[354] This is recorded by Tirmidhi 3499.
[355] This is recorded by Abu Dawud 1522.
[356] as-Safat, 180.

of reward." They then wipe their faces with their hands at the end of it because of his statement, upon him be peace and blessings, *"When you supplicate to Allah, supplicate with your palms and do not supplicate with the back of them. When you have finished, wipe your face with them."*[357] *He, upon him be peace and blessings, on raising his hands in supplication would not lower them – and in a narration, he would not return them – until he had wiped his face with them."*[358]

Allah, Exalted is He, is the facilitator.

---

[357] This is recorded by Abu Dawud 1485 and ibn Majah 3866.
[358] This is recorded by Tirmidhi 3386.

Section 15 – Invalidators[359] of Prayer

There are sixty eight invalidators, which he has mentioned by number to be approximate and not to be precise.

1,2. A word even if it he utters it forgetfully or mistakenly

A word invalidates even if it is not beneficial such as, "O". It invalidates if he utters it forgetfully believing himself not to be in prayer or having uttered it mistakenly such as intending to say, "O, People" but instead saying, "O, Zayd". It invalidates even if he is ignorant of it being an invalidator and even if he is sleeping, according to the chosen position. This is because of his statement, upon him be blessings and peace, *"This prayer, no human speech is suited to be in it"*[360]. Minimal movement is exempted because of the inability to avoid it.

3. Supplication with that which resembles our speech

This is, for example, "Allah, clothe me in such and such a garment", "feed me such and such", "clear my debt", or "grant me such and such a woman", according to the correct position. These invalidate because it is possible to obtain them from slaves, as opposed to his statement, "Allah, grant me well being, pardon me, and sustain me."

4. Salaam with the intention of greetings even if it forgetfully

This invalidates even if he does not say, "upon you" and even if it is forgetfully, because it is communication.

---

[359] Invalid is the opposite of rectified. In worship invalid and nullified are the same but in transactions such as sale are different

[360] This is recorded as part of long traditions by Muslim 1199; Abu Dawud 930; and Nasa'i 1219, and the wording is that of Muslim and Nasa'i.

5, 6. Replying to salaams verbally or by shaking hands

Verbally invalidates because it is human speech and shaking hands invalidates because it has the meaning of speech.

7. Excessive movement

Minimal movement does not invalidate. The separator is that excessive is that which an observer has no doubt that the person is not in prayer, but if it is unclear, it is minimal, according to the most correct position. Other than this has also been said in explaining it, such as three consecutive movements is excessive and less than it is minimal.

Raising the hands on desiring to bow is offensive but raising, with us, does not invalidate, according to the correct position.

8. Turning the chest away from the direction of prayer

This is because he has left the obligation of direction except due to ritual impurity escaping or formation of rows as protection facing the enemy during fear prayer.

9. Eating something from outside of his mouth even if it is small

This is, for example, a sesame seed, because of the possibility of avoiding it.

10. Eating that which is between his teeth whilst being the size of a chickpea

This invalidates if it is large such as the size of a chickpea even if it is with minimal movement, because of the possibility of avoiding it, as opposed to a small amount with minimal movement which follows his saliva. If it is with excessive movement, it is invalid by the movement.

11. Drinking

This invalidates because it negates prayer. If he raises his head to the sky and a hailstone or a raindrop falls into his mouth which then reaches his stomach, his prayer is invalid.

12. Clearing the throat without an excuse

This invalidates because it contains letters. If it is due to an excuse such as phlegm that prevents him from reciting, it does not invalidate.

13. Grumbling

This is such as blowing soil away and annoyance.

14. Groaning

This is *ah* with a *sukun* on the *ha*, shortened on the form *d'a*.

15. Sighing

This is to say, *"uwwah"*. There are many variations such as elongation, without elongation with stress on the *waw* with *fatha*, and the *ha* with *sukun* and with *kasra*.

16,17. Crying loudly due to pain or misfortune but not due to mention of Heaven or Hellfire

This is by letters being heard. The qualification "due to pain on his body or misfortune due to losing a loved one or wealth" applies to groaning onwards because it has the meaning of speech. It is not invalid by mention of Heaven and Hellfire, by agreement, because they indicate humility.

18. Responding[361] to someone having sneezed by saying "Allah have mercy on you"

This invalidates with them both, as opposed to Abu Yusuf.

19. Replying to an inquirer about a partner for Allah, Glory be to Him, with "There is no god but Allah"

This is a person asking, "Is there another god with Allah?" and the worshipper replies, "There is no god but Allah". This invalidates with them both, as opposed to Abu Yusuf who says that it is praise that does not alter by his determination. They both say that it has become a reply, thus he is speaking with something that negates.

20. Replying to an inquirer about bad news with, "We belong to Allah, and surely to Him we shall return"

21. Replying to an inquirer about happy news with, "Praise is to Allah"

22, 23. Replying to an inquirer about strange news with, "There is no god but Allah" or "Glory be to Allah"

24. Anything from the Koran by which he intended a response

Examples include
- "O John! Hold fast to the Book!"[362] for a person seeking a book or something similar

---

[361] *Tashmit* with a *shin* is more eloquent than with a *sin* which is a supplication for goodness – Maraqi Falah.
[362] Maryam, verse 12.

- "Bring us our breakfast"[363] for an inquirer about bringing something
- "These are the limits set by Allah"[364], prohibiting a person who has asked permission to take something

If he does not intend a reply by it but intending to inform that he is in prayer, it does not invalidate by agreement.

25. A person in dry ablution seeing water

Likewise, it is invalid for a person following him with the imam not having seen it. It invalidates if he is able to use it before him sitting the extent of the testification, as we shall qualify in the coming legal issues. It is also invalid by the cessation of any excuse that legitimises dry ablution.

26. Completion of the time period for the person wiping on footgear

Clarification of this has preceded.

27. Removal of the footgear

This invalidates even if it is with minimal movement because of its presence before the final sitting the extent of the testification.

28. An illiterate[365] person learning a verse

This is if he is not following a reciter whether he learnt it by receiving it or remembering it.

---

[363] al-Kahf, verse 62.

[364] al-Baqarah, verse 229. This phrase also occurs in other Koranic verses.

[365] Ummi is an attachment to the Arab nation that was devoid of knowledge and writing being like a newborn child – Maraqi Falah.

29. A naked person finding covering

Prayer is required of him in it. This removes completely impure covering and that which the owner does not permit.

30. A person motioning being able to bow and prostrate

This is because of the strength of the remainder. Thus it is not built on weak.

31. Remembering a missed prayer for the person of order

The invalidity is suspended. If he prays five whilst being aware of the missed prayer and makes it up before the time for the fifth leaves, the description of that which he prayed is invalid and it becomes optional. If, however, he has not made it up until the time for the fifth had left, it is valid and its invalidity is lifted.

32. Substitution with a person not eligible to be an imam

This is, for example, an illiterate and an excused person.

33. Sunrise at dawn

This is because of the arrival of that which is incomplete on that which is complete.

34. Passing of the sun from its zenith for the two 'Eid prayers

35. Entrance of midafternoon time for Friday prayer

This is because the condition of validity is missed, being the time.

36. Splint coming off having healed

This is because of the appearance of the previous ritual impurity.

37. Cessation of the excuse of the excused person

This is ceasing by a nullifier. Its cessation is known by a complete time being free of it.

38, 39. Ritual impurity intentionally or by the action of something else

Ritual impurity intentionally, i.e. not escaping from him, invalidates, because with it he builds. The action of something else is like a date falling and causing him to bleed.

40. Unconsciousness

41. Insanity

42, 43. Sexual impurity that has occurred by looking or by a wet dream from a firmly seated sleeping person

44. Standing parallel to a desirable woman in a complete prayer, combining prohibiting, in one place, without a barrier, with the imam having intended to lead her

The following conditions apply
- a desirable woman even if she is nonmarriageable for him or a wife who is desired even in the past, such as a disfigured old woman
- standing parallel if it is with her shin and ankle, according to the most correct position
- for the performance of an integral with Muhammad or its length with Abu Yusuf
- in a complete prayer, even if it is by motions — funeral prayer is not invalid because there is no prostration in it

- combining prohibiting by them both following an imam or her following him
- in one place, even legally by her standing on something less than a fathom[366]
- without a barrier the size of an arm length or a gap the extent of a man
- him not indicating to her to move back – if she does not move back by his indication, her prayer and not his prayer is invalid; furthermore, he is not required to step ahead of her because of its offence
- the imam having intended to lead her – if he did not intend her, she is not in prayer thereby standing parallel being negated

45. **The appearance of the nakedness of a person from whom ritual impurity escaped, according to primary narration, even if he is compelled to do so for purity**

Examples include a woman uncovering her forearm for ablution or a man uncovering nakedness after ritual impurity escaping, according to the correct position.

46. **His reciting, going and returning for ablution**

This is the recitation of a person for whom ritual impurity has escaped whilst going for ablution or returning to complete prayer because he has performed an integral with ritual impurity, or walking going and returning. Reciting glorifications does not invalidate, according to the most correct position.

47. **His remaining for the length of the performance of an integral after ritual impurity escaping in a waking state**

---

[366] This is the height of an average person, i.e. approximately 6ft.

This is if there is no excuse. Thus, if he remains due to congestion, for his nosebleed to stop, or due to a firmly seated sleep in which he had a nosebleed, he builds. He raises his head from the bow or prostration in which ritual impurity escaped with the intention of purification and not with the intention of completing the integral thereby avoiding invalidation by it. He places his hand on his nose as concealment.

48. His passing water near him for other than it

This invalidates if it is more than two rows and intentionally with the presence of a tool. He can pierce a bucket, open a door, repeating washing, the sunnas of purity, according to the most correct position, purifying his garment from his ritual impurity, and removing impurity from it.

49. His leaving the mosque believing ritual impurity

This is because of the presence of a negator without an excuse, but not if he does not leave the mosque. Likewise, it is invalid if he leaves the residence, the house, the graveyard, or the 'Eid prayer place, by juristic preference, with the intention of rectification.

50. His passing rows or his barrier in other than the mosque

This is that which has its ruling, as we have mentioned, which is the desert. If there is no row in front of him or he prays individually and there is no barrier in front of him, the extent of his place of prostration is overlooked for him form all sides, according to the correct position. This invalidates if he believes ritual impurity escaped whilst it was not the case, such as if water leaked from a man's nose believing it to be blood whereupon his prayer is invalid.

Likewise, it is invalid if he does not return to his imam whilst he is still in it. If he has finished it, he has the choice to either complete it at his place or return – they differ over the best.

51. His leaving his place believing that he is not in ablution

52. that the time period of his wiping has passed

53, 54. that he has a missed prayer on him, or that there is an impurity on him even if he does not leave the mosque or something similar

This is because he has turned away by leaving it and not for rectification – this being the difference between it and believing ritual impurity to have escaped.

You now are aware by that which we have mentioned the conditions of building due to uncontrollable ritual impurity escaping, thus removing the need to have a separate section.

The best is restarting, thereby removing from the difference and acting upon the consensus.

55. Correcting other than his imam

This is because he is educating without necessity. Correcting his own imam is permitted even if he has recited the obligatory amount or moved to another verse, according to the correct position, to rectify their prayer.

56. Uttering takbir with the intention of moving to a prayer other than his prayer

This is because he has obtained that which he intended and he has left that which he was in. This is like an individual who intends following or the opposite, or like a person moves by the takbir from one obligatory prayer to another obligatory prayer, an optional prayer, or the opposite, with its intention.

We have indicated that if he utters takbir intending to restart the very prayer he is in without pronouncing the intention, it is not invalid, unless he is a latecomer because of the difference between the rule of the individual and the latecomer. If that which has passed does not invalidate, he is required to sit at that which is the end of his prayer. If he leaves it relying on that which he believed, his prayer is invalid. However, sitting at the end of that which he believed he began with does not invalidate it.

In it is also an indication that a person making up a missed fast, if he intends after beginning it to begin in another fast, it does not harm.

The invalidity of that which has been mentioned is qualified by them happening before the final sitting the length of the testification, whereupon it is invalid by agreement. However, if the negator happens just before the salaam but after sitting the length of the testification, the chosen position is the validity of the prayer because leaving it by the action of the worshipper is necessary, according to the correct position. It is also said that it is invalid based on that which is said that it is obligatory with the Imam. There is no text from the Imam, rather it is the deduction of Abu Sa'id Birda'i from the twelve points because the Imam, when he said that the invalidity of prayer is only by leaving an obligatory component and only leaving by an action is left, he judged that it is obligatory due to that. With them both it is not obligatory because if it was the case, it would have been specified as with a devotional act but it has not been specified because of the validity of the leaving by speech and intentional ritual impurity. This indicates that it is necessary and not obligatory. If these occurrences happen with no obligatory component left, it has become the same as after the salaam. Karkhi deemed Birda'i to be incorrect in his deduction because of the absence of specification of that which is a devotional act, being the salaam. The basis of it is the presence of an alternator. However this requires further research.

57. Elongating the *hamza* in the takbir

We have already discussed this.

58. Reciting that which he has not memorised from a copy of the Koran

This is even if he is not holding it because he is receiving from another person. However, if he has memorised it and he is not carrying it, it is not invalid because of the absence of movement and receiving.

59, 60. Performance of an integral or the possibility with the nakedness exposed or with a preventative impurity

Performance of an integral such as the bow or the time passing in which an integral could be performed invalidates because of the presence of a negator. If he pushes away the impurity the moment it touches and there is no trace of it or he covers his nakedness the moment it is uncovered, it does not harm him.

61. The follower preceding by an integral that the imam has not performed with him

This, for example, is if he bows and raises his head before the imam without repeating it with him or after him, and uttering salaam. If he does not utter salaams with the imam and precedes him with in the bow and the prostration in each unit, he makes up a unit without reciting because he has caught the beginning of the prayer of the imam, catching up whilst making up before the imam completes. However, he missed the first unit by leaving following the imam in the bow and the prostration. Thus, his bow and prostration in the second is making up for the first, in the third for the second, and in the fourth for the third. He makes up after it a unit without reciting. The complete elaboration is in the original.

62. Following the imam in the forgetfulness prostration for the latecomer

This is if his separation has been emphasised by standing after the imam's salaam or before his sitting the length of testification and having added a prostration to his unit. The imam then remembers a forgetfulness prostration whereupon he follows him, thereby his prayer being invalid. His prayer is invalid because he followed after the presence of separation and it being necessary. We have qualified the latecomer standing by it being after the imam's sitting the length of testification because if it is before it, it does not suffice him since the imam still has an obligatory component on him where the latecomer does not become separate, thereby his prayer being invalid.

63. Not repeating the final sitting after performing a core or recitation prostration that he remembered after the final sitting

This is because the final sitting is only considered after the completion of the integrals. The final sitting is to conclude it and there is no contradiction, and the final sitting is lifted by the recitation prostration, according to the chosen position.

64. Not repeating an integral that he performed sleeping

This is because the condition for its validity is performing it waking, as has preceded.

65. Loud laughter of the imam of the latecomer even if he did
not intend it

66. Intentional ritual impurity

This is other than loud laughter. This and the previous point
invalidate if they are after the final sitting the length of the
testification with the Imam because of the invalidity of the part in
which it occurred. The same amount is invalid in the prayer of the
latecomer and thus building the missed part on it is not possible.

67. Uttering salaams after two units in other than a two unit
prayer, such as sunset and a four unit prayer for a resident,
believing that he is a traveller whilst he is a resident; that it
is Friday prayer; that it is tarawih whilst it is night prayer

68. or that he has recently become Muslim, or that he grew up
as an ignorant Muslim believing the obligatory prayer to be
two units for other than a two unit prayer

This is because it is an intentional salaam in a conclusive manner
before its time. Thus, the prayer is invalid.

Section 16 – That Which Does Not Invalidate the Prayer

If a person looked at something written and understood it, whether it is Koran or something else and whether he intended understanding or not, it is bad etiquette but his prayer is not invalid because he has not uttered speech.

If he eats that which is between his teeth which is less than a chickpea without excessive movement, it is offensive but does not invalidate because of the difficulty of avoiding it. If he swallows sugar that has melted in his mouth, it is invalid. If he swallows before prayer and finds its sweetness in it, it is not invalid.

If a person passes in his prostration place, it is not invalid, whether it is a woman, a dog, and a donkey because of his statement, upon him be blessings and peace, *"Nothing breaks the prayer and repel as much as you can, for indeed he is a devil"*[367]. The legally responsible passer-by is sinful because he has done it intentionally due to his statement, upon him be blessings and peace, *"If the passer-by in front of the worshipper knows what is on him, standing for fourty is better for him than passing in front of him"* [368] - the two Shaykhs have narrated it. The narration of Bazzar mentions *"fourty autumns"*. The offence is passing the prostration place, according to the most correct position, in a large

---

[367] This is recorded by Abu Dawud 719. In the next tradition, Abu Dawud records that a young Qurayshi man passed in front of Abu Sai'd Khudri, Allah be pleased with him, whilst praying who repelled him. He returned and he repelled him three times. When he had finished he said, "Nothing breaks the prayer but the Messenger of Allah, upon him be blessings and peace, said, "Repel as much as you can, for indeed he is a devil."" Abu Dawud then commented, "If two reports from the Prophet, upon him be blessings and peace, conflict, that which his companions after him acted upon is analysed."

[368] This is recorded by Bukhari 510; Muslim 1132; Abu Dawud 701; Tirmidhi 336; and Nasa'i 757. The narrations of Bukhari, Muslim, and Tirmidhi record that Abu Nadr, one of the narrators of this tradition commented, "I do not know whether he said fourty days, months, or years." However, the tradition of Bazzar in the text clarifies.

mosque and a desert, in a small mosque generally, and less than a fathom that he is praying on, but not beyond that in a street because of the restriction that it causes on passers-by.

Prayer is not invalid by looking at the private part of a divorced woman or an unrelated woman with desire, according to the chosen position, because it is minimal movement, even though taking back is affirmed by it. If he kisses her or touches her, his prayer is invalid because it has the meaning of sexual intercourse, and sexual intercourse is excessive movement. If she is praying and he penetrates between her thighs even if he does not ejaculate, kisses her even without desire, or touches her with desire, her prayer is invalid. If she kisses him but does not desire her, his prayer is not invalid.

Section 17 – Offensive Actions

Offensive is the opposite of beloved. If the prohibition is questionable, the offence is severe except due to something that changes it. If the proof is not a prohibition but indicates leaving that is not definitive, it is slight. Slight offence is closer to permissibility and severe offence is closer to prohibition. Prayer is necessarily repeated with it being valid for leaving a necessary component, but it is recommended to be repeated by leaving something else. *Tajnis* mentions that every prayer performed with offence is repeated but not in the offensive manner. The explanation of his statement, upon him be blessings and peace, *"After a prayer, the likes of it is not prayed"*[369] is prohibition of repeating due to whispers, and it does not cover repeating due to offence – Sadr Islam Bazdawi mentions it in *Jam'i Saghir*.

There are approximately seventy seven things that are offensive for a worshipper.

1, 2. Leaving a necessary component or a sunna intentionally

He started with this because it a universal principle that applies to many particulars. This includes leaving being motionless in the integrals and preceding the imam because of the threat in it according to that which is in the two authentic collections, *"Each one of you should fear when he raises his head before the imam that Allah makes his head the head of a donkey, or Allah makes his form the form of a donkey"*[370]. Likewise, it includes the hands passing the ears, having them beneath the shoulders, and covering the feet in prostration intentionally for men.

---

[369] This is mentioned by Zayla'i in *Nasb Raya*, 115 who catgeorised it as a raised strange tradition, and added that ibn Abu Shayba recorded it as a *mawquf* tradition from 'Umar ibn Khattab and 'Abdulla ibn Mas'ud.

[370] This is recorded by Bukhari 691; Muslim 963 to 965; Tirmidhi 582; Nasa'i 829; and ibn Majah 961.

3. Futile movement with his garment and his body

This is because it negates humility which is the soul of prayer. It is offensive because of His statement, Exalted is He, *"Successful indeed are the believers; who are humble in their prayers."*[371] and his statement, upon him be blessings and peace, *"Allah dislikes for you futile movement in prayer, obscene language in fast, and laughter at graveyards."* He, upon him be blessings and peace, saw a man stroking his beard in prayer whereupon he said, *"Had his heart been humble, his limbs would have been stilled."*[372] Futile movement is an action that has no benefit to it and no wisdom that necessitates it. The meaning of futile movement here is an action that is not from the actions of prayer because it negates it.

4. Arranging stones except for prostration once

Jabir ibn 'Abdullah said, *"I asked the Prophet, upon him be blessings and peace, about touching stones who said, "Once, and that you refrain from it is better for you than one hundred camels with dark black pupils.""*

5. Cracking the fingers

This is offensive even once and is cracking them or pulling them thereby producing sound because of his statement, upon him be blessings and peace, *"Do not crack your fingers whilst in prayer"*[373]

6. Interlocking them

---

[371] al-Mu'minun, 1and 2.

[372] This is the tradition of Abu Hurayra which Suyuti recorded in Jam'i Saghir 7447 and categorised it as weak.

[373] This is recorded by ibn Majah 965.

This is because of the statement of ibn 'Umar about it, *"That is the prayer of those who have incurred wrath."*

7. Clasping the waist

This is because it is prohibited in prayer.[374] According to the most famous and most correct interpretation it is placing his hand on his waist because it contains leaving the sunna of folding the hands and impersonating tyrants.

8. Turning with his neck

It is not offensive with his eyes. This is because of the statement of 'Aisha, Allah be pleased with her, *"I asked the Messenger of Allah, upon him be blessings and peace, about a man's turning in prayer. He said, "It is a seizing that the Devil seizes from the prayer of the slave.""*[375] – Bukhari narrates it, and his statement, upon him be blessings and peace, *"Allah still comes towards the slave whilst he is in his prayer as long as he does not turn away. If he turns away, he leaves him."*[376] It is offensive to spit unless he is compelled whereupon he takes it in his garment or spits it beneath his left foot if he is praying outside of the mosque because of that which is in Bukhari, *"When one of you stands for prayer, he should not spit in front of himself because he is conversing with Allah, Exalted is He, as long as he is at his place of prayer nor on his right because there are two angels on his right. He should spit on his left or under his feet."*[377] – in one narration, *"or under his left foot"*. The two authentic collections

---

[374] This is reference to the tradition of Abu Hurayra as recorded in Abu Dawud 947, "The Messenger of Allah prohibited clasping the waist in prayer". Abu Dawud adds, "meaning that he places his hands on his waist."

[375] This is recorded by Bukhari 751 and 3291; Abu Dawud 910; Tirmidhi 590; and Nasa'i 1197 to 1200.

[376] This is recorded by Abu Dawud 909 and Nasa'i 1196.

[377] This is recorded by Bukhari 416 and Muslim 1223 to 1230.

mention, *"Spitting in the mosque is a sin and its expiation is burying it."*[378]

9. Canine posture

This is placing his buttocks on the ground whilst erecting his knees because of the statement of Abu Hurayra, Allah be pleased with him, *"The Messenger of Allah, upon him be blessings and peace, prohibited me from pecking like a rooster, sitting like a dog, and turning around like a snake."*

10. Spreading out the forearms

This is because of the statement of 'Aisha, Allah be pleased with him, *"The Prophet, upon him be blessings and peace, prohibited the Satanic posture and that a man spreads out his forearms like a predatory animal."*[379] – Bukhari narrated it.

11. Folding his sleeves

This is because of the prohibition against it due to the harshness in it that negates humility.

12. Prayer in trousers or loincloth with the ability to wear a shirt

This is because of the neglect, laziness, and lack of etiquette that it contains. The recommended is for a man to pray in three garments, a loincloth, a shirt, and a turban, and for a woman in a shirt, a scarf, and a veil.

13. Replying to salaam by indicating

---

[378] This is recorded by Muslim 1231 to 1232.

[379] This is recorded by Muslim 1110 and Abu Dawud 783 as part of a long tradition.

This is because it has the meaning of salaam. *Dhakira* mentions that there is no problem for the worshipper to reply to the person speaking to him with his head – the report with it has come from 'Aisha, Allah be pleased with her. There is no problem for a man to speak to a worshipper – *"and the angels called to him as he stood praying in the retreat"*[380]

14. Sitting cross-legged without an excuse

This is because of leaving the sunna of sitting. It is not offensive out of it because the majority of the sitting of the Prophet, upon him be blessings and peace, was cross-legged, and likewise 'Umar ibn Khattab, Allah be pleased with him. Sitting cross-legged is inserting the shins in the thighs such that they become four.

15. Tying his hair

This is tying it on the nape or on the hand because he, upon him be blessings and peace, passed by a man praying with his hair tied whereupon he said, *"Leave your hair to prostrate with you."*

16. Tying the head with a handkerchief or folding his turban on his head whilst leaving the centre uncovered

It is also said that it is covering his face with his turban such that he covers his nose. This is because the Prophet, upon him be blessings and peace, prohibited *i'itijar* in prayer.

17. Gathering his garment

This is raising it in front of him or from behind him when he intends to prostrate. It is also said that it is to gather his garment and fasten it at his centre. This is because of the haughtiness in it that negates humility and because of his statement upon him be

---

[380] Al-'Imran, verse 39.

blessings and peace, *"I was ordered to prostrate on seven bones and not to gather hair or a garment"*[381] – agreed upon.

18. Draping

Draping is offensive out of arrogance and neglect, but with an excuse, it is not offensive. It is to place a garment on his head or his shoulder, or his shoulders alone and drape its sides without tying it. This is because of the statement of Abu Hurayra, Allah be pleased with him, that he, upon him be blessings and peace, prohibited draping and that a man covers his mouth.[382] Thus, veiling the lower face by covering the mouth and nose in prayer is offensive because it resembles the action of Zoroastrians during their worship of fire. There is no offence of draping outside of prayer.

19. Inserting in a garment such that he does not leave a hole from where he can bring out his hands

This is complete wrapping. The Messenger of Allah, upon him be blessings and peace, said, *"If one of you has two garments, he should pray in them. If he only has one garment, he should wear it. He should not wrap himself like Jews."*[383]

20. Having the garment under his right armpit and placing its both sides on his right shoulder

This is offensive as is the opposite because covering the shoulders is recommended in prayer. Thus, leaving it is slightly offensive without necessity.

21. Reciting in other than the state of standing

---

[381] Refer to footnote 263.

[382] This is recorded by Abu Dawud 643 and Tirmidhi 378. The tradition of Tirmidhi does not mention "and that a man covers his mouth".

[383] This is recorded by Abu Dawud 635.

This is, for example, completion of reciting during bowing. It is offensive to recite the prescribed remembrances during the movements after completing the movement because there are two faults which are leaving it from its place and attaining it in other than it.

22. Lengthening the first unit in every two units of an optional prayer

This is offensive unless it has been narrated from the Prophet, upon him be blessings and peace, or recorded from a companion, such as al-A'la, al-Kafirun, and al-Ikhlas in witr because in terms of recitation it is attached to optional prayers. Imam Abu Yusr said that it is not offensive because the matter of optional prayers is easier than obligatory prayers.

23. Lengthening the second unit over the first unit in all prayers

The offence is in lengthening by three or more verses but not in lengthening the third unit because it is beginning an optional prayer. It is offensive in obligatory prayers, by agreement, and in optional prayers, according to the most correct position, attaching them to obligatory prayers in that which specifying in facilitation has not been reported.

24. Repeating a chapter in one unit of an obligatory prayer

Likewise, it is offensive to repeat in two units, if he has memorised other than it and he intended it, because of the absence of narration. If he has not memorised it, it is necessary for him to recite it because of the necessity of attaching a chapter to al-Fatiha. If he forgets, he does not leave it because of his statement, upon him be peace and blessings, *"If you begin a chapter, recite it accordingly."* He has qualified it with obligatory prayer because repeating is not offensive in optional prayers due to its affair being wider. *He, upon him be blessings and peace, stood until dawn with one verse, repeating it in his night vigil.*[384] Furthermore, a group of the early Muslims used to spend their nights with a verse of punishment, a verse of mercy, a verse of hope, or a verse of fear.

25. Reciting a chapter before that which he had recited

Ibn Mas'ud, Allah be pleased with him, said, "Whoever recites the Koran inverted, he is inverted." The practice that has been established for educating children is only to facilitate memorisation with the short chapters. If he recites in the first unit *"Say, I take refuge with the Lord of men"* without intending, he repeats it in the second unit with there being no offence in it so as to avoid the offence of reciting inverted. If he concludes the Koran in the first unit, he recites from al-Baqarah in the second because of his statement, upon him be peace and blessings, *"The best of people is the person arriving and the person departing"*,[385] i.e. the person who concludes and the person who starts.

26. Separating it with one chapter between two chapters that he had recited in two units

This is because of the resemblance to preference and avoiding that it contains. Some have said that it is not offensive if the chapter is long just as if there were two brief chapters between them. Moving to a verse from its chapter is offensive even if he separates by a verse, and combining between two chapters that have chapters or a chapter between them. *Khulasa* mentions that this is not offensive in optional prayers.

27. Smelling scent

---

[384] This is recorded by Nasa'i 1011 and ibn Majah 1350.
[385] This is recorded by Tirmidhi 2948.

This is if it is intentional because it is not from the actions of prayer.

28. Fanning himself with his garment or a fan once or twice

This is because it negates humility even if it is minimal movement.

30, 31. Turning his fingers or toes from the direction of prayer in prostration or other than it

This is because of his statement, upon him be blessings and peace, *"He should turn his limbs to the direction of prayer as much as he is able,"* It is offensive in other than prostration because it involves removing them from their sunna place.

32. Leaving placing the hands on the knees in the bow

Likewise, it is offensive to leave placing them on the thighs between prostrations and during testification, and leaving placing the right on the left during standing, because he has left the sunna.

33. Yawning

This is because it from laziness and satiation. If it overcomes him, he should control it as much as he able even by holding his lip with his tooth, or by placing the back of his right hand or sleeve whilst standing and his left hand in other than it because of his statement, upon him be blessings and peace, *"Allah loves sneezing and dislikes yawning. Thus, if one of you sneezes, he should repel as much as he is able. He should not say, "ha ha" because that is from the Devil who is laughing at him"*[386] One narration mentions, *He should put his hand on his mouth because the Devil enters in it."*

34. Closing his eyes

---

[386] This is recorded by Bukhari 3289 and Abu Dawud 5028.

This is unless there is a benefit because of his statement, upon him be blessings and peace, *"When one of you stands in prayer, he should not close his eyes."* It causes his sight to miss the recommended place and each limb and body part has a portion of worship. In addition, by looking at something that will cause his humility to be lost and distract his mind, it is possible that closing the eyes is better than looking.

35. Raising them to the sky

This is because of his statement, upon him be blessings and peace, *"What is the matter people who raise their gazes towards the sky. They will stop or their gazes will be dazzled."*[387]

36. Stretch out

This is because it is from laziness.

37. Minimal movement

This negates prayer and has many individual types such as plucking a hair, firing from a bow once in fear prayer, and walking in his prayer.

38, 39. Picking lice and killing it

This is without an excuse. If it is distracting him by biting, as with an ant and a flea, picking it is not offensive. However, he should avoid its blood because of the statement of Imam Shaf'i, Allah be pleased with him, that its shell and blood is impure. With us, throwing its shell in the mosque is not permitted.

---

[387] This is recorded by Bukhari 750; Abu Dawud 912; Nasa'i 1277; and ibn Majah 1044 to 1045. .

40, 41. Covering his nose and mouth

This is because of that which we have narrated.

42. Putting something in his mouth that does not melt that prevents him from the sunna reciting

Likewise, it is offensive if it distracts him, such as gold.

43. Prostrating on the coil of his turban

This is without necessity, such as heat, cold, or hardness of the ground. It is offensive if it is on the forehead because it is a barrier that does not prevent prostration. However, if it is on the head and he prostrates on it without his forehead touching the ground, his prayer is not valid – many ordinary Muslims do this.

44. Prostrating on a picture

This is offensive if it is a life form because it resembles worshipping it.

45. Restricting on the forehead in prostration without an excuse to the nose

This is severely offensive because of leaving the necessary component of attaching the nose.

46. Prayer on the street

This is because it occupies the right of the public and blocks them from passing.

47. Prayer in a Turkish bath

48. Prayer in a toilet

49. Prayer in a graveyard and the likes of it

This is because the Messenger of Allah, upon him be blessings and peace, prohibited from praying in seven locations, at the rubbish dump, the slaughterhouse, the graveyard, the pathway, the Turkish bath, camel resting places, and above the House of Allah.[388] He only prays in a Turkish bath due to necessity. There is no problem with prayer in the changing rooms and the sitting area of the worker.

50. Praying on another person's land without his consent

If he has the misfortune of praying on another person's land which is not cultivated or a pathway, if he is a Muslim, he prays on it, and if he is an unbeliever, he prays on the pathway.

51. Praying near impurity

This is because anything that is near to something has its rule and we have been instructed to distance ourselves form impurities and their locations.

52, 53. Praying whilst repelling the two filths and wind

These are urine and faeces. This is even if it occurs during it because of his statement, upon him be blessings and peace, *"It is not permitted for anyone who believes in Allah and the Last Day to pray whilst holding in until he finds relief."*[389]

54. Praying with a non-preventative impurity unless he fears missing the time or the group prayer, otherwise breaking it is recommended

---

[388] This is recorded in Tirmidhi 346 to 347 and ibn Majah 746 to 747.
[389] This is recorded by Abu Dawud 90 to 91.

Clarification of a non-preventative impurity has preceded, whether it is on his garment, his body, or his place, removing from the disagreement. If he fears missing the time or the group prayer, he prays in that state because removing prayer from its time is prohibited and group prayer is emphasised or necessary. The case of his statement, upon him be blessings and peace, *"it is not permitted"* is the necessity of breaking for completion.

55. Prayer in dishevelled clothes

Dishevelled means a garment that is not protected from dirt and is unkempt. It is also said that it is that which a person would not go to important people with. 'Umar, Allah be pleased with him, saw a man having done that. He said, "What do you think if I had sent you to someone, would you have passed with these clothes of yours?" He said, "No." 'Umar said, "Allah is more worthy that you adorn yourself for Him."

56. Praying with his head uncovered but not due to humility and beseeching

This is offensive out of laziness because he of leaving respect, but not due to humility and beseeching. *Tajnis* mentions that is recommended for him. Jalal Suyuti, Allah, Exalted is He, be merciful with him, said that they differed over humility, is it from the actions of the heart like fear, is it from the action of the limbs like being motionless, or is it an expression for both. Razi said that the third is more appropriate. 'Ali, Allah be pleased with him, mentioned that humility is in the heart. A group of the early Muslims mentioned that humility in prayer is being motionless in it. Baghawi said that humility is close to submission except that submission is in the body and humility is in the body, sight, and voice.

57. In the presence of food that his nature inclines to

This is because of his statement, upon him be blessings and peace, *"There is no prayer in the presence of food nor whilst he is repelling the two filths"*[390] – Muslim narrated it. That which is narrated in Abu Dawud, *"Prayer is not delayed for food or for other than it"*[391] is interpreted as delaying it from its time because of his direct statement, upon him be blessings and peace, *"When the dinner of one of you is presented whilst the prayer is being established, begin with the dinner, and he should not hasten until he has completed it"*[392] – the two Shaykhs narrated it. Bringing it forward has only been instructed so that humility does not go by occupying his thought with it.

58, 59. In the presence of everything that occupies the mind, such as adornment, and diminishes humility, such as games and amusement

Hence, the Prophet, upon him be blessings and peace, prohibited coming to the prayer, hastily and at speed.[393] That is not the intent of the instruction to hasten to Friday prayer, rather going with tranquillity and dignity

60, 61. Counting verses and glorification with the hand

A verse is a set sentence of the Koran, and is used with the meaning of a sign. With the hand by folding the fingers is a qualification for

---

[390] This is recorded by Muslim 1246 to 1247 and Abu Dawud 89.

[391] This is recorded by Abu Dawud 3758.

[392] This is recorded by Bukhari 673 and Muslim 1244.

[393] This is a reference to the tradition of Abu Hurayra as recorded by Bukhari 636 and Muslim who said, *"I heard the Messenger of Allah, upon him be blessings and peace, say, "When the prayer is established, do not come to it hastily. Come to it walking with tranquillity on you. Whatever you catch, pray and whatever you miss, complete.""* This tradition is also recorded by Abu Dawud 572; Tirmidhi 327 to 329; Nasa'i 862; and ibn Majah 775.

offence in counting verses and glorification with Abu Hanifa, Allah be pleased with him, as opposed to them both,. Signalling with the fingertips at their place is not offensive, nor calculating in the heart, by agreement, such as the number of glorification in glorification prayer which is known. By the tongue invalidates, by agreement. It is not offensive outside of prayer, according to the correct position.

62. The imam standing completely in the prayer niche[394]

Standing outside of it and prostrating in it is not offensive. The offence is because his state becomes confusing to the worshippers. If space is restricted, there is no offence.

63. The imam standing on a place alone

This is if it is the extent of an arms length, according to the relied upon position. It is narrated from Abu Yusuf that it is the height of an average man – Shams Aimma Halawani chose it.

64. The imam standing on the ground alone

In both legal issues, being alone is the qualification. Thus, the offence is negated if one person stood with him, because of the prohibition in both of them, as the report has come with.

65. Standing behind a row in which there is a gap

This is because of the instruction to fill the gaps of the Devil and because of his statement, upon him be blessings and peace, *"Whoever fills a gap in the row, ten good deeds are recorded for him, ten bad deeds are wiped from him, and ten degrees are raised for him."*

---

[394] Prayer niche is named *mihrab* because it wages war against the soul and the Devil by standing in it – Maraqi Falah.

66. Wearing a garment that has pictures on it

This is pictures of life forms because it resembles a person carrying a statue.

67-70. Praying with an animal picture above his head, behind him, in front of him, or parallel to him unless it is small, with the head removed, or not a life form

This is because it resembles its worship. The worst offence is in front of him, then above him, then to his right, then to his left, and then behind him. It is not offensive if it is small such that it does not appear to a person standing without reflection, such as that which is on the dinar. This is because it is not normally worshipped. If he prayed and he had dirhams with him that had pictures of a king on it, there is no problem because this is insignificant to the sight. It is not offensive if it is large with the head removed because it is not worshipped without a head, or not a life form, such as a tree, because it is not worshipped. If he sees a picture in a house, effacing or altering it is permitted for him.

71, 72. The worshipper having a furnace or a stove with live charcoal in it in front of him

This is because it resembles Zoroastrians during their worship of it. Candles, lamps, and lanterns are not offensive, according to the correct position because it does not resemble worship.

73. Praying in front of a group of people sleeping

This is offensive if he fears the emission of something that will make them laugh, nervous, harm them, or if he faces a face, otherwise there is no offence. This is because 'Aisha, Allah be pleased with her, said, *"The Messenger of Allah, upon him be blessings and peace, used to pray all of night vigil prayer whilst I was stretched*

*out in front of him and the direction of prayer. Then when he wanted
to pray witr, he woke me up and prayed witr.* ^395

74. Wiping the forehead of dirt that does not harm him during prayer

This is because it is a type of futile movement. If it harms him,
there is no problem for him in prayer and after completion —
likewise wiping sweat.

75, 76. Specifying a chapter not reading other than it, except for ease for himself or taking blessings from the recitation of the Prophet, upon him be blessings and peace, which is not offensive

This is offensive for other than al-Fatiha because it is specified, as
being necessary, as well as the specific sunnas. This is such that he
does not recite anything else because it contains leaving the
remainder.

Following the recitation of the Prophet, upon him be blessings and
peace, is recommended, such as as-Sajdah and al-Insan at Friday
dawn^396, occasionally.

We have mentioned in the original a number of chapters that the
Prophet, upon him be blessings and peace, recited with its chain.
The following are the basis.

- Dawn
He used to recite Ya Sin at dawn.
He used to recite at dawn al-Waqi'ah and a similar chapter.
He recited al-Rum at dawn. ^397

---

395 This is recorded by Muslim 1140 to1143 and Abu Dawud 711 to 712.
396 This is recorded by Bukhari 891; Muslim 2031 to 2035; Abu Dawud 1074 to
1075; and Nasa'i 956 to 957.

He was on a journey and prayed dawn. He recited al-Falaq and al-Nas in it.

He prayed dawn with them with the shortest two chapters of the Quran and was brief. When he completed prayer, Muadh said to him, "Messenger of Allah, you prayed a prayer the likes of which you have never prayed before." He said, "Did you not hear the crying of the child behind me in the row of women. I wanted to give respite to his mother."

He recited in dawn az-Zilzal.[398]

He prayed dawn at Mecca and began with al-Mu'minun until he reached the mention of Aaron and Moses. He then bowed.[399]

He used to recite in dawn Qaf.[400]

He would not recite at dawn with less than twenty verses and he would not recite at nightfall with less than ten verses.

- Noon and Midafternoon

The Messenger of Allah, upon him be blessings and peace, used to recite al-Layl, at midafternoon similar to that, and at dawn longer than that.[401]

He used to recite at dawn al-'Ala and at noon longer than that.[402]

He used to recite in noon and midafternoon al-Buruj, at-Tariq, and similar chapters.[403]

He used to pray noon with us. We would hear verse after verse of Luqman and adh-Dhariyat.[404]

He prayed noon and prostrated. We thought that he had recited Ha Mim Sajdah.

---

[397] This is recorded by Nasa'i 948.

[398] This is recorded by Abu Dawud 816.

[399] This is recorded by Bukhari as a comment in the Book of Azan; Muslim 1022; Abu Dawud 649; Nasa'i 1008; and ibn Majah 820.

[400] This is recorded by Muslim 1024 to 1028; Tirmidhi 306; and ibn Majah 816.

[401] This is recorded by Muslim 1029; Abu Dawud 806; and Nasa'i 981.

[402] This is recorded by Muslim 1030.

[403] This is recorded by Abu Dawud 805; Tirmidhi 307; and Nasa'i 980.

[404] This is recorded by Nasa'i 972 and ibn Majah 830.

He used to recite at noon and midafternoon al-A'la and al-Ghashiya[405]

He prayed noon and raised his voice. He recited ash-Shams and al-Layl. Ubayy ibn K'ab said to him, "Messenger of Allah, have you been instructed with anything in this prayer?" He said, "No, but I wanted to set a time for you."

- Sunset

He recited al-A'raf at sunset.[406]

He used to recite at sunset al-Anfal.

He used to recite with them at sunset Muhammad.

The final prayer he prayed with them was sunset. He recited in the first unit al-'Ala and in the second al-Kafirun.

He recited in sunset al-Tin.

He recited in sunset ad-Dukhan.[407]

He prayed sunset and recited al-Qari'ah.

He used to recite in sunset prayer on Friday night al-Kafirun and al-Ikhlas.[408]

He used to recite in the final nightfall on Friday night al-Jumu'ah and al Munafiqun.

- Nightfall

From Jubayr ibn Mut'im, "I heard the Prophet, upon him be blessings and peace, reciting in nightfall al-Tin."[409]

From Abu Rafi who said, "I prayed nightfall with Abu Hurayra. He recited al-Inshiqaq and prostrated. I spoke to him. He said, "I prostrated behind Abu Qasim.""[410]

---

[405] This is recorded by Nasa'i 973.

[406] This is recorded by Nasa'i 991.

[407] This is recorded by Nasa'i 989.

[408] This is recorded by ibn Majah 833 without mentioning Friday.

[409] This is recorded by Bukhari 767; Muslim 1037 to 1039; Abu Dawud 1221; Tirmidhi 310; Nasa'i 1001; and ibn Majah 834 all of whom mention the tradition as that of Bara ibn 'Azib, Allah be pleased with him.

[410] This is recorded by Bukhari 768; Muslim 1299 to 1330 and 1304 to 1306; Abu Dawud 1408; and Nasa'i 969.

The Prophet, upon him be blessings and peace, used to recite at the final nightfall al-Buruj and at-Tariq,
He used to order lightening and he would lead us with as-Saffat.[411]

From ibn 'Umar who said, "There is not a small or large chapter from the mufassal except that I heard the Prophet, upon him be blessings and peace, lead the people with it in the prescribed prayer.[412]

This ends that which we have quoted from Jalal Suyuti, Allah, Exalted is He, be pleased with him, so that people who preserve the honourable sunna that reaches them can follow it. You are aware of the details in reciting from the mufassal at the times with us. Allah is the facilitator.

77. Leaving taking a barrier at a location that passing is expected in front of the worshipper

This is because of his statement, upon him be blessings and peace, *"When one of you prays, he should pray to a barrier and he should not leave anyone to pass in front of him."[413]*. This is whether he is in the desert or elsewhere, thereby removing the passer-by from falling into sin.

---

[411] This is recorded by al-Nasa'i 827.
[412] This is recorded by Abu Dawud 814.
[413] This is recorded by ibn Majah 954.

Section 18 – The Barrier

If a person intending prayer believes that a passer-by will pass, it is recommended that he insert a barrier because of that which we have narrated and because of his statement, upon him be blessings and peace, *"Each one of you should have a barrier, even with an arrow."*[414]

Its height should be an arms length or more because the Messenger of Allah, upon him be blessings and peace, was asked about the barrier of a worshipper who said, *"like the rear[415] of the camel bags."*[416] This is the stick that is at the back of the ride which is parallel to the head of the rider on the camel. This has been explained as being an arms length or more. Its minimum thickness is a finger because anything less perhaps will not manifest to an observer, thus the objective is not attained.

The sunna is that he draws near to it because of the statement of the Prophet, upon him be blessings and peace, *"When one of you prays to a barrier, he should draw near to it, thus the Devil will not break his prayer for him."* [417] He has it to the direction of one of his eyebrows and he does not intend it completely because of that which was narrated from Miqdad, Allah be pleased with him, that he said, *"I did not see the Messenger of Allah, upon him be blessings and peace, pray to a pillar or a tree except that he had it to his right or left eyebrow. He would not intend it directly"*[418], i.e. he would not face it directly but would incline away from it.

If he does not find something to erect, a group of the early scholars forbade a line but the later scholars permitted it because the sunna is more worthy to be followed. This is because of that which is narrated

---

[414] This is mentioned by Zayla'i in *Nasb Raya,* 81 who mentions that Bukhari records it in his *Tarikh Kabir* under the biography of ibn M'abad Juhani.
[415] Rear is *mu'khira* and stressing the *kha* is a mistake – Maraqi Falah.
[416] This is recorded by Nasa'i 747.
[417] This is recorded by Abu Dawud 695 and Nasa'i 749.
[418] This is recorded by Abu Dawud 693.

in the Sunan from the Prophet, upon him be blessings and peace, that he said, *"If he does not have a stick with him, he should draw a line."*[419] Thus, generally it becomes apparent because the objective is gathering the mind by binding the imagination by it so that it is not distracted. He has it either lengthwise as a stick inserted in front of him, or, as they also said, he has it horizontally like a crescent. If the ground is hard, that which is with him is placed lengthwise as if it has been inserted and then fallen – this is that which Faqih Abu J'afar, Allah, Exalted is He, be merciful with him, chose. Hisham said, "I performed pilgrimage with Abu Yusuf and he would throw his whip in front of him." The imam's barrier is a barrier for the person behind him because the Prophet, upon him be blessings and peace, prayed at Abtah to a small spear[420] that was planted for him whilst the people did not have a barrier.

If he takes it or not, it is recommended to leave repelling the passer-by because the basis of prayer is on tranquillity and the instruction to ward off in the tradition is a clarification of the allowance, like the instruction to kill the two black ones in prayer[421]. As a result, an allowance has been made in repelling the passer-by with an indication with the head, eye, or something else, as the Prophet, upon him be blessings and peace, did with the two children of Umm Salama, or by glorifying because of his statement, upon him be blessings and peace, *"When something happens to one of you in prayer, he should glorify."*[422] Combining between indicating and glorifying is offensive because there is sufficiency in one of them.

The man repels him by raising his voice with recitation even if it is increasing on his original audibility. The woman repels by indication or clapping with the back of the fingers of her right hand on the palm

---

[419] This is recorded by Abu Dawud 689 and ibn Majah 943.

[420] *'Anaza* is a small spear that has a metal tip to it – Maraqi Falah.

[421] This is a reference to the tradition of Abu Dawud, *"Kill the two black ones in prayer, the snake and the scorpion."*

[422] This is recorded by Bukhari 684 and Muslim 949.

of her left hand because they can clap. She does not raise her voice with reciting or glorifying because it is a tribulation, thus repelling by it is not sought from them.

The worshipper does not fight the passer-by in front of them. That which is mentioned from his statement, upon him be blessings and peace, *"When one of you is praying, he should not leave anyone to pass in front of her and he should repel as much as he can. If he refuses, he should fight him because he is a devil."*[423] is interpreted that fighting was permitted at the beginning of Islam whilst negating movement to the prayer was legitimate in it at that time and subsequently it was abrogated, as we have mentioned.

---

[423] This is recorded by Muslim 1128 to 1131; Abu Dawud 697 and 700; and Nasa'i 758.

Section 19 – Non-offensive Actions for the Worshipper

Tying his waist is not offensive because it protects the nakedness and is preparation for worship. Thus, if he wears an outer garment without fastening it around his waist, he has done badly. It is said that in other than an outer garment it is offensive because it is the practice of the Jews and Christians.

Wearing a sword or something similar is not offensive if he is not disturbed by its movement. If it disturbs him, it is offensive in other than war.

Not inserting his hands in his tunic and its slit is not offensive, according to the chosen position because the mind is not occupied.

Facing a copy of the Koran or a hung sword is not offensive because they are not worshipped. Allah, Exalted is He, said, *"They should take precaution and their weapons."*[424] Likewise, facing the back of a person talking is not offensive, according to the chosen position, because it does not resemble the worship of pictures. Additionally, ibn 'Umar prayed to the back of Naf'i. Also, facing candles or lanterns is not offensive, according to the correct position, because it does not resemble the worship of Zoroastrians.

Prostration on mats with pictures of life forms that he does not prostrate on is not offensive because he degrades them by stepping on them.

Killing all types of snakes is not offensive for the prayer itself. However, if it is due to fear of jinn, he should refrain from the white snake that moves straight because it broke the pact of the Prophet with whom the jinn took a covenant not to enter the homes of his community and not to reveal themselves. The one who breaks a pact is

---

[424] al-Nisa, 102.

treacherous and harm by killing and striking is feared from it and the likes of it from its species. He, upon him be blessings and peace, said, *"Kill the striped snake and the snake without a tail. Beware of the white snake because it is from the jinn."*[425]

Killing a snake and a scorpion whose harm a worshipper fears is not offensive, even if he kills them with two strikes and by turning away from the direction of prayer, according to the most apparent position. The qualification with fear of harm is because with safety excessive movement is offensive. Abu Layth, Allah be pleased with him, mentions in *Sab'iyyat* that seven things, if a worshipper sees them, there is no problem in killing them, snake, scorpion, *wazagha*[426], hornet, locust, flea, and lice. Bedbug, mosquito, and biting ant are added. However, avoiding the blood of lice touching is better so that he does not carry an impurity that prevents with Imam Shaf'i, Allah be pleased with him. We have already mentioned the offence in picking and killing lice in prayer with the Imam. He said that burying it is preferred to killing it. Muhammad has said the opposite and Abu Yusuf has said that they are both offensive.

There is no problem with shaking his garment with minimal movement so that it does not stick to his body in bowing, thus avoiding the appearance of the form of his limbs. There is no problem with protecting it from dust.

There is no problem with wiping dust or grass from his forehead after completing the prayer, thereby cleaning it from the description of disfiguring and dirtying.

There is no problem with his wiping before completing the prayer if it harms him or disturbs him from humility in prayer, such as sweat.

---

[425] This is recorded by Abu Dawud 5252.

[426] This is a lizard from the gecko species that is insectivorous and inhabits warm regions.

There is no problem with looking from the corner of his eyes, right and left, without turning his face away. The best is leaving it without a need because it involves leaving etiquette by looking to the prostration place and other places, as has preceded.

There is no problem praying on rugs, carpets, and felt if he finds the firmness of the ground. Likewise, there is no problem in placing a cloth that he prostrates on, protecting from heat, cold, and harmful hardness. The best is prayer on the ground without a barrier or anything that it produces such as palm leaves and grass in mosques which is better than carpets because of its nearness to humility.

There is no problem in repeating a chapter in two units of an optional prayer because optional prayer is more expansive. It has been mentioned that he, upon him be blessings and peace, stood with one verse repeating it in his night vigil.
Allah facilitate for the likes of it by His bounty and His generosity.

Section 20 – Actions That Necessitate Breaking the Prayer

Breaking prayer is necessary, even obligatory, if a distressed person with an important matter afflicting him calls for help. Thus, if an oppressor clutches him, he falls in water, or an animal pounces on him and he calls for help from the worshipper or another person and he is able to ward of from him, it is necessary.

Breaking prayer is not necessary by one of his parents calling him without calling for help because breaking prayer is only permitted for necessity. Tahawi said that this is in obligatory prayer. If he is in an optional prayer, if one of his parents knows that he is in prayer and calls him, there is no problem in not replying, but if he did not know, he replies.

Breaking is permitted, even if it is an obligatory prayer, for fear of theft of an item equivalent to one dirham, because it is wealth, and he, upon him be blessings and peace, said, *"fight for your wealth"*[427] Likewise, he is permitted to break for less than that, according to the most correct position, because he is detained for a *daniq*.[428] He is also permitted to break if his pot boils over, if she is afraid for her child, or if an unbeliever requested that Islam be presented to him. Breaking is permitted even if the amount belongs to other than the worshipper to ward off injustice and prohibit wrongdoing.

Breaking is permitted for fear of a wolf or something similar on livestock or something similar, or fear that a blind person or someone similar who does not have awareness will fall in a well or something similar such as a ditch or from a roof. If he feels it is highly probable that he will fall, breaking the prayer is necessary, even if it is an obligatory prayer.

---

[427] This is recorded by Nasa'i 4087.

[428] A *daniq* is equivalent to one sixth of a dirham.

Delaying prayer from its time and breaking it if she is in it is necessary for a midwife if she feels it is highly probable that the child will die or one of its limbs will be damaged, or his mother by leaving her. If this is not the case, there is no problem in delaying the prayer and seeing to the child because of the excuse, just as the Prophet, upon him be blessings and peace, delayed prayer from its time on the Day of the Trench.

Likewise, delaying the current prayer is permitted for a traveller who is moving in open lands, if he fears from thieves, highway robbers, predatory animals, or a flood, as is the case with warriors if they are not able to motion riding, due to the necessity.

Likewise, delaying making up missed prayer is permitted for an excuse such as earning a livelihood for his dependants, even though making them up is necessary immediately. However, making up fasts is made up delayed as long as the next Ramadan has not approached. There is a difference over recitation prostration and an unrestricted vow, it is said that they are extended and it is said that they are restricted.

The person who intentionally out of laziness leaves prayer is beaten severely until blood pours from him and, after that, he is detained. He is not neglected but his state inspected through admonition, rebuking, and also beating until he prays or dies whilst detained. This is his worldly punishment.

However, in the afterlife, if he dies on Islam as a sinner by leaving it, he has a lengthy punishment in a valley in Hellfire that is severest in heat and the deepest pit. In it is a well called *habhab,* and wells to which pus flows that is prepared for the person who leaves prayer. His description is in the tradition of Jabir, in his statement, upon him be blessings and peace, *"between a man and unbelief is leaving the prayer"* – Ahmad and Muslim narrated it.[429]

---

[429] This is recorded by Tirmidhi 2618 to 2620; and ibn Majah 1078.

Likewise, a person who leaves the Ramadan fast out of laziness is beaten and detained until he fasts.

He is not killed by merely leaving prayer and fast whilst admitting that they are obligatory, unless he denies that prayer and fast are obligatory because he has rejected that which is known of the religion by consensus. Likewise, he is killed if he belittles one of them, such as revealing that he has broken his fast during the daytime hours of Ramadan without an excuse, out of indifference, or uttered a statement that indicates it. His ruling is that of an apostate. Thus, his doubt is clarified and he is detained. He is then killed if he persists.

Section 21 – Witr

Having completed clarifying actions obligatory by knowledge, the discussion is the active obligatory actions.

In Arabic language, it means odd, as opposed to even, and is with *fath* and *kasr*. In Sacred Law, it is a specific prayer that he described by his statement witr is necessary, according to the most correct position. This is the final statement of the Imam. It is reported from him that it is sunna, which is the statement of them both. It is reported from him that it is obligatory. The scholars have unified the narrations that it is obligatory by action being that which is not left, necessary by belief, and sunna by proof because it is established by it.

The basis of it being necessary is his statement, upon him be blessings and peace, *"Witr is true, thus whoever does not perform witr is not from me; witr is true, thus whoever does not perform witr is not from me; witr is true, thus whoever does not perform witr is not from me."*[430] – Abu Dawud and Hakim reported it and he[431] authenticated it.

Its number is three units with it being conditional that it be performed with one salaam because the Messenger of Allah, upon him be blessings and peace, used to perform witr with three, only uttering salaam at its end – Hakim authenticated it and said that it is on the condition of the two Shaykhs.

He necessarily recites al-Fatiha and a chapter in every unit of it because of that which is narrated that he, upon him be blessings and peace, recited in the first of it, i.e. after al-Fatiha, *"Glorified is the name of Your Lord Most Exalted"*, in the second *"Say, "O Unbelievers!"*, and in the third *"Say, "He Allah is One"* and the two protectors. This is acted upon on occasions, thereby acting upon both traditions not in a necessary manner. He sits necessarily at the end of the first two units of

---

[430] This is recorded by Abu Dawud 1419.
[431] i.e. Hakim.

it because of the report. He restricts to the testification because of the resemblance to the obligatory and he does not recite the opening supplication on standing to the third because it is not the beginning of another prayer. When he completes reciting the chapter in it, i.e. in the third unit, he raises his hands parallel to his ears, as we have mentioned, unless he is making it up so that his negligence in it is not seen by raising his hands in the presence of someone who sees him. He then utters takbir because he is moving to the state of supplication.

After takbir he recites the supplication standing because the Prophet, upon him be blessings and peace, used to recite the supplication in witr before the bow. With the Imam, he places his right on his left but from Abu Yusuf, he raises them as ibn Mas'ud used to raise them to his chest whilst their palms were to the sky. Farj, the slave of Abu Yusuf, said, "I saw my master Abu Yusuf raising his hands in supplication when he would enter the supplication in witr" – ibn Abu 'Imran said, "Farj was trustworthy". Kamal said, "His basis is the general nature of the proof of raising for supplication. However, it is refuted that it is specific to that which is not in the prayer because of the consensus that there is no raising in the testification supplication." I say, "There is a problem with this because of the statement of ibn Ma'ud which has just been mentioned."

Mabsut mentions from Muhammad ibn Hanafiyya who said, "Supplication is four:
1. Hopeful supplication in which he has the centre of his palms to the sky.
2. Fearful supplication in which he has the back of his hands to his face like a person seeking protection from something.
3. Humble supplication in which he clenches the small finger and the ring finger, circles the thumb and the middle finger, and points with index finger.
4. Secret supplication which is that which a person does to himself."

This is mentioned in *M'iraj Diraya*.

Because of that which we narrated he supplicates before bowing throughout the year. He does not supplicate in other than witr, which is dawn because of the statement of Anas, *"The Messenger of Allah, upon him be blessings and peace, supplicated in dawn after bowing, supplicating against Arab tribes, R'il, Dhakwan, and 'Usayya when they killed the reciters, who were seventy or eighty men. He then left it once he had dominated them."*[432] This indicates its abrogation. Ibn Abu Shayba narrated, *"When 'Ali, Allah be pleased with him, supplicated in dawn, the people censured him for that. He said, "We are only seeking victory against our enemy."*" *Ghaya* mentions, "If a calamity afflicts the Muslims, the imam supplicates in the audible prayer – this is the statement of Thawri and Ahmad, The majority of the tradition scholars said, "Supplication at a calamity is legislated in all prayers."" Thus, the Prophet, upon him be blessings and peace, not supplicating in dawn, after his victory against those, is because of the absence of a calamity that requires supplication after it. Hence, its legislation is continuous, and this is the interpretation of the supplication of the companions, Allah be pleased with them, who supplicated after his passing away, upon him be peace and blessings – this is our school, and the majority are on this. Abu J'afar Tahawi, Allah be pleased with him, said, "Supplication is not recited with us in dawn without a calamity. If a tribulation or calamity occurs, there is no problem with it as the Messenger of Allah, upon him be blessings and peace performed it." – i.e. after the bow, as has preceded.

Qunut has the meaning of supplication in witr and is with the wording that is narrated from ibn Mas'ud. He says:

Allah, i.e. O Allah; *we seek Your assistance*, i.e. we request from You help in worship of You; *we seek Your guidance*, i.e. we seek from You guidance to that which pleases You; *we seek Your forgiveness*, i.e. we seek from You concealment of our defects, so do not disgrace us; *and we repent to You* – repentance is turning away from sins, and legally is

---

[432] This is recorded by Bukhari 1002 to 1003 and Nasa'i 1071.

remorse at the sin that has passed, removing from it instantly, determination to leave returning in the future thereby venerating the affair of Allah, Exalted is He. If a human right is attached to it, there must be his forgiveness and pleasing him. *We believe*, i.e. we confirm, whilst believing in our hearts and pronouncing on our tongues. Thus, we say that we believe *in You*, in that which came from You, in Your angels, Your scriptures, Your messengers, the Last Day, and the good and evil of destiny. *We place our trust*, i.e. we depend, *in You* by resigning our affairs to You because of our incapacity. *We praise you with all goodness*, i.e. we praise You with all goodness whilst affirming all of Your blessings, out of kindness from You. *We thank you* by turning all the favours You have bestowed upon us for the purpose that You created it for. Glory be to You, we cannot enumerate praise of You, You are as You praised Yourself; *and we do not reject[433] you*, i.e. we do not deny any favour from You to us nor do we attribute it to other than You. *And we renounce* – with the connecting particle established – i.e. we throw away[434], we fling, and we remove the yoke of unbelief from our necks and the yoke of all that does not please You; *and we leave*, i.e. we separate, *from those who rebel against you* by him denying Your favour and worshipping other than You. We avoid him and his characteristic by assuming him to be nonexistent, absolving Your honour because every particle in existence is witness that You are the One who bestows favours, the Kind, the Existent, the One deserving all types of praise, the Singular, and the One worshipped. The person who opposes this is the repelled wretch.

Allah, You alone do we worship – returning to praise and specifying His essence for worship, i.e. we do not worship other than You, because bringing forward the object is for restriction. *And to You we pray* – prayer is singled out for mention because of its nobility by it

---

[433] *Kufr* is the opposite of thanks and is originally from concealment. It is said, "He rejected the favour" if he did not give thanks for it, as if he concealed it by denying it. Their statement, "You rejected so an so" is with the omission of the construct state, the original being that you rejected his favour. From this is "and we do not reject You". Maraqi Falah

[434] It is said, "the horse removed its halter, i.e. threw it away – Maraqi Falah

incorporating all worship – *and prostrate* – specifying after specifying because it is the nearest of states of the slave to the worshipped Lord. *To You we strive* – this is a reference to his statement in the tradition, relating from Him, Exalted is He, *"Whoever comes to me striving, I come to him rushing"*[435], *and hasten*[436] – we are quick in attaining Your worship with energy. *We hope*, i.e. we long, *for Your mercy*, i.e. its continuation, its reinforcement, and the vastness of Your gifts by fulfilling Your service and acting in Your obedience. You are generous and you do not let down the person who hopes in You. *We fear Your punishment* whilst avoiding that which You have prohibited us from, thus we do not feel secure from Your plot. We are between hope and fear, which is an reference to the true school, because feeling secure from the plot is unbelief just like despair from mercy. He has combined between hope and fear because the affair of the powerful one is that his favour is hoped for and his punishment is feared. The tradition mentions, *"The two do not come together in the heart of a believing slave except that Allah gives him that which he hopes for and secures him from that which he fears."*[437] Thus, due to your bestowing the favour of faith on us and facilitating action of the pillars, whilst executing Your order and not restricting to the heart and the tongue which is the desire of liars and people of falsehood, we believe and say, *indeed, Your real*[438] *punishment is overtaking*[439], i.e. catching, *the unbelievers*, meaning that Allah, Gory be to Him and Exalted is He, is inflicting it on them.

---

[435] This is recorded by Bukhari 7405 and Muslim 6952.

[436] *Hafad* means speed, as a result of which servants are called *hafada* because of their speed in serving their masters. *Nahfid* is with a *fatha* on the *nun* and a *damma* is permitted. It is with a *fa* that has *kasra*. Thus, it is said *hafada*, but *ahfada* is a dialect of it. If he replaces the *dal* with a *thal*, his prayer is invalid because it is unrelated speech that has no meaning. Maraqi Falah.

[437] This is recorded by Tirmidhi 983 and ibn Majah 4261.

[438] *Jidd*, i.e. real is with a *kasra* on the *mim*, by agreement, and is confirmed in the Marasil of Abu Dawud. Thus, no attention is paid to the one who said that *jidd* is not read. Maraqi Falah.

[439] *Mulhiq* with a *kasra* on the *ha* is more eloquent, but it is said, with a *fatha*.

Because Nasa'i narrated with a fair chain that in the witr supplication tradition *"and Allah bless and send peace on the Prophet"*[440], we bless him, Allah bless him "and his family" – as the Faqih Abu Layth, Allah be merciful to him, chose that he blesses the Prophet, upon him be blessings and peace, in the witr supplication.

The follower recites the witr supplication like the imam, according to the most correct position. The imam and worshippers read it silently – this is the correct position. However, it is recommended that the imam recites it audibly in non-Arab lands so that they learn it, just as 'Umar, Allah be pleased with him, read the praise audibly when a delegation came to him from 'Iraq. Thus, some of them expanded that if the worshippers do not know it, the best for the imam is audible so that they learn, otherwise silently is best.

If the imam begins the supplication, "Allah, guide us ..." as we shall mention, after the statement that has preceded, "Allah, we seek Your assistance ...", Abu Yusuf, Allah be merciful to him, said that he follows him and also reads it with him. Muhammad says that he does not follow him in it nor in the witr supplication that is "Allah, we seek Your assistance and we seek Your forgiveness", but utters amen to his supplication.

A group of scholars said that there is nothing specific for the supplication. The best is that he reads, after the preceding supplication, the witr supplication of Hasan ibn 'Ali, Allah be pleased with them both, who said, *"The Messenger of Allah, upon him be blessings and peace, taught me words that I read in witr"* – and in one wording *"in the witr supplication"* – Hakim narrated it. In it he said, *"When I raise my head and only prostration remains, "Allah, guide me with those who You have guided, give me wellbeing with those whom You have given wellbeing, take care of me with those whom You have taken care of, bless me in that which You have given me, save me from the evil of that which You have decreed, for You decree and nothing is decreed against You, and*

---

the person whom You protect is not lowly. You are blessed and exalted."[441] – Tirmidhi has classified it as fair. Bayhaqi has added after *"You protect"*, *"the person whom you oppose is never honoured."* As you can see, it is in the singular form in it and in the narration from him, upon him be blessings and peace, during his dawn witr supplication when he would do it. Kamal ibn Humam said that they brought it from a tradition in relation to the imam which is general and witr supplication is not specified. Thus they read it with the plural *nun* "Allah, guide us, give us wellbeing, take care of us, etc." I say that amongst them is the author of *Durar wal Ghurar* and *Burhan*.

The supplication is: *Allah, guide us* – the narration of Hasan is "guide me" as we have pointed out. The origin of guidance is message and clarification, such as His statement, Exalted is He, *"You do indeed guide to the right path."*[442] However, his statement, Exalted is He, *"You do not guide whom you like, but Allah guides whom He will"*[443], it is from Allah, Exalted is He, facilitation and direction. Thus, the believers seeking guidance whilst already being guided has the meaning of seeking firmness in it or the meaning of an increase in it. *Through Your grace* not being necessary on You – this addition is not in the witr supplication of Hasan, "Allah guide me" – *amongst those whom You have guided. Give us wellbeing* – *'afiya* is safety from sicknesses, tribulations, and troubles and *mu'afa* is that Allah protects you from people and protects them from you – *amongst those whom You have given wellbeing. Take care of us* – this is when you pay particular attention and look at the benefit for it just as a guardian looks at the affair of an orphan because He, Glory be to Him, looks at the affairs of those whom He has taken care of through His providence – *amongst those whom You take care of* from Your closest slaves. *Bless us in that which You have given* – blessing is an increase in good. Thus, you have sought to ascend above the previous two states. He then returns to the state of fear and majesty saying *and save us* which is from protection

---

[441] This is recorded by Abu Dawud 1425; Tirmidhi 464; and Nasa'i 1746 to 1747.

[442] al-Shura, 52.

[443] al-Qasas, 56.

through providence by repelling *the evil of that which You have decreed* by us fleeing to You. *For You decree* with whatever You will *and nothing is decreed against You* because You are the Owner, the One, having no partner in the dominion. Thus, we seek Your protection *for the person who You protect is not lowly* because of Your might and the authority of your subjugation, *and the person who You oppose is not mighty* – "*that is because Allah is the ally of the believers, and the disbelievers have no ally*"[444], "*and whomever Allah abases none will be able to honour.*"[445] *Blessed are you,* sanctified are You and you are above blemish, thus it is a specific description that is only used for Allah, *our Lord,* i.e. O our master, our owner, our object of worship, our rectifier. Baydawi said that blessed is Allah is His affair is exalted in His ability and His wisdom which then has the meaning of *and Exalted are you.* The basis for mentioning "blessed are you" first is that is specific to Him, Glory be to Him. *Blessings and peace be on* the Prophet *our master Muhammad, his family, and his companions* because of that which we have narrated.

Faqih Abu Layth, Allah, Exalted is He, be pleased with him, said that whoever is not proficient in the mentioned witr supplication says, "Allah, forgive me" repeating it three times, or says, "Lord, Give us what is good in this world and what is good in the Hereafter, and keep us from the torment of the Fire" – Tajnis mentions that this is the choice of our scholars, or says, "Lord, Lord, Lord" thrice – Sadr Shahid mentioned it. Hence, these are three chosen statements.

If he follows a person who recites a supplication in dawn, such as a Shafi, stands with him during his supplication silently, according to the most apparent position, because of the necessity of following him in the standing. However, with them both he stands silently, but with Abu Yusuf he recites it with him because he is following the imam and the supplication is disputed thus becoming like the takbirs of the two

---

[444] Muhammad, 11.
[445] Hajj, 18.

'Eids and the witr supplication after the bow. He leaves his hands at his sides because it is a remembrance that is not sunna.

If he forgets the witr supplication in the third unit of witr and remembers it in the bow or in the raising from the bow, he does not supplicate, according to the correct position, not in the bow in which he remembered it nor after raising from it. He prostrates for forgetfulness.

If he recites witr supplication after raising his head from the bow, he does not repeat the bow. He prostrates for forgetfulness because the witr supplication was removed from its original location and his delaying the necessary component.

If the imam bows before the follower completes reciting the witr supplication or before beginning it and fears missing the bow with the imam, he follows his imam. This is because occupying himself with that causes him to miss the necessary requirement of following, thus it is best. If he does not fear missing partnership in the bow, he recites the witr supplication, thereby combining the two necessary components.

If the imam leaves the witr supplication, the follower brings it if he is able to have partnership with the imam in the bow, so that he combines between the two necessary components according to his ability. If he is not able to have partnership, he follows him, because following him is best.

If he catches the imam in the bow of the third unit of witr, he has caught the witr supplication legally. Thus, he does not bring it in that which he makes up just as they agree that the latecomer who recited the witr supplication with him in the third unit does not recite witr supplication in that which he makes up because it is not legislated. Abu Fadl equates him to a doubter, which will come in Supplication Prostration.

It is recommended to pray witr in a group only in Ramadan – the consensus of the Muslims is on this. This is because it is optional from one perspective and group prayer in optional prayers other than tarawih is offensive, thus caution is leaving it in witr outside of Ramadan. Shams A'imma mentions that this is for that which is in the form of announcement. However, if one person follows one or two with one, it is not offensive. There is a difference of agreement if three follow one. If four follow one, it is offensive by agreement.

Witr prayer with the group in Ramadan is better than performing it individually at the end of the night, according to the choice of Qadikhan. He, Allah be merciful to him, said that it is the correct position because once group prayer is permitted, it is best, and because 'Umar, Allah be pleased with him, used to lead them in witr. Others have authenticated its opposite. Nihaya mentions after relating this, "Our scholars have chosen that he prays witr in his house not in a group because the companions did not gather for witr in a group in Ramadan since 'Umar, Allah be pleased with him, used to lead them in it and Ubayy ibn K'ab did not used to lead them. Fath and Burhan indicate that the statement of Qadikhan is more dominant because he, upon him be blessings and peace, prayed witr with them in it and clarified the excuse for leaving.[446] Whoever fails to pray the group prayer for it, his best prayer is at the end of the night and group prayer is difficult at that time. Thus, it does not indicate that the best is leaving group prayer in it at the beginning of the night."

If he prays witr before sleep and then prays night vigil prayer, he does not repeat witr, because of his statement, upon him be blessings and peace, *"There are no two witrs in a night."*[447]

---

[446] This is a reference to the tradition of Bukhari 1129; Muslim 1783 to 1784; Abu Dawud 1373; and Nasa'i 1605.
[447] This is recorded by Abu Dawud 1439; Tirmidhi 470; and Nasa'i 1680.

Section 22 – Optional Prayers

He has used the expression optional prayers and not sunnas because optional prayers are more general as every sunna is an optional prayer but not the opposite.

Nafl, in Arabic language, is an increase, and in Sacred Law is an action that is not obligatory, nor necessary, nor sunna from worship. Sunna, in Arabic language, is a general path whether pleasing or not, and in Sacred Law is a traversed path in religion which is not obligatory or necessary. Qadi Abu Zayd, Allah be pleased with him, said, "Optional prayers are legislated to repair faults that have occurred in the obligatory prayer, because the slave, even if his rank is lofty, is not free of deficiency." Qadikhan said, "Sunna before the prescribed prayed is legislated to sever the desire of Satan because he says, "Whoever does not obey me in leaving that which is not prescribed on him, how will he obey me in leaving that which is prescribed on him.""

Sunna is recommended and emphasised. Emphasised sunnas include the following.

1. Two units before dawn prayer

These are the strongest sunna such that Hasan narrated for Abu Hanifa, Allah be pleased with him, "If he prays them sitting without an excuse, it is not permitted." Marghaynani narrated from Abu Hanifa, Allah be pleased with him, that they are necessary. He, upon him be blessings and peace, said, *"Do not leave them, even if horses drive you away."*[448] He, upon him be blessings and peace, said, *"The two units of dawn are more beloved to me than*

---

[448]

the world and all that is in it[449] – in one variant, *"better than the world and all that is in it."*[450]

There is a difference over the best after the two units of the sunnas of dawn. Halawani said, "The two sunnas of sunset, then those after noon, then those after nightfall, then those before noon, then those before midafternoon, and then those before nightfall." It is said, "Those after nightfall, and those before noon, after it, and after sunset are all equal." It is said, "Those after noon are the most emphasised" – Hasan said it is the most correct position, and he began Mabsut with it.

---

[449]

[450]

Section 23 – Optional Prayer Sitting and Prayer on an Animal

- **Optional prayer is permitted sitting whilst having the ability to stand**

He has mentioned optional prayer to cover emphasised sunna and other than it. It is valid if he prays it sitting whilst having the ability to stand. In fact, a consensus of the scholars has been related about it. However, on the non-relied upon position it is said that the sunnas of dawn are exempted because it is said that it is necessary and due to the strength of its emphasis and the tarawih is exempted on other than the correct position because the most correct position is that it is valid sitting without an excuse. Therefore, nothing is exempted from the validity of optional prayer sitting without an excuse according to the correct position because he, upon him be peace and blessings, would pray after witr sitting and would sit in most of his prayers at night out of ease.[451] In a narration from 'Aisha, Allah be pleased with her, "*Then when he wanted to bow he stood and recited verses. He then bowed and prostrated and returned to sitting.*"[452] M'iraj Diraya says that this is recommended in every optional prayer prayed sitting to conform to the sunna. If he does not recite on standing and prostrates and bows it suffices him. However, if he does not stand but bows it does not suffice him because it is neither bowing standing nor bowing sitting as mentioned in *Tajnis*.

- **However he has half the reward of the standing person except due to an excuse**

He, i.e. the person praying optional prayer sitting, has half the reward of the standing person because he, upon him be peace and blessings,

---

[451] The meaning of this is recorded by Muslim 1710 to 1711
[452] This is recorded by Muslim 1704 to 1707 and Abu Dawud 954 and 1340.

said, "*Whoever prays standing it is best. Whoever prays sitting has half the reward of the standing person. Whoever prays sleeping has half the reward of the sitting person.*"[453] This however applies to the one who is able. As for the person incapable due to an excuse his prayer motioning is better than the prayer of the standing, bowing, prostrating person because it is the effort of the incapable. Furthermore, there is a consensus that the prayer of the sitting person with an excuse equals the prayer of the standing person in reward as mentioned in *Diraya*. I say that in fact it is higher than it because it is also the effort of the incapable and the intention of a person is better than his action.

- ### He sits like the person reciting the testification according to the chosen position

The person praying optional prayer sitting sits like the person reciting the testification if he has no excuse. Therefore, he places the left foot on its side and sits on it whilst keeping the right foot up according to the chosen position and fatwa is upon it. However, *Shaykh Islam* mentions that the best for him is to sit in the standing position with his legs drawn up because most of the prayer of the Messenger of Allah, upon him be peace and blessings, towards the end of his life was sitting with his legs drawn up, i.e. in the optional prayers. Also, the person sitting with his legs drawn up has more of his limbs facing the direction of prayer because the shins both face as with the standing position. It is narrated from Abu Hanifa, Allah be pleased with him, that he sits however wants because since it has been permitted for him to leave the original standing by extension he can leave the manner of sitting. The manner of sitting for the sick person is not restricted in any way.

- ### It is permitted to complete it sitting after having begun it standing without offence according to the most correct position

---

[453] This is recorded by Abu Dawud 951 and Nasa'i 1661.

It is permitted to complete it, i.e. the person able to complete his optional prayer, sitting whether he is in the first or the second, after he has begun standing with Abu Hanifa, Allah be pleased with him, because standing is not an integral in optional prayer thereby leaving it is permitted. With them both it is not permitted because beginning is binding which thereby resembles a vow. However, with Abu Hanifa his vow binds him to a general prayer which is complete by standing with all the integrals. Beginning only requires safeguarding of the optional prayer which does not necessitate standing. He therefore may complete it sitting without any offence according to the most correct position because remaining is easier than beginning and his beginning sitting is not offensive therefore by extension his remaining is not. In addition, *he, upon him be peace and blessings, used to begin the optional prayer and would then move from standing to sitting and sitting to standing* – 'Aisha, Allah be pleased with her, narrated it.

- ## He prays optional prayer riding outside of the city motioning towards any direction that his animal turns

He prays optional prayer, i.e. optional prayer is permitted for him, in fact it is recommended for him, riding outside of the city. This means outside of the built-up area so that it covers outside of the village and the encampment. This is the place where if a traveller enters he shortens his prayer. This is irrespective of whether he is a traveller or he has left for a need to a certain area according to the most correct position. It is said that if he leaves a distance of a mile and it is also said that if he leaves a distance of two farsakh[454] it is permitted for him otherwise it is not. It is narrated from Abu Yusuf that it is also permitted within a city on an animal motioning towards any direction. He begins prayer wherever his animal turns because of the place of need. His inability to stop the animal for the prohibition is not a condition according to primary narrations because of the statement of Jabir, *"I saw the Messenger of Allah, upon him be peace and blessings,*

---

[454] One farsakh is three Hashimi miles as mentioned in Lanes Lexicon.

praying his optional prayer on his animal towards any direction motioning. However, he would lower the two prostrations in the two units." – ibn Hibban narrated it in his authentic collection. If he moves his feet or strikes his animal it is not a problem as long as he is not excessive.

• He builds by descending but not by mounting

He builds by descending on what has passed if he does not produce excessive movement such as if he folds his legs and slides down because his prohibition took place permitting bowing and prostrating as originals by his descent after it. Thus, motioning for them riding is an allowance. This differentiates between the permissibility of his building and the sick person not building with bowing and prostrating whilst motioning because the prohibition of the sick person does not include them due to his inability to do them. Hence, building is not permitted after his mounting on what has passed from his prayer on the ground according to primary narrations because beginning it on the ground required all conditions. However, whilst riding the conditions of facing the direction of prayer, single place, purity and actual bowing and prostration is missed.

• Even if it is the regular optional prayers

Motioning on an animal is permitted even if is the regular emphasised optional prayers or other than it, even the dawn sunna.

• From Abu Hanifa, Allah be pleased with him, that he descends for the dawn sunnas because they are more emphasised than other than them

ibn Shuj'a, Allah be pleased with him, says that it is possible that this is to highlight the best option, meaning that the best is to descend for the two units of dawn as is mentioned in *'Inaya*. We have mentioned that this is on the narration that they are necessary.

- **It is permitted for the person praying optional prayer to lean on something if he is tired without offence**

It is permitted for the person praying optional prayer to lean on something such as a stick, wall or servant if he is tired because it is an excuse as it is permitted to sit without offence.

- **If it is without an excuse it is offensive according to the most apparent position due to bad etiquette**

This is opposed to sitting without an excuse after sitting as we have mentioned.

- **Impurity on the animal does not prevent validity of prayer even if it is on the saddle and stirrups according to the most correct position**

Excessive impurity on the animal does not prevent validity of prayer even if the impurity is more than a dirham on the saddle and stirrups according to the most correct position. This is the statement of most of our scholars due to necessity.

- **The prayer of the walking person is not valid by consensus**

This is the consensus of our imams because of the difference in place.

Section 24 – Obligatory and Necessary Prayers on an Animal and a Litter

Obligatory, necessary prayers such as witr, vow, the two Eid prayers and making up what he began as an optional prayer and then broke, funeral prayer and a recitation prostration whose verse is recited on the ground is not valid on an animal except due to a necessity. This has been mentioned by His statement, *"if you are exposed to danger, while on foot or riding."*[455] Necessary prayer is attached to it. Necessity includes

- fear of a thief against his person, animal or clothes if he were to dismount and his friends do not stand for him,
- fear of a predatory animal against his person or his animal,
- presence of rain and mud at the place whereby the face would disappear in it, soil it or anything he spread out would be ruined. Mere wetness does not permit that. The person who does not have an animal prays standing in the mud motioning.
- unruliness of the animal
- absence of a person who could seat him on his animal even if it is not unruly because of his inability by agreement. Repeating is not necessary by the cessation of the excuse. It is permitted for the sick person who by dismounting and mounting increases his sicknesses or delays its healing to motion for the obligatory prayers on the animal standing facing the direction of prayer if it is possible – otherwise it is not. The same is the case if the place is covered in clay. If the person unable to mount finds a helper it is the issue of the person able through the ability of another who is unable with him as opposed to them both. This is the same as a woman who is not able to dismount without a non-marriageable person or husband. The person stabilising for

---

[455] Baqara 239.

his wife or his non-marriageable companion is the same as a woman if his son does not take his place.

Prayer in a litter which is on an animal is like prayer on it in the rule that you are aware of whether it is moving or stationary. If he stops it and places wood or something similar beneath the litter such that its, i.e. the litter, firmness remains to the ground through what he has placed beneath it it is, i.e. the litter has become, in place of the ground. Hence, obligatory prayer is valid in it standing but not sitting with bowing and prostration.

Section 25 – Prayer on a Ship

Obligatory and necessary prayer on it whilst it is moving sitting without an excuse for him and whilst he is able to disembark is valid with the Greatest Imam Abu Hanifa, Allah be pleased with him, but with bowing and prostration and not motioning. This is because in most instances standing there will be dizziness and the dominant is like the actual. However, standing on it and disembarking is better if possible because it is more distant from the doubt of disagreement and more tranquil for his heart.

They both said, i.e. Abu Yusuf and Muhammad, Allah, Exalted is He, be pleased with them both, it is not valid sitting except due to an excuse. This is the most apparent position because of the tradition of ibn 'Umar that the Prophet, upon him be peace and blessings, was asked about prayer on a ship and said, *"Pray on it standing unless you fear drowning."* He also said the same to J'afar. This is because standing is an integral and is not left without a certain and not speculative excuse. However, the evidence of the Imam is stronger and is therefore followed because ibn Sirin said, *"We prayed with Anas on a ship sitting and had we wanted to we could have gone on land"* and Mujahid said, *"We prayed with Janada on a ship sitting and had we wanted to we could have stood."* Zahidi said that the traditions of ibn 'Umar and J'afar are interpreted as recommended. Hence, the strength of his evidence is clear because it conforms to two followers, ibn Sirin and Mujahid, and two companions, Anas and Janada. Thus, the statement of the Imam, Allah, Exalted is He, be merciful to him, is followed.

An excuse is like dizziness and the inability to disembark. It is not permitted, i.e. prayer is not valid, on it by motioning for the person able to bow and prostrate by agreement because of the absence of a legitmiser actually and legally.

The ship moored at sea by anchors and mountains which despite that a wind violently rocks is like a moving ship in its rule and the difference in it that you are aware of otherwise, i.e. if it does not rock it violently it is like a stationary ship at shore according to the most correct position.

He has mentioned the stationary ship with its rule by saying that if it is moored to shore his prayer on it is not permitted sitting whilst having the ability to stand because of the negation of the necessitator for its validity by consensus according to the correct position. This excludes the statement of some of them that it is also on the difference. Thus if he prays on the ship tied to shore standing and a part of the ship was on the firmness of the ground the prayer is valid being like the prayer on a bed otherwise, i.e. if no part of it settles on the ground prayer on it is not valid according to the chosen position – as is mentioned in *Muhit* and *Bada'i* – because it is then like an animal. The apparent of *Hidaya* and *Nihaya* is the validity of prayer on a ship tied to shore standing in all situations, i.e. whether it settles on the ground or not. If he is not able to disembark without harm he prays on it because of the difficulty.

If it is moving the worshipper turns on it towards the direction of prayer because of his ability to fulfil the obligatory component of facing the direction of prayer when beginning prayer. Whenever the ship changes direction from it, i.e. the direction of prayer, the worshipper turns with its change of direction to it, i.e. to the direction of prayer, during the prayer. If he is unable he refrains from prayer until he is able to complete it facing the direction of prayer. If he leaves facing the direction of prayer it does not suffice him according to all of their statements.

Section 26 – Tarawih

- **Tarawih is sunna for men and women**

Tarwiha originally is sitting. Then the four units at the end of which is a sitting came to be known by it.

Hasan narrated its attribute from Abu Hanifa by his statement, "*Tarawih is sunna*" as mentioned in *Khulasa* and is emphasised as is mentioned in *Ikhtiyar*. Asad ibn 'Amr narrated from Abu Yusuf that he said, "*I asked Abu Hanifa about Tarawih and what 'Umar, Allah be pleased with him, did. He said, "Tarawih is an emphasised sunna and 'Umar did not make it up from himself, nor was he an innovator nor did he instruct it except by from a basis with him and a pledge from the Messenger of Allah, Allah be pleased with him.*""

It is an individual emphasised sunna on men and women. It being sunna has been established by the action of the Prophet, upon him be peace and blessings, and his statement, "*Upon you is my sunna and the sunna of the guided caliphs after me.*"[456] Furthermore, 'Umar, 'Uthman and 'Ali, Allah be pleased with them, persisted on it. The Prophet, upon him be peace and blessings, said in a tradition, "*Allah has made obligatory upon you its fast and I have established a sunna for you in its night worship.*"[457] This is a refutation of some Shi'a who claim it is a sunna for men and not for women and the claim of some people that it is a sunna of 'Umar because the correct position is that it is the sunna of the Prophet, upon him be peace and blessings. Group prayer in it is also sunna but collectively as will be explained.

- **Its prayer in a group is a collective sunna**

This is a collective sunna because it is established that, he upon him be peace and blessings, prayed in a group eleven units with witr through

---

[456] This is recorded by Abu Dawud 4607, ibn Majah 42 to 44 and Darimi .

[457] This is recorded by Nasa'i 2212 and ibn Majah 1328.

announcement and did not treat it like other optional prayers. He then explained the reason for leaving it which was his fear, upon him be peace and blessings, that it would be made obligatory upon us.[458] Sadr Shahid said that group prayer is a collective sunna in it such that if some people performed it in the mosque in a group and the remaining people in the locality performed it individually at home they have not left the sunna since it has been narrated from a number of companions that they remained behind. It is mentioned in *Mabsut* that if a person prays at home he has not sinned because ibn 'Umar, 'Urwa, Salim, Qasim, Ibrahim and Naf'i did that. Thus, the action of these indicates that group prayer in the mosque is sunna collectively because it is unimaginable that ibn 'Umar and those who followed him would leave the sunna.

If he prays with a group at home the correct position is that he has attained one of the two virtues because performing it in the mosque has a virtue that is not there when performing it at home – the same is the rule with obligatory prayers.

- **Its time is after nightfall prayer**

This is the correct position until daybreak.

- **Bringing witr before tarawih is valid as is delaying it after it**

Bringing it before is valid because it follows nightfall prayer. However, delaying it after it is best. Hence, if it becomes clear that the night prayer but not the tarawih and witr was invalid they repeat the night prayer and then tarawih without witr with Abu Hanifa because it falls as a general optional prayer since it took place in other than its place – this is the correct position. A group of our colleagues including Isma'il the ascetic said that all of the night is a time for it whether before or

---

[458] The meaning of this is recorded by Bukhari 1129, Muslim 1783 and Abu Dawud 1373.

after nightfall prayer and before or after witr because it is night worship.

- **Delaying tarawih to a third of the night or half of it is recommended**

This means just before a third of the night or just before half of the night.

They differed about performing it after half. Some have said that it is offensive because it follows nightfall and thus is like nightfall sunnas.

- **Delaying it until after it is not offensive according to the correct position**

Others have said that delaying after half of the night is not offensive because intrinsically the best night prayer is at its end. However, the best is that tarawih is not delayed to it out of far of missing it.

- **It is twenty units with ten salaams**

It is twenty units by consensus of the companions with ten salaams as is the inherited practice. Hence, he utters salaams after every two units. If he connects them and sits after every even number the most correct position is that if he intended that it is offensive but valid and it suffices him for all of them. However, if he only sat at the end of four it substitutes for one salaam thus being in place of two units according to the correct position.

- **Sitting after every four for its time length is recommended as it is between the fifth sitting and witr**

This is because it is the inherited practice from the early Muslims and it has been narrated from Abu Hanifa as such. In addition, the name tarawih originates from that. They have a choice during the sitting between glorification, reciting, prayer individually and silence.

- **Completing Koran is sunna in it once in the month according to the correct position**

This is the statement of the majority. Hasan has narrated it from Abu Hanifa, Allah be merciful to him, that he recites in every unit ten verses or similar to it. It is also narrated from Abu Hanifa, Allah be merciful to him, that he used to complete in Ramadan sixty one completions, every day one completion, every night one completion and in every tarawih one completion. He also prayed the Koran in two units and prayed dawn with nightfall ablution for forty years.

- **If the people become impatient of it he recites an amount that does not turn them away according to the chosen position**

This is because the best in our time is that which does not turn the group away as is mentioned in *Ikhtiyar*. *Muhit* mentions that the best in our time is to read with that which does not cause the people to turn away from group prayer because increasing the people is better than lengthening the recitation – and the fatwa is on this. The ascetic said that he recites as in sunset, i.e. the short *mufassal* after Fatiha. Restricting to less than three verses or one long verse after Fatiha is offensive because of leaving the necessary component.

- **Blessings on the Prophet, upon him be peace and blessings, is not left in every testification of it even if the people are impatient according to the chosen position**

This is because it is an emphasised sunna with us and obligatory on the statement of some *mujtahid* scholars with whom it is not valid without it. He should also beware of babbling, leaving distinct reciting and leaving straightening out during the integrals and other than them as is done by people having no fear. This is the case even if the people are impatient towards that because that is the essence of laziness from them. Thus, they are not turned towards in it.

- **Nor is the praise and glorification in the bow and prostration left**

The praise is not left at the beginning of every even number. Likewise glorification is not left because it is obligatory with some and an emphasised sunna with us.

- **He does not bring the supplication if the people are impatient**

The imam does not bring the supplication at the salaam if the people are impatient of it. However, he does not completely leave it. Thus, he supplicates with it shortened thereby attaining the sunna.

- **Tarawih is not made up by missing it individually or as a group**

It is not made up if it is completely missed from its time according to the most correct position because making up is from the unique features of obligatory prayers. If he does make it up it is an optional recommended prayer and not tarawih.

It is a sunna of the time and not of the fast according to the most correct position. Hence, whoever becomes eligible for prayer at the end of the day tarawih is sunna for him, such as the menstruating women when she becomes clean and the traveller and sick person who are not fasting.

Section 27 – Prayer in the Kaaba

We have previously mentioned that amongst the conditions of prayer is facing the direction of prayer which is the Kaaba. The condition is facing a part of the site of the Kaaba or its vertical axis because the direction of prayer is the name for the fixed site of the Kaaba to the heavens with us as is mentioned in 'Inaya. Its building is not the direction of prayer. Hence, when the building ceased the Companions, Allah be pleased with them, prayed towards the site and it is not narrated from them that they took a barrier. Hence,

- **Obligatory and optional prayers are valid in it**

This means inside it, i.e. towards any part of it that he turns because of His statement, Exalted is He, *"to purify Our house"*[459] The order to purify for prayer in it is apparent that it is valid in it.

- **Likewise above it even if he does not take a barrier. However it is offensive because of bad etiquette by him rising over it**

Obligatory and optional prayers are valid above it even if the worshipper does not take a barrier because of that which we have mentioned. However, prayer is offensive for him above it because of bad etiquette by him rising over it and leaving its exaltation.

- **It is valid for whoever has his back to other than the face of his imam in it or above it**

Hence, if his face is to the back or side of his imam, his back to the side or back of his imam, his side to the face or side of his imam facing other than his direction or his face to the face of his imam following

---

[459] Baqara, 125.

him is valid in all seven of these combinations. However, it is offensive if his face faces the face of his imam without a barrier between them because of the offence that has previously been mentioned due to it resembling statue worship. Every direction is a direction of prayer however being ahead and behind is only apparent when the directions are unified whilst they differ within the Kaaba.

- **If he has his back to the face of his imam it is not valid**

This means that his following is not valid. This is a clear statement of that which is known by necessity previously to clarify the rule and that is because he is ahead of his imam.

- **Following is valid outside of it of an imam in it whilst the door is open**

Following is for the person outside of it of an imam inside it whether he has a group with him in it or not whilst the door is open. This is like him standing in the prayer niche in mosques other than it – the qualification here is conventional. Hence, if he hears the relay whilst the door is closed there is nothing preventing his following from being valid as has preceded.

- **It is valid if they circled around it whilst the imam is outside of it except for the person closer to it in the direction of his imam**

All of their following is valid except it is not valid for the person closer to it than his imam whilst in the direction of his imam because he is ahead of his imam. However, the following of the person closer to it than his imam who is not in his direction is valid because being ahead and behind only appears on the same side that both are turning towards.

Section 28 – Traveller Prayer[460]

Linguistically, travel means to cross a distance. In Sacred Law, it is a set distance by specific travel.

- **The minimum travel by which rules alter is the travel of three days from the shortest days of the year at an average pace with breaks**

The laws are the necessity of shortening prayer which is like the allowance of dropping. Know that is two types, an actual allowance and a figurative allowance[461]. Examples of the first are breaking fast and uttering blasphemous words under compulsion and examples of the second are drinking alcohol under compulsion and shortening prayer on a journey. In the first the slave has a choice between performing the allowance and acting upon the original thereby being rewarded. However, in the second there is no choice for him because the action can only be the allowance and the original has been dropped. Hence, completing the prayer does not entail reward because reward in the action of a slave is from what is upon him even by choice between it and something easier than it such as a person wearing footgear who has a choice between keeping them on and wiping and removing them and washing. Thus prayer on a journey is only two units from the four unit prayers and once he has prayed them nothing remains upon him. So there is no reward for him in completing the four units because of his opposing that which was individually obligatory upon him, behaving bad by delaying the salaams and imagining that the additional two were obligatory. Nor is there reward for him in being patient on being killed and not drinking alcohol under compulsion, in fact he sins because of his patience. Naming these and naming shortening on a journey an allowance is figurative because the actual allowance

---

[460] Traveller prayer is the genitive construction of a thing to its condition. However, it is also said that it is to its place or the verb to its subject.

[461] This is also known as *rukhsa tarfiy*.

establishes with it a choice for the slave between coming towards the allowance and bringing the original such as wiping the footgear as we have mentioned, breaking fast in Ramadan and dropping of the necessity of Friday prayer, the two 'Eids and the sacrificial animal whilst there is no choice for him between drinking alcohol under compulsion and being patient on being killed nor between completing the four unit prayer and shortening it on a journey.

Estimation is by days and not by stages or farsakhs – this is the most correct position.

An average pace is during daytime because night is not the place for moving, in fact it is for rest. Moving must be during daytime with breaks. Hence the traveller dismounts in it to eat, drink, carry out any needs and pray. The majority of the day takes the rule of all of it. Thus, if he leaves intending a place and set off early on the first day and moved until before noon until he reached the stage where he dismounted for rest and spent the night there. He then set off early on the second day and moved until after noon and dismounted and then set off on the third day and moved until noon where he reached his intended location Shams Aimma said that the correct position is that he is a traveller.

- **Average is the movement of camels and walking on foot on land, whatever is appropriate to it in mountainous terrain and moderate winds at sea**

Whatever is appropriate to it is considered in mountainous terrains because it involves climbing, descending, mountain passes and rugged terrains. Thus camel movement and walking on foot will be less than their movement on flat ground. Hence if with that movement he crosses a distance which is not distant from the beginning of the first day and dismounted after noon it is counted for him according to what we have mentioned as a day. If he spends the night then wakes up in the morning and does the same until after noon and then dismounts it is a second day. The quickest movement which is the movement of the donkey is not considered nor the slowest movement which is the movement of chariots pulled by animals. The best matters are moderate ones which here is the movement of camels and on foot as we have mentioned.

At sea moderate winds are considered according to fatwa. Hence if he moves most of the day by it it is like all of it even if the distance is less than on flat ground.

- **Whoever intends a journey shortens the four unit obligatory prayer even if he is sinful by his journey when he passes the houses of his place and also passes the open space connected to it**

The traveller shortens the four unit obligatory in belief prayers. Thus there is no shortening of the two or three unit prayers, witr which is an active obligatory prayer or the sunnas. If he is in a state of stopping, stability and safety he brings the sunnas but if he is moving or fearful he does not bring them – this is the chosen position. 'Aisha, Allah be pleased with her, said, "*Prayer was made obligatory as two units which was then increased in residence and affirmed in travel*"[462] except sunset which is the daytime witr, Friday prayer because of its sermon and dawn because of its lengthy recitation.

With us whoever intends a journey shortens even if he is sinful by his journey such as a slave fleeing his master or a highway robber because of the absolute nature of the allowance text.

He shortens when he passes the houses of his place even if they are in an encampment from the side that he left from. If he is only parallel to it on one of its sides it does not harm him.

It is a condition that he also crosses the open space connected to his place as it is a condition that he crosses the outlying area which is the

---

[462] This is recorded by Muslim 1570 to 1572.

houses around the city which have the rule of the city. Likewise, it is a condition to pass villages that are connected to the outlying area of the city according to the correct position.

- **If the open space is separated by farmland or a short distance passing it is not a condition**

It has previously been mentioned that the short distance is 300 to 400 feet. Likewise, it is not a condition to cross it but to cross the open space if the village is connected to the open space and not the outlying area as is mentioned in Qadikhan. However, Nihaya, Fatwa Walwalijiya and Tajnis and Mazid contradict this by saying, "He shortens by leaving the city buildings. The open space of a city is not part of the city in terms of travelling but is part of the city for the validity of Friday prayer. The difference is that Friday prayer is from the interests of the city and the open space of the city is part of the city in whatever is from the needs of the city which includes Friday prayer. Shortening the prayer is not from the needs of the inhabitants of the city thus the open space of the city is not part of the city in this rule, i.e. shortening the prayer."

- **The open space is the area that has been allocated for the interests of the city such as horse training and burying the deceased**

This includes removing earth. Gardens are not considered from the city buildings even if they are connected to its buildings and even if city dwellers inhabited them for all of or part of the year. The homes of the guardians and farmers are not considered by agreement.

- **Three things are conditional for the validity of the intention of travel, independent ruling, maturity and the journey distance not being less than three days. Hence the person who has not passed the buildings of his place or has passed but is a child or is a follower whilst the person being** followed in the journey has not intended such as a woman with her husband, a slave with his master, a soldier with his leader or intends less than three days does not shorten

The woman is a follower of her husband if he has paid her advanced dowry. If he has not paid it she is not attached to him even if he has entered her because it is permitted for her to prevent him from sexual relations and eviction for the dowry with Abu Hanifa, Allah be merciful to him. The slave does not include the mukatab but does include umm walad and mudabbar. The soldier is a follower of his leader if he is paid. Followers also include the employee with the employer, the student with his teacher, the prisoner and the kidnapped with the person who has forced him on the journey and the blind person with the person voluntarily guiding him. If he is paid the consideration is the intention of the blind person.

He does not shorten if he intends less than three days because he does not become a traveller with less than it in Islamic Law.

- **Intention of residency and travel is considered from the original and not the follower if he knows the intention of the person followed according to the most correct position**

The intention of the original such as the husband, master and leader is considered and not of the follower such as the woman, slave and soldier if he is aware. Hence, he is not required to complete by the original intending residency until he knows as with divine injunction and removal of a trustee. Hence, if he prays opposed to him before knowing it is valid according to the most correct position.

- **Shortening is an original with us. Thus, if he completes four units and sat the first sitting his prayer is valid with offence otherwise it is not valid unless he intends residency when he stands for the third**

If he completes four units whilst having sat the first sitting the length of testification his prayer is valid because of the presence of the obligatory in its place which is sitting after two units. The last two units become optional for him. It is offensive because of delaying the necessary component which is the salaam from its place if he intended. However, if he was forgetful he prostrated for forgetfulness. Otherwise, i.e. if he has not sat the length of testification after the first two units his prayer is not valid because he has left the obligatory sitting from its place and the mixing of an optional prayer with an obligatory prayer before its completion. It is valid if he intended residency when he stood to the third in a place where residency is valid for him because he becomes a resident by intention and his obligatory prayer changes to four. Leaving the necessary first sitting does not invalidate as with reciting in one unit because he is able to correct the obligatory reciting in the last two by the intention of residency.

- **He continues shortening until he enters his city or intends residency of half a month at a city or village**

The traveller who has consolidated his journey by having passed three days as a traveller shortens until he returns to his city, i.e. his original abode, or intends residency of half a month. This was estimated by ibn 'Abbas and ibn 'Umar, Allah be pleased with them. If he does not consolidate his journey by wanting to return to his abode before the passing of three days he completes by merely returning even if he has not reached his abode. This is because he has broken his journey because it is leaving as opposed to travelling which does not exist with mere intention until he travels because it is action.

- **He shortens if he intends less than it or does not intend and remains years**

He shortens if he intends less than it, i.e. than half a month or does not intend anything and remains on that for years whilst intend to leave the following day or after a week because 'Alqama ibn Qays remained like that at Khawarizm for two years shortening prayer.

- **Intention of residency is not valid in two towns where he has not specified overnight stay at one of them nor in a desert for other than encampment dwellers nor for our forces at enemy territory nor at our territory whilst besieging rebels**

Intention of residency is not valid in two towns where he has not specified overnight stay at one of them with each one being an original by itself. If it follows such as a village upon the inhabitants of whom Friday prayer is obligatory residency is valid by entering either of them. Likewise, it is valid if he specifies overnight stay at one of the two towns because residency is attached to the place of overnight stay.

Intention of residency is not valid in a desert for other than encampment dwellers because the place is not suitable for him. Encampment[463] is a home of came and goat fur and wool but the meaning is more general than that. However, the intention of residency is valid for encampment dwellers according to the most correct position in a desert.

Intention of residency is not valid for our forces at enemy territory even of they have besieged a city because their state fluctuates between remaining and fleeing.

Intention of residency is not valid for our forces at our territory whilst besieging rebels because of the fluctuation as we have mentioned even if the upper hand is clearly with us over them.

- **If a traveller follows a resident in the time it is valid and he completes it as four**

---

[463] Encampment is *akhbiya* which is the plural of *khaba* without *hamza* such as *kasa* and *aksiya*.

If a traveller follows a resident who is praying a four unit prayer even in the final sitting in the time his following is valid. He completes it as four following his imam and because the changer has connecter to the cause which is the time even if the time has left before he has completed it or the imam has left the first sitting according to the correct position.

- **It is not valid after it**

The traveller following the resident is not valid after it, i.e. after the time leaving even if the prohibition of the resident was before the time leaving because his obligatory prayer does not change after its leaving.

- **It is valid in both of them the other way round**

Following is valid the other way round by the resident following the traveller in both of them, i.e. in the time and after it leaving because he, upon him be peace and blessings, prayed with the Meccans whilst he was a traveller and said, "Complete your prayers because we are a travelling people."[464] Furthermore, his sitting is obligatory and is stronger than the first for the resident. The residents complete individually without reciting and prostration forgetfulness and following them is not valid.

- **It is recommended for the imam to say, "Complete your prayer because I am a traveller"**

It is recommended for the imam to say this as we have narrated after the two salaams according to the most correct position. It is also said that he says it after the first salaam. It is only recommended because it is not specified as a change for the state of the imam because of the permissibility of question before prayer or after they have completed prayer.

---

[464] The meaning of this is recorded by Abu Dawud 1229.

- **It is befitting that he says that before entering the prayer**

It is befitting that the imam say that before entering the prayer to remove confusion from the offset.

- **The resident does not recite in that which he completes after his travelling imam has completed according to the most correct position**

The resident follower does not recite because he has caught the beginning of his prayer with the imam and the obligatory reciting has been fulfilled as opposed to the latecomer.

- **The missed prayer of travel and residency is made up as two and four**

The missed prayer of residency and the missed prayer of travel is made up as two and four respectively because making up is according to the original. This is as opposed to the missed prayer of the sick and healthy person because the sick person when he gets better makes up with bowing and prostrating and but if he becomes sick he makes up by motioning the missed prayers of his healthy state because the bowing and prostrating have dropped dues to the excuse and their necessity when able whilst making up.

- **The consideration in it is the end time**

The consideration in it, i.e. the requirement of four in residency and two in travelling is by the end time. Thus, if at its end he is a traveller he prays two units and if he is a resident he prays four because it is the consideration in the cause in non-performance prior during the time. Thus, prayer is required of him if he becomes fit for it at the end time by maturity, Islam, recovery from insanity and unconsciousness and cleanliness from menstruation and postnatal bleeding and is dropped because of his unsuitability by insanity, lengthy unconsciousness, postnatal bleeding and menstruation.

- **The original abode is only cancelled by its like**

Hence, it is not cancelled by residency or travel abode because a thing can only be cancelled by a thing like it or superior to it and not by a thing lesser than it. A prior journey is not a condition for the establishment of an original abode by consensus or for a residency abode according to primary narrations. If he does not move his family but acquires new family at another town it does not cancel his original abode and each one of them is an original abode for him.

- **Residency abode is cancelled by its like, by travel and by the original**

Residency abode is cancelled by leaving on a journey after it and by returning back to the original abode because of what we have mentioned.

- **Original abode is that place where he was born, married or did not marry but intended to live there and not to move from it**

- **Residency abode is a place at which he intended residency half a month or more**

This is a place that is suitable for it as we have previously mentioned. The point of this is that he completes prayer when he enters it whilst he is a traveller before invalidating it.

- **The scholars did not consider the travel abode which is where he intends residency less than half a month**

This is a place where he intends residency less than half a month whilst he was a traveller. Hence, his residency abode does not invalidate by it nor does his journey invalidate.

Section 29 – Dropping Prayer and Fast

- **If the sick person dies whilst unable to pray motioning bequeathing it is not required of him even they are few**

Bequeathing it is not required of him even if they are few because they are less than prayer of a day and night because of that which we have narrated. This is because he is unable to find time for it according to the statement of those who interpret acceptance of excuse as the permissibility of delaying. Those who interpret it as dropping is obvious.

- **Likewise is fast if the traveller and sick person break fast and die before residency and health**

Likewise is the rule of fast in the month of Ramadan if the traveller and sick person break fast and die before residency for the traveller and before health for the sick person because they were unable to find a number of other days. Hence bequeathing it is not required.

- **He must bequeath that which he was able and remained upon him**

He must, i.e. the person who broke his fast in Ramadan even without an excuse, bequeath that which, i.e. the compensation of that which he was able by finding a number of other days if he broke fast with an excuse. If he broke fast without an excuse and did not find a number of other days he must compensate all that he broke because the fault was from him. However pardon is hoped for him by the grace of Allah through compensation of that which was on him and remained upon him until death overtakes him. This includes obligatory fast, expiation, shunning wives, offence in ihram and vow.

- His executor pays for him from a third of that which he left half a s'a of wheat or its value for every day of fast and for every prayer time including witr

His executor, i.e. the person who deals with his finances whether inheritance or bequest, pays for him from a third of that which the inheritee leaves because his right is in a third of his finances on his sickbed. The right of the inheritor is in two thirds. Thus it is not executed forcibly on the inheritor except from the third if he bequeaths it. It is not required of the inheritor to pay it if he does not bequeath it. It is permitted if he donates it as we will mention. The same is the case with the debt of fitr zakat, compulsory maintenance, land tax, military tax, financial expiations, pilgrimage bequest, vow charity and finally vow seclusion from the needs of the city which includes Friday prayer.

Section 30 – Doubt

- **Prayer is invalid by doubt about the number of its units if it is before its completion and it is the first time that doubt has occurred or doubt is not normal for him**

Doubt is equality in two matters such as being unsure between three and four. It invalidates if it is the first time it has occurred after maturity in any prayer – this is the statement of most scholars. Fakhr Islam said that it is the first time that it occurs to him in this prayer – ibn Fadhl chose it. Imam Sarakhsi held that it means that forgetfulness is not normal for him and not that it means that he has never forgotten. Thus his rule is that of the person who began with doubt. Hence he mentions that doubt is not normal for him thus invalidating by it. This is because of his statement, upon him be peace and blessings, *"If one of you doubts in his prayer how many he has prayed he should restart his prayer."*[465] This is interpreted as if it is the first time doubt has occurred to him as we shall mention with the other narrations and because he is able to drop that which he is on with certainty. This is the same as the person who doubts whether he has prayed or not whilst the time remains; he must pray.

- **If he doubts after his salaam it is not considered unless he is certain of having left**

If he doubts after his salaam or his sitting the length of the testification before salaam about the number of units his doubt is not considered. There is nothing on him viewing his state as being good. However if he is certain that he has left he does that which he has left. If a trustworthy person informs him after the salaam that he is short one unit but with the worshipper he has completed he does not consider his informing. If two trustworthy people inform him his doubt is not considered and he must take their statement. If the imam and followers differ if he is

---

certain he does not take their statement but if some of them are with him he takes his statement.

- **If the doubt is a lot he acts upon his strongest probability**

He investigates and takes this because of his statement, upon him be peace and blessings, *"If one of you doubts he should investigate the correct and complete according to it."*[466] This is interpreted as if the doubt is a lot because of the previous narration.

- **If he has no strong probability he takes the minimum**

This is because of his statement, upon him be peace and blessings, *"When one of you forgets in his prayer and does not know whether he has prayed one or two he should build on one. If he does not know whether he has prayed two or three he should build on two. If he does not know whether he has prayed three or four he should build on three. He prostrates twice before uttering salaam"*[467] i.e. for forgetfulness. Since all three narrations that we have mentioned with the three issues are established with them they dealt with it by combining by interpreting each one in a manner that has a basis as is mentioned in Fath Qadir.

- **He sits after every unit he believes to be the end of his prayer**

This is so that he does not leave the obligatory sitting whilst the path to being certain in not leaving it is straightforward. Likewise, he sits at every sitting that he believes to be necessary.

466

467

He has doubt about ritual impurity but is certain of purity he is pure but the other way around he is ritually impure. He has doubt about some of his ablution and it is the first time it has occurred to him he washes that part. If his doubt is a lot he does not consider it. Likewise, if he doubts whether he has uttered takbir for opening whilst he is in prayer, whether impurity has touched him, whether he has broken his ablution or whether he has wiped his head or not if it is the first time it has occurred to him he restarts but if it is a lot he continues. 'Attabiyya mentions that if he has doubt whether he has uttered takbir it is said that if it is in the first unit he repeats it but if it is in the second he does not.

Section 31 – Recitation Prostration

Recitation prostration is from construction of the rule to its cause which is the primary form in construction because it is for specification. The strongest form is specification by primal cause with the cause because it occurs due to it. Its condition is purity from ritual impurity and filth – thus dry ablution is not permitted for it without an excuse, facing the direction of prayer and covering the nakedness. Its pillar is placing the forehead on the ground. Its attribute is that it is necessary instantly in prayer and over time in other than prayer. Its rule is that the necessity is dropped in this world and the attainment of reward in the afterlife.

- **Its cause is recitation on the reciter and the listener according to the correct position**

This is on the reciter by agreement. Listening is a condition for the action of reciting for him. Hence prostration is necessary on a deaf person who recites it but does not hear.

- **It is necessary over time if it is not in prayer**

The recitation prostration is necessary because it is either an explicit order, contains the haughtiness of unbelievers towards it or following the prophets and each of these is necessary. It is necessary over time with Muhammad and is a narration from the Imam – this is the chosen position. With Abu Yusuf, and it is a narration from the Imam, it is necessary instantly. This is the case if it has not become necessary by reciting it in prayer because it has become a part of the prayer which cannot be made up outside of it. Thus it is necessary instantly in it. However other than it is necessary over time.

- **However it is slightly offensive to delay it**

Delaying the prostration from its time is slightly offensive according to the most correct position if it is not offensive because over a long time he could forget it.

- **It is necessary on the person who recites a verse even in Persian**

Prostration is necessary for the morally responsible person for prayer, not following and in other than bowing, prostration and testification because of the prohibition in them of reciting. It is obligatory even if he recites it in Persian by agreement whether he understands or not because it is Koran from one perspective.

- **Reciting the recitation word with the word before or after it from its verses is like the verse according to the correct position**

Thus it necessitates prostration like reciting a complete verse. It is said that it is not necessary unless he recites most of the recitation verse. Mukhtasar Bahr mentions that if he recites *"but prostrate yourself"*[468] and stops without reciting *"and draw near"*[469] he must prostrate.

- **Its verses are fourteen being in al A'raf, ar-Ra'd, an-Nahl, al-Isra', Maryam, al-Hajj, al-Furqan, an-Naml, as-Sajdah, Sad, Ha-Mim as-Sajdah, an-Najm, al-Inshiqaq and al-'Alaq**

Prostration is necessary for the following

1. al-A'raf at His statement, Exalted is He, *"Those who are with your Lord are not too proud to worship Him, but they praise Him and fall down in prostration before Him."*[470]

---

[468] al-'Alaq 19.
[469] al-'Alaq 19.
[470] al-A'raf 206.

2. ar-Ra'd, "*And to Allah prostrate all who are in the heavens and the earth, willingly or unwillingly, and their shadows too, in the mornings and in the evenings.*"[471]

3. an-Nahl, "*To Allah prostrates everything that is in the heavens, every thing walking on the earth, and the angels, and they are not proud. They all fear their Lord, High above them, and they do all that they are commanded.*"[472]

4. al-Isra', "*Those who were given knowledge before it, when it is recited to them, fall down upon their faces in prostration. And say: "Transcendent is our Lord, the promise of our Lord shall be fulfilled!" They fall down upon their faces weeping, and it increases them in humility.*"[473]

5. Maryam, "*These are those upon whom Allah has bestowed His favours: the Prophets from among the descendants of Adam and of those whom We carried with Noah; the descendants of Abraham and of Israel, and of those whom We guided and chose. When the signs of the All-Merciful were recited to them they would fall down in prostration, and tears.*"[474]

6. al-Hajj, "*Have you not seen that to Allah prostrate all who are in the heavens, and who are on the earth, and the sun and the moon, and the stars, and the mountains, and the trees, and the beasts and many of mankind, while many deserve punishment? And whomever Allah abases none will be able to honour. Allah does what He will.*"[475]

7. al-Furqan, "*And if it is said to them: "Prostrate yourselves to the All-Merciful," they said: "And who is the All-Merciful? Shall we prostrate ourselves to whatever you bid us?" And it increases them in aversion.*"[476]

8. an-Naml, "*So that they worship not Allah, Who brings forth the hidden in the heavens and the earth, and knows what you conceal*

---

[471] ar-Ra'd 15.

[472] an-Nahl 49 to 50.

[473] al-Isra' 107 to 109.

[474] Maryam 58.

[475] al-Hajj 18.

[476] al-Furqan 60.

and what you reveal. Allah; there is no God save Him, the Lord of the formidable Throne."[477] This is on the general reading with emphasis but at His statement, Exalted is He, "*O prostrate*" on the reading of Kasa'i with lightness. Mujtaba mentions that Farra said that prostration is only necessary in Naml on the rading of Kasa'i, i.e. with lightness and it is appropriate not to be necessary with emphasis because its meaning is the Devil has made their deeds seem fair to them so that they worship not Allah. However the most correct position is that it is necessary on both readings because it has been recorded in the 'Uthamni copy as mentioned in Diraya.

9. as-Sajdah, "*Only those believe in Our signs who, when they are reminded of them, fall down prostrate and extol the praise of their Lord, and are not proud.*"[478]

10. Sad, "*And David guessed that We had tried him, and he sought forgiveness of his Lord, and he bowed himself and fell down prostrate and repented. So We forgave him that; and he was given nearness to Us and an excellent end.*"[479] This is better than that which Zayla'i said that it is necessary at His statement, Exalted is He, "*and he bowed himself and fell down prostrate and repented*"[480] and with others at His statement, "*and an excellent end*"[481] as we shall mention.

11. Ha-Mim as-Sajdah, "*If they show arrogance, those who are in Allah's presence glorify Him night and day, and are never wearied*"[482] from His statement, Exalted is He, "*Among His signs are the night and the day, and the sun and the moon. Do not prostrate yourselves before the sun and the moon, but prostrate yourselves before Allah who created them, of you would worship Him. If they show arrogance, those who are in Allah's presence*

---

[477] an-Naml 25 to 26.
[478] as-Sajdah 15.
[479] Sad 24 to 25.
[480] Sad 24.
[481] Sad 25.
[482] Ha-Mim as-Sajdah 38.

glorify Him night and day, and are never wearied."[483] This is according to our school and is narrated from ibn 'Abbas and Wa'il ibn Hujr. However with Shafi' it is at His statement, Exalted is He, "*if you would worship Him*"[484] which is the school of 'Ali and is narrated from ibn Mas'ud and ibn 'Umar. Our scholars have preferred the first position based on taking caution when the schools of the companions differ. This is because if prostration is necessary at His statement, "*you would worship*" delaying to His statement, Exalted is He, "*never wearied*" does not harm and he has fulfilled the necessary component. However if it is necessary at His statement, Exalted is He, "*never wearied*" the intended prostration before it would be attained before it is necessary and before the existence of the cause of it being necessary which would create a deficiency in the prayer if it was in the prayer whereas there is no deficiency at all based on what we say. This is a sign of mastery in legal science as is mentioned in Bahr from Bada'i. The same is the case with that which I mentioned before in Sad otherwise there would be a contradiction. This is the basis that we promised.

12. an-Najm, "*Do you marvel then at this discourse, and laugh: instead of weeping, while you amuse yourselves? Rather prostrate yourselves before Allah, and worship Him.*"[485]

13. al-Inshiqaq, "*Why do they not believe, and when the Koran is recited to them, do they not prostrate?*"[486]

14. al-'Alaq, "*No! Never obey Him! But prostrate yourself and draw near.*"[487]

We shall also mention the benefit of this collection.

---

[483] Ha-Mim as-Sajdah 38 to 39.

[484] Ha-Mim as-Sajdah 38.

[485] an-Najm 59 to 62.

[486] al-Inshiqaq 20 to 21.

[487] al-'Alaq 19.

- Prostration is necessary on the person who listens even if he did not intend listening except the menstruating woman, the woman in postnatal bleeding, the imam and his follower

Prostration is necessary on the person who listens to the Arabic recitation whether he understands or not – this is narrated from leading companions. The menstruation woman and the woman in postnatal bleeding are exempted. Hence nothing is necessary on them by reciting or listening but it is necessary by listening from them and from the sexually impure as it is necessary upon the sexually impure and by listening from an unbeliever and from a discerning child. It is not necessary on the imam and his follower by listening from a follower of the listening imam or another imam. However it is necessary on the person who is not in prayer by listening from the follower according to the most correct position.

- If they hear it from other than him they prostrate after prayer

If the followers and the imam hear it from other than the follower they prostrate after prayer because the cause has been realised and the removal of a preventor by doing it in prayer.

- It does not suffice them if they prostrate in it but their prayer is not invalid according to primary narration

It does not suffice them because of its deficiency but it does not invalidate because it is from its type according to primary narration which is the correct position.

- It is necessary by listening to Persian if he understands it according to the relied on position

Prostration is necessary by listening to recitation in Persian if he understands it – this is with them both. It is necessary with Abu Hanifa even if he does not understand its meaning if he is told it is a prostration verse. The basis of the difference is whether Persian is Koran from every angle or not. If he does understand it is necessary out of caution.

- ## Authentication differs about its necessity by listening from a sleeping or insane person

This is about its necessity on the listener. Shaykh Islam says that it is not necessary because of the absence of a valid recital due to the absence of discernment. Tatarkhaniyya mentions that if he hears it from a sleeping person it is said it is necessary but the correct position is that it is not necessary. Khaniya mentions that the correct position is that it is necessary. Khulasa mentions that if he hears it from a bird it is not necessary – this is the chosen position – but if he hears it from a sleeping person the correct position is that it is necessary – the same is in Qadikhan. If he is informed that he has recited it in his sleep it is necessary upon – this is the most correct position. Diraya mentions that it is not on him – this is the correct position. The recital of a drunken person necessitates upon himself and the listener. It is not necessary on a dumb or deaf person or a writer of a prostration by seeing a person prostrating and writing because of the absence of a recital and listening.

- ## It is not necessary by listening from a bird and an echo

Recitation prostration is not necessary by listening from a bird according to the correct position. However it is said that it is necessary and Hujja mentions that it is the correct position because he has heard the speech of Allah. The same difference exists by listening to it from a trained chimpanzee. It is not necessary by listening to an echo[488].

---

[488] An echo is that which replies to you and is like your voice in mountains, deserts and the likes.

- It is performed in bowing and prostrating in prayer other than the prayer bowing and its prostrating

Siyam (Fasting)

Section 1 – Offensive, Non-offensive and Recommended Actions

- Seven things are offensive for the fasting person

1. Tasting something

This is because it exposes the fast to becoming invalid even if optional according to the school.

2. Chewing without an excuse

This, for example, is a woman who finds a person to chew food for her child such as a menstruating woman not keeping fast. However if she finds no alternative there is no problem with chewing it for the preservation of the child. There is a difference of opinion if he fears excessive price in purchasing an edible food that can be tasted. A woman can taste food if her husband has bad character to know its saltiness. However if he is of good character it is not allowed for her. The same is for the slave girl. I say, the same is the employee.

3. Chewing mastic[489]

This is mastic of which nothing reaches the stomach with the saliva because he will be accused of breaking fast by chewing it whether male or female. Imam 'Ali, Allah be pleased with him, said, "Beware of that whose rejection hastens to the mind even if you have an excuse for it."

---

[489] *'Alak* is mastic which is an aromatic resin obtained from the mastic tree and used as an astringent and to make varnishes and lacquers. It is also said that it is frankincense.

It is recommended for women in other than fasting and is offensive for men except when alone – however, it is said it is permitted for them.

4. Kissing

5. Contact

This is even if he feels safe from ejaculating or making love according to primary narration

Kissing, sexual and other contact is offensive for him because it exposes the fast to becoming invalid due to the consequence of the action. Sexual kissing by chewing her lip is offensive as mentioned in Thahiriyya.

6. **Gathering saliva in the mouth and then swallowing it**

This is offensive if intentional thereby avoiding uncertainty.

7. **That which he believes will weaken him such as phlebotomy and cupping**

Any action that weakens the fast is offensive. This includes a strenuous task because it exposes the fast to becoming invalid.

- **Nine things are not offensive for the fasting person**

These have been mentioned even though they are understood to provide evidence.

1. Kissing and Contact

This is whilst feeling safe from ejaculating and making love because of that which is narrated from 'Aisha, Allah be pleased with her, that *he, upon him be peace and blessings would kiss and make contact whilst he* *was fasting* – the two Shaykhs narrated it.[490] This is primary narration. It is mentioned from Muhammad that he regarded sexual contact as offensive which is the narration of Hasan from the Imam because it is not free of difficulty. Jawhara mentions that it is said that contact is offensive even whilst feeling safe. It is that his genitals touch her genitals.

2. Oiling[491] the moustache

This is because there is nothing in it that negates the fast.

3. Eyeliner

This is because *he, upon him be peace and blessings, used eyeliner whilst he was fasting.*[492]

4. Cupping

This is that which does not weaken from the fast.

5. Phlebotomy

This is like cupping. Shaykh Islam mentioned that the condition for it to be offensive is weakness that needs breaking the fast.

6. Using toothstick at the end of the day which is in fact sunna as with the beginning of it even if it is moist or soaked in water

---

[490] This is recorded by Bukhari 1927; Muslim 2576; Abu Dawud 2382 and Tirmidhi 729.

[491] *Dahn*, oiling, is the verbal noun but *duhn*, oil, is the concrete noun taking the place of the verbal noun.

[492] This is recorded by ibn Majah 1678.

This is because of his statement, upon him be peace and blessings, *"From amongst the best traits of a fasting person is the toothstick."*[493] Kifaya mentions that *the Prophet, upon him be peace and blessings, would use the toothstick at the beginning of the day and at its end whist he was fasting.* Jami' Saghir of Suyuti mentions, *"Using the toothstick is sunna. Hence, use the toothstick at any time you want."*[494] This is also because of his statement, upon him be peace and blessings, *"A prayer with a toothstick is better than seventy prayers without a toothstick."* It is general because it is described in a general manner which is applicable to the midafternoon of the fasting person as is mentioned in *Fath*.

It is not offensive even if it is green and moist or soaked with water because of the unqualified nature of that which we have narrated.

7. **Rinsing the mouth and nose for other than ablution**

8. **Performing ritual bath**

9. **Wrapping in a wet cloth for cooling according to fatwa**

This is done for cooling and removing heat. This is the statement of Abu Yusuf because the Prophet, upon him be peace and blessings, *poured water over his head whilst he was fasting from thirst or heat* – Abu Dawud narrated it[495] and ibn 'Umar, Allah be pleased with them both, used to wet a cloth and wrap it around him whilst he was fasting. This also assists in worship and removes natural unease. However Abu Hanifa regarded it as offensive because it displays unease in performing worship.

- **Three things are recommended**

---

[493] This is recorded by ibn Majah 1677.
[494] This is recorded by Suyuti in Jami' Saghir 4839 who traces it to Daylami in Musnad Firdaus and classifies it as fair.
[495] This is recorded by Abu Dawud 2365.

1. Predawn meal

This is because of his statement, upon him be peace and blessings, *"Eat the predawn meal because there is blessing in the predawn meal"*[496] and because it provides strength and additional reward. However it should not be excessive because it takes away from the purpose as is done by wealthy people.

2. Delaying it

This is because of his statement, upon him be peace and blessings, *"Three are from the character of the Messengers, hastening breaking the fast, delaying the predawn meal and placing the right on the left in prayer."*

3. Hastening breaking the fast on other than a cloudy day

On a cloudy day he should be cautious thereby protecting his fast from being invalid. The recommended hastening is before the appearance of the stars as Qadikhan has mentioned. The blessing is with even water. He, upon him be peace and blessings, said, *"Predawn meal is blessing so do not leave it even if one of you swallows a mouthful of water. Allah and His angels bless those who eat the predawn meal"* – Ahmad, Allah be merciful with him, narrated it.

---

[496] This is recorded by Bukhari 1923; Muslim 2549; Tirmidhi 708; ibn Majah 1692 and Darami 1696.

Section 2 – Occurrences

This includes sickness, travel, compulsion, pregnancy, breastfeeding, hunger, thirst and old age. These permit breaking fast.

Hence it is permitted for

- **Person who fears an increase in sickness or a delay in healing**

The person who is sick is permitted if he fears an increase in sickness in quantity or quality. Sickness is a state that produces a change in nature towards weakness occurring first internally followed by its effects manifesting. This is whether he has a sore eye, injury, headache, etc. Likewise if he fears a delay in healing he is permitted to break fast because it could lead to ruin thus being necessary to avoid. The soldier who knows with certainty or high probability that he will fight because of the presence of the enemy in front of him and fears that he will be weakened from fighting but is not a traveller may break fast before the battle. There is no problem for the person who has fever cycles or menstruation habit from breaking fast on the probability of its presence. However if it is not present there is a difference of opinion in the requirement of expiation – the most correct position is that it is not required of them. Likewise there is no expiation if villagers on hearing a drum on the thirtieth day believing it to be 'Eid broke their fast but then found out that it was for other than it.

- **Pregnant woman or breastfeeding mother who fears mental retardation, death or sickness for herself or her child whether by birth or breastfeeding.**

She can take medicine if a doctor advises that it will prevent diarrhoea of the breastfeeding child. Thus she may break fast for this excuse. This is because of his statement, upon him be peace and blessings, *"Allah has removed from the traveller the fast and half the prayer and from the pregnant woman and the breastfeeding mother the fast.*"[497] Whoever qualifies with the woman paid to breastfeed is rejected.

The considered fear for the permissibility of breaking fast is known in two ways:

10. That which is based on high probability from experience

High probability has the status of certainty from a past experience.

11. Advice of a doctor

This is a Muslim skilled trustworthy doctor in diseases as is mentioned in Burhan. Kamal says that it is a Muslim skilled doctor not known to be sinful. However it is said that his trustworthiness is a condition.

- **The person who has severe thirst or hunger from which death is feared**

Breaking fast is permitted if death, mental retardation or partial sensory loss is feared. However this is if he has not exhausted himself because if this is the case expiation is required – it is also said that it is not.

- **The traveller can break fast**

The traveller who began his journey before dawn break can break his fast since he is not permitted to break his fast by beginning it after he woke up as a fasting person. This is opposed to the person who suffers sickness after it who can break his fast. The traveller can break his fast because of His statement, Exalted is He, *"but if any one of you is ill or*

---

[497] This is recorded by Abu Dawud 2408; Tirmidhi 715 and ibn Majah 1667.

on a journey, let him fast the same number of days later on"[498] and because of that which we have narrated .

- However his fast is better if it does not harm him and most of his friends have not broken their fast or contributed to the expenses. If they have contributed or have broken their fast breaking his fast is best conforming to the group[499]

His fast is better if it does not harm him because of His statement, Exalted is He, "*but to fast is better for you.*"[500]

- The person who dies before the cessation of his excuse is not required to bequeath

This person is not required to bequeath the expiation of that for which he has broken fast if he dies before the cessation of his excuse such as sickness, travel, and other legitimising excuses for breaking fast that have preceded because he has missed catching a number of days later on.

- He makes up that which he is able to make up for the length of residency and health

If he catches a number of days he makes up that which he is able to make up. If he does not make up he is required to bequeath the length of residency from travel and health from sickness and the cessation of the excuse by agreement according to the correct position.

The difference is in the person who vows to fast a month if he gets well and then is well for one day. He is required to bequeath feeding for the whole month with them both but with Muhammad he makes up that which he was well in.

---

[498] al-Baqara 184.
[499] This is mentioned in Jawhara.
[500] al-Baqara 184.

- **Succession is not conditional in making up**

This is because of the unqualified nature of the scriptural text. However succession and not delaying beyond the period of ability is recommended hastening towards good and meeting the responsibility.

Note:

There are four successive by scriptural text
1. Performing Ramadan
2. Shunning the wife expiation
3. Killing expiation
4. Oath expiation

The optional ones are
1. Making up Ramadan
2. Compensation for shaving due to an ailment on the head of the person wearing ihram
3. Tamattu'
4. Qiran
5. Hunting penalty

There are three not mentioned in the Koran but are established by reports
1. Fasting expiation for breaking fast intentionally in Ramadan which is successive
2. Optional fast which is optional
3. Vow which has types. He either vows a number of successive specific days, unspecific days and that which is required by a seclusion vow which is successive even if he does not state that unless he explicitly states in the vow that they are not successive

- **If another Ramadan comes it precedes making up and there is no compensation in delaying to it**

If he has not made up the missed fast he performs the current before making up legally. Thus if he intends it as a missed fast it is only considered as a current fast as has preceded. There is no compensation in delaying to it because of the unqualified nature of the scriptural text.

- Breaking fast is permitted for an elderly[501] man or woman

- Compensation is required of them for each day half sa' of wheat as with the person who vowed perpetual fast and became weak

Compensation is required as with the person who became incapable of fulfilling the perpetual vow but not for any other excused person. The compensation for each day is half sa' of wheat or its value on the condition that the old person's inability remains until death. If he is a traveller and died before residency compensation is not necessary for him breaking fast on the journey. The person who vowed a perpetual fast and became weak due to being occupied with earning livelihood breaks his fast and compensates because of certainty that he is unable to make up.

- If he is unable to compensate because of difficulty he asks Allah's forgiveness and pardon

If a person who is permitted to pay compensation and is unable to he asks Allah's forgiveness and pardon, i.e. he seeks his pardon for his shortcoming towards Him.

- If an oath or killing expiation is necessary and he does not find that by which he expiates such as freeing and he is an old person or not having fasted compensation is not valid

---

[501] They are referred to as *fani* which is a reference to them approaching extinction or that their strength has perished and are unable to perform.

Compensation is only permitted for a fast that is primary by itself and not as a substitute for other than it. Thus if an oath, killing, shunning wife or breaking fast expiation is necessary and he does not find that by which he expiates such as freeing, feeding and clothing and he is an elderly person or not having fasted whilst being able to fast until he became old compensation is not valid because fast here is a substitute for other than it which is financial expiation. Thus fast is only referred to when he is unable to expiate financially. If he bequeaths the expiation it is executed from one third.

Permission for food is permitted in compensation being two satiating meals for a day just as possession is permitted. This is different to zakat fitr where possession must occur as with zakat. Know that that which is legislated with the terms feeding or food possession and permission is permitted but that which is legislated with the terms giving or paying possession is conditional.

- **Breaking fast is permitted for the optional person without an excuse according to one narration**

This narration is from Abu Yusuf. Kamal said that my belief is that it is soundest because of that which Muslim narrated from 'Aisha, Allah be pleased with her, that she said, "*The Prophet, upon him be peace and blessings, entered one day and said, "Do you have anything?" We said, "No." He said, "I am therefore fasting." On another day he came whereupon we said, "Messenger of Allah, some hays[502] has been gifted to us." He said, "Show me it because I woke up fasting." He then ate."[503]*Nasa'i continues, "*However I will fast a day in place of it*" – Abu Muhammad Abdul Haqq has authenticated this addition.

---

[502] *Hays* is a meal of dates mixed with clarified butter and a preparation of dried curd which is kneaded vehemently or rubbed and pressed with the hand until they mingle together.
[503] This is recorded by Muslim 2714 to 2715 and Nasa'i 2324 to 2332.

Karkhi and Abu Bakr mention that he can only break fast for an excuse – this is primary narration – because if that which is narrated that he, upon him be peace and blessings, said, *"When one of you is invited for food he should respond. If he is not fasting he should eat but if he is fasting he should pray."*[504] – i.e. he should leave. Qurtubi said that this tradition has been established from him, upon him be peace and blessings, and had breaking fast been permitted breaking fast would have been best to respond to the invitation that is sunna – this has been authenticated in Muhit.

Know that invalidating fast and prayer without an excuse after having begun them both optionally is offensive but is not impermissible because the proof is not unquestionable in meaning though making up is required. However if an excuse arises it is permitted for the optional person to break fast by agreement.

- **Hospitality is an excuse according to the most apparent position for the guest and the host**

This is before zenith but not after it unless not breaking fast involves filial disobedience and not for anyone else because of the emphasis. If a person swears a divorce that he will break his fast the relied upon position is that he breaks the fast even after zenith but he has not broken it to preserve the right of his brother.

- **He has glad tidings by this great news**

He says in Tajnis and Mazid that if a man rises fasting optionally and enters on one of his brothers who asks him to break his fast there is no problem in him breaking it because of the statement of the Prophet, upon him be peace and blessings, *"Whoever breaks fast for the right of*

---

[504] This is recorded by Abu Dawud 2460 and ibn Majah 1751. Abu Dawud mentions in his narration that Hisham, one of the narrators, said, *"Prayer is supplication"*. The narration of ibn Majah states, *"Whoever is invited to food whilst fasting should respond. If he wants he eats and if he wants he leaves."*

his brother the reward of one thousand days fast is recorded for him and when he makes up a day the reward of two thousand days fast is recorded for him." This is also transmitted in Tatarkhaniyya, Muhit and Mabsut.

- **If he breaks fast anyhow making up is on him unless he began optionally on five days, the two 'Eids and tashriq days when making them up is not required by invalidating them according to primary narration**

There is no difference between our colleagues in the necessity of making up if the optional person breaks his fast thereby preserving that which has passed from being invalid. If he began fast optionally on the five days making them up is required according to primary narration from Abu Hanifa, Allah be pleased with him, because he is instructed to break its fast. Completing it is not permitted because in actually beginning he has committed a prohibited act by turning away from the hospitality of Allah, Exalted is He. Hence he is instructed to break it. However it is narrated from Abu Yusuf and Muhammad that making up is on him, i.e. even if breaking fast is necessary.

In that which we have mentioned is an indicator that an optional prayer that he broke because he began it at, for example, sunrise should be made up as has preceded.

And Allah is the One who facilitates by His greatest favour towards the soundest religion.

Section 3 – Vow

This includes fast, prayer and other vows.

- **If he vows something he is required to complete it**

If he vows some devotional act he is required to complete it because of His statement, Exalted is He, *"then they should complete their rites"*[505] and his statement, upon him be peace and blessings, *"Whoever vows to obey Allah should obey him but whoever vows to disobey Allah should not disobey him"*[506] – Bukhari narrated it. Consensus is on it being necessary to complete it and this is the basis of those who claim it is obligatory. *Nathara* is of the form *daraba* but according to one language *qatala*.

- **If three conditions come together**

The vow is required if three conditions come together in the vow.

12. Its type is necessary

It is necessary by itself even if it is performing it is prohibited because of its quality such as sacrifice day fast.

13. It is aspired

This is that it is aspired intrinsically and not for something else such as ablution.

14. It is not necessary

It is not necessary before his vow by the requirement of Allah, Exalted is He, such as the five prayers and witr.

---

[505] al-Hajj 29.

[506]

A fourth condition is added that the vow is not impossible such as his statement, "For Allah on me is yesterday's fast today" which is not required of him. Likewise if he says, "today yesterday" and his statement is after zenith.

- **Hence ablution is not required by his vow, nor recitation prostration or visiting the sick**

Ablution is not required by his vow nor Koranic recitation because ablution is not aspired intrinsically since it is legislated as a condition for other than it such as the validity of prayer.

Recitation prostration is necessary by the requirement of the Lawmaker.
Visiting the sick is not from the type that is necessary and requirement of the slave is considered by the requirement of Allah, Exalted is He, because he may follow and not innovate – this is according to primary narration. According to another narration from Abu Hanifa he said that if he vows to visit a sick person today his vow is valid but if he vows to visit so and so nothing is required of him. This is because visiting the sick is a devotional act - he, upon him be peace and blessings, said, "*The one who visits a sick person is in the fields of Heaven until he returns.*"[507] Visiting a specific sick person does not carry the meaning of a devotional act as intended by the person making the vow. ngth of residency from travel and health from sickness and the cessation of the excuse by agreement according to the correct position.

The difference is in the person who vows to fast a month if he gets well and then is well for one day. He is required to bequeath feeding for the whole month with them both but with Muhammad he makes up that which he was well in.

- **Succession is not conditional in making up**

507

This is because of the absolute nature of the scriptural text. However succession and not delaying beyond the period of ability is recommended hastening towards good and meeting the responsibility.

Note:

There are four successive by scriptural text
    5. Performing Ramadan
    6. Shunning the wife expiation
    7. Killing expiation
    8. Oath expiation

The optional ones are
    6. Making up Ramadan
    7. Compensation for shaving due to an ailment on the head of the person wearing ihram
    8. Tamattu'
    9. Qiran
    10. Hunting penalty

There are three not mentioned in the Koran but are established by reports
    4. Fasting expiation for breaking fast intentionally in Ramadan which is successive
    5. Optional fast which is optional
    6. Vow which has types. He either vows a number of successive specific days, unspecific days and that which is required by a seclusion vow which is successive even if he does not state that unless he explicitly states in the vow that they are not successive

- **If another Ramadan comes it precedes making up and there is no compensation in delaying to it**

If he has not made up the missed fast he performs the current before making up legally. Thus if he intends it as a missed fast it is only considered as a current fast as has preceded. There is no compensation in delaying to it because of the absolute nature of the scriptural text.

- Breaking fast is permitted for an elderly[508] man or woman

- Compensation is required of them for each day half sa' of wheat as with the person who vowed perpetual fast and became weak

Compensation is required as with the person who became incapable of fulfilling the perpetual vow but not for any other excused person. The compensation for each day is half sa' of wheat or its value on the condition that the old person's inability remains until death. If he is a traveller and died before residency compensation is not necessary for him breaking fast on the journey. The person who vowed a perpetual fast and became weak due to being occupied with earning livelihood breaks his fast and compensates because of certainty that he is unable to make up.

- If he is unable to compensate because of difficulty he asks Allah's forgiveness and pardon

If a person who is permitted to pay compensation and is unable to he asks Allah's forgiveness and pardon, i.e. he seeks his pardon for his shortcoming towards Him.

- If an oath or killing expiation is necessary and he does not find that by which he expiates such as freeing and he is an old person or not having fasted compensation is not valid

Compensation is only permitted for a fast that is primary by itself and not as a substitute for other than it. Thus if an oath, killing, shunning wife or breaking fast expiation is necessary and he does not find that by

---

[508] They are referred to as *fani* which is a reference to them approaching extinction or that their strength has perished and are unable to perform.

which he expiates such as freeing, feeding and clothing and he is an elderly person or not having fasted whilst being able to fast until he became old compensation is not valid because fast here is a substitute for other than it which is financial expiation. Thus fast is only referred to when he is unable to expiate financially. If he bequeaths the expiation it is executed from one third.

Permission for food is permitted in compensation being two satiating meals for a day just as possession is permitted. This is different to zakat fitr where possession must occur as with zakat. Know that that which is legislated with the terms feeding or food possession and permission is permitted but that which is legislated with the terms giving or paying possession is conditional.

- **Breaking fast is permitted for the optional person without an excuse according to one narration**

This narration is from Abu Yusuf. Kamal said that my belief is that it is soundest because of that which Muslim narrated from 'Aisha, Allah be pleased with her, that she said, *"The Prophet, upon him be peace and blessings, entered one day and said, "Do you have anything?" We said, "No." He said, "I am therefore fasting." On another day he came whereupon we said, "Messenger of Allah, some hays[509] has been gifted to us." He said, "Show me it because I woke up fasting." He then ate."[510]*Nasa'i continues, *"However I will fast a day in place of it"*– Abu Muhammad Abdul Haqq has authenticated this addition.

Karkhi and Abu Bakr mention that he can only break fast for an excuse – this is primary narration – because if that which is narrated that he, upon him be peace and blessings, said, *"When one of you is invited for food he should respond. If he is not fasting he should eat but if he is fasting*

---

[509] *Hays* is a meal of dates mixed with clarified butter and a preparation of dried curd which is kneaded vehemently or rubbed and pressed with the hand until they mingle together.
[510] This is recorded by Muslim 2714 to 2715 and Nasa'i 2324 to 2332.

he should pray."[511] – i.e. he should leave. Qurtubi said that this tradition has been established from him, upon him be peace and blessings, and had breaking fast been permitted breaking fast would have been best to respond to the invitation that is sunna – this has been authenticated in Muhit.

Know that invalidating fast and prayer without an excuse after having begun them both optionally is offensive but is not impermissible because the proof is not unquestionable in meaning though making up is required. However if an excuse arises it is permitted for the optional person to break fast by agreement.

- **Hospitality is an excuse according to the most apparent position for the guest and the host**

This is before zenith but not after it unless not breaking fast involves filial disobedience and not for anyone else because of the emphasis. If a person swears a divorce that he will break his fast the relied upon position is that he breaks the fast even after zenith but he has not broken it to preserve the right of his brother.

- **He has glad tidings by this great news**

He says in Tajnis and Mazid that if a man rises fasting optionally and enters on one of his brothers who asks him to break his fast there is no problem in him breaking it because of the statement of the Prophet, upon him be peace and blessings, *"Whoever breaks fast for the right of his brother the reward of one thousand days fast is recorded for him and when he makes up a day the reward of two thousand days fast is recorded for him."* This is also transmitted in Tatarkhaniyya, Muhit and Mabsut.

---

[511] This is recorded by Abu Dawud 2460 and ibn Majah 1751. Abu Dawud mentions in his narration that Hisham, one of the narrators, said, *"Prayer is supplication"*. The narration of ibn Majah states, *"Whoever is invited to food whilst fasting should respond. If he wants he eats and if he wants he leaves."*

- If he breaks fast anyhow making up is on him unless he began optionally on five days, the two 'Eids and tashriq days when making them up is not required by invalidating them according to primary narration

There is no difference between our colleagues in the necessity of making up if the optional person breaks his fast thereby preserving that which has passed from being invalid. If he began fast optionally on the five days making them up is required according to primary narration from Abu Hanifa, Allah be pleased with him, because he is instructed to break its fast. Completing it is not permitted because in actually beginning he has committed a prohibited act by turning away from the hospitality of Allah, Exalted is He. Hence he is instructed to break it. However it is narrated from Abu Yusuf and Muhammad that making up is on him, i.e. even if breaking fast is necessary.

In that which we have mentioned is an indicator that an optional prayer that he broke because he began it at, for example, sunrise should be made up as has preceded.

And Allah is the One who facilitates by His greatest favour towards the soundest religion.

Section 4 – Spiritual Retreat

In language it is remaining and persisting on something. It is transitive with the verbal noun *'akf* and intransitive with the verbal noun *'ukuf.* The transitive has the meaning of hindering and preventing. From it is His statement, Exalted is He, *"and hindered the sacrificial animals"*[512] and from it is also spiritual retreat (*'itikaf*) in the mosque because it is hindering and preventing the soul. The intransitive is coming to something in a persistent manner. From it is His statement, Exalted is He, *"worshipping idols which they had."*[513]

- **It is residing with its intention in a mosque in which group prayer is performed for the five prayers**

Legally it is residing with its intention, i.e. intention of spiritual retreat. It is in a mosque in which group prayer is performed for the five prayers because of the statement of 'Ali and Huthayfa, Allah be pleased with them both, "Spiritual retreat is only in a group mosque." It also involves waiting in the most complete manner for group prayer.

- **Hence it is not valid in a mosque in which group prayer is not performed according to the chosen position**

This is if it is not performed for the five prayers. However it is narrated from Abu Yusuf that the necessary spiritual retreat is not permitted in other than the group mosque but the optional is permitted.

This is in relation to men.

- **He only leaves for a legal, natural or essential need such as the mosque collapsing, an oppressor expelling forcibly,**

---

[512] al-Fath 25.
[513] al-'Araf 138.

family division, fear for himself or his belongings from *vigilantes*

He does not leave from it, i.e. from his place of spiritual retreat. This includes the woman in spiritual retreat in her home mosque. He may leaves for a legal reason such as Friday prayer and the two 'Eid prayers. Thus he leaves at a time that allows him to catch it with its prior sunnas. He then returns. If he completes his spiritual retreat in the Friday mosque it is valid but offensive. He also leaves for a natural reason such as urinating, relieving oneself, removing impurity and performing ritual bath from sexual impurity due to a wet dream because he, upon him be peace and blessings, used to only leave his place of spiritual retreat for human needs. He also leaves for an essential need such as the mosque collapsing, fulfilling testimony that he has been specified for and an oppressor expelling forcibly because he would miss that which was intended from it.

- **He immediately enters another mosque**

He only leaves to perform spiritual retreat elsewhere. He only occupies himself with going to another mosque.

- **If he leaves for a moment without an excuse the necessary is invalid**

There is no sin on him. It is also invalid by unconsciousness and insanity if they last for days except the first day if he remains and completes it in the mosque. He makes up other than it after the cessation of the insanity and unconsciousness even if the insanity stretches according to hidden analogical deduction. They both said that if most of the day passes it is invalid otherwise not.

- **Other than it ends by it**

This means that other than the necessary ends by leaving. This is the optional which has no limit.

- **The person in spiritual retreat eats, drinks, sleeps and agrees sales that he needs for himself or his dependants in the mosque**

These only take place in the mosque because of the necessity of spiritual retreat. Hence if he leaves for these things his spiritual retreat is invalid. Thahiriyya mentions that it is said that he leaves after sunset for eating and drinking.

- **Bringing merchandise in it is offensive**

This is because the mosque is freed of human rights. Hence it should not be made like a shop.

- **Trade agreement is offensive**

This is because he is devoted to Allah, Exalted is He, so he does not occupy himself with worldly matters. Hence sewing and the likes of it is offensive in it. All sales are offensive for a person not performing spiritual retreat.

- **Silence is offensive if he believes it to be a devotional act**

This is because it is prohibited since it is the fast of the People of the Book which has been abrogated. There is no problem if he does not believe it to be a devotional act but protects his tongue from uttering that which does not benefit. However he should persist in Koranic recitation, remembrance, traditions, knowledge, studying, the Prophetic life, upon him be peace and blessings, prophetic stories, upon them be blessings and peace, narrations of the pious and writing religious matters. Speaking ill is not allowed for the person not in spiritual retreat. Permitted speech is offensive because it consumes good deeds as fire consumes firewood if he entered the mosque for that at the beginning.

- **Intercourse and foreplay is prohibited**

This is because of His statement, Exalted is He, *"and do not approach them whilst you are in the mosques."*[514] Touching and kissing are attached to it because sexual intercourse is prohibited in it thus it passes to foreplay as with ihram, shunning the wife and confirmation of non-pregnancy. This is opposed to fast because abstaining from sexual intercourse is the integral in it and the prohibition is established **within** it so that integral is not missed. Hence it does not pass to foreplay because that which is established by necessity is estimated accordingly.

- **Intercourse and ejaculating by foreplay invalidates**

Spiritual retreat invalidates whether intentional, forgetful or compelled by night or day because he has a reminding state as with pray and pilgrimage as opposed to fast. If he ejaculates by thinking or looking his spiritual retreat does not invalidate.

- **Nights are also required by vowing spiritual retreat of days**

Nights are also required, i.e. as days are required, because mentioning days in the plural includes within it the nights that **follow** it. The first night is included. Hence he enters the mosque before sunset of the first night and leaves after sunset on its last days.

- **Days are required by vowing successive nights even if he does not make succession conditional according to primary narration**

This is because the basis of spiritual retreat is on succession. The effect is that which is intrinsically separate is not required to be connected

---

[514] al-Baqara 187

without scriptural proof and that whose parts are connected is not allowed to be separated without scriptural proof.

- **Two nights are required by vowing two days**

Thus he enters at sunset as we have mentioned because dual has the meaning of plural and thus it is attached to it here out of caution.

- **The intention of days specifically and not nights is valid**

The intention of spiritual retreat if he intends specifically days is valid and not nights if he intends spiritual retreat of less than a month. This is because he has intended his actual words hence his intention applies for example if he says, "I vow spiritual retreat of twenty days" and he intended daytime specifically of it his intention is valid.

- **If he vows spiritual retreat of a month and he vowed the month specifically or the nights specifically his intention does not apply unless he states an exemption**

This is by agreement because month is a noun for a set period that includes days and nights and is not a general noun as with ten for a number of ones. Hence it does not apply to anything less than that number at all just as ten does not apply to five for example actually or figuratively. However if he says, "a month with days and not nights" he is required as he said – this is apparent – or if he exempts by saying, "except nights" because exemption is referring to the remainder after the exemption and becomes as if he has said, "thirty days." If he exempts days nothing is upon him because the remainder are the nights alone and it is not valid in them because they negate its condition which is the fast. This is from Fath Qadir with the help of the Protector and Helper.

- **Spiritual retreat is established by the Book and Sunna**

Spiritual retreat is established by the Book because of that which we have recited from His statement, Exalted is He, "*and do not approach them whilst you are in the mosques.*"[515] The construction is to mosques that are specific for devotional acts and leaving permitted intercourse for its sake is a proof that it is a devotional act. It is established by the Sunna because of that which Abu Hurayra and 'Aisha, Allah be pleased with them both, *that the Prophet, upon him be peace and blessings, used to perform spiritual retreat in the last ten of Ramadan since he came to Medina until Allah, Exalted is He, received him.*[516] Zuhri, Allah be pleased with him, said, "How amazing are people that they have left spiritual retreat whilst the Messenger of Allah, upon him be peace and blessings, would do something and leave it but did not leave spiritual retreat until he was taken."

He then indicates its basis by a type of logic by saying

- **It is from amongst the noblest actions if it is from sincerity**

This is if it is from sincerity for Allah, Exalted is He, because he is waiting for prayer and is like a worshipper. It is a state of nearness and devotion and its virtues are countless.

- **Amongst its virtues are**

1. **He empties his heart of worldly matters**

This is by him being occupied with turning towards worship exclusively for it.

2. **He surrenders himself to the Master**

---

[515] al-Baqara 187.

[516]

This is by referring his affair to His **mighty presence**, depending on His generosity and standing at His door.

3.   He regularly worships Him in His abode

He approaches Him to approach His mercy as He indicates in the tradition, "*Whoever approaches Me.*"[517] He remains in His abode, Glorified and Exalted is He, and it is befitting the owner of a house to be generous to his guest out of courtesy, mercy and excellence from him and as an act of kindness to him for having taking refuge with him.

4.   He protects himself in His fortress

Thus his enemy does not reach him with his plot and subjugation because of the strength of the power of Allah, His subjugation and the might of His help and victory. You see a flock devoting themselves at the door of their leader whilst he is one of them. They strive to serve him and stand in front of him humbly for their needs to be fulfilled. He then is sympathetic to them through his goodness and protects them from their enemy with the might of his power and the strength of his force.

He has pointed out attaining the intended, removed the veil of error, lowered the covering and brought forth the truth by the overflowing gift through that which he has indicated by his statement

- 'Ata said, "The likeness of the person in spiritual retreat is like a man who regularly goes to the door of an important person. The person in spiritual retreat says, "I will not leave until He forgives me.""

He is the teacher, Gnostic of Allah, Exalted is He, the mujtahid imam 'Ata ibn Abu Rabah, the follower. He was the pupil of ibn 'Abbas,

---

517

Allah be pleased with them both, and one of the teachers of the greatest imam, Allah be merciful to him. Abu Hanifa said, "I have not seen anyone with more understanding than Hammad or anyone more comprehensive in knowledges than 'Ata ibn Abu Rabah." Most of the narrations of the greatest imam Abu Hanifa are from 'Ata who heard ibn 'Abbas, ibn 'Umar, Abu Hurayra, Abu Sa'id, Jabir and 'Aisha, Allah be pleased with them. He died in the year 115 whilst he was 80 years old as mentioned in 'Ilam Akhbar.

He said, Allah be merciful to him and benefit us with his blessings and help, "The likeness of the person in spiritual retreat is like a man who regularly goes" – i.e. goes back and forth and stands, "at the door of an important person" – such as an important king, minister or leader – "for a need" – that he is able to normally grant. "The person in spiritual retreat says," – with his body language even if his tongue does not utter it – "I will not leave" – standing at the door of my master, asking him all of my needs and those difficulties that have afflicted me and have become my companions and have distanced me from my beloved brothers, in fact from my nearest ones – "until He forgives me" – my sins that are the cause of my distance and the descent of my difficulties. He pours forth from His kindness on me that which is befitting His importance and His generosity, generosity towards the one who has taken refuge within His impenetrable fortress and the protection of His sanctuary.

This is an indicator that the slave who has all these requests stands as a lowly slave stands at the door of his master, free of any actions and attachment to virtue, turning to Him, Glorified is He, with the greatest ways of approach, stretching out the palms of need, persisting in supplication and requests, prostrate at the doorsteps of the door of Allah, Exalted is He, hoping for His intercession tomorrow with Him with that which He has promised. He is a guarantor for all good.

Section 5 – Visiting the Grave of the Prophet

Visiting the Prophet, upon him be peace and blessings, is from the best devotional acts and the most rewarded recommended actions. In fact it is close to being from the rank of necessary actions because he, upon him be peace and blessings, encouraged it and strongly recommended it.

He said, "Whoever has the ability and does not visit me has been harsh to me."

He said, "Whoever visits my grave my intercession is established for him."

He said, "Whoever visits me after my passing it is as if he visited me in my lifetime."

Amongst those beliefs that is confirmed with the scholars is that he, upon him be peace and blessings, is alive, provided with sustenance and enjoying all pleasures and worship except that he is veiled from the eyes of those who are deficient from the noble states.

It is befitting the person who intends visiting the Prophet, upon him be peace and blessings, to send as much blessings as possible because he hears them and they reach him. Their virtues are so well known as not to require mention.

When he sees the walls of Illuminated Medina he sends blessings on the Prophet, upon him be peace and blessings, and then says, "Allah, this is the sacred precinct of your Prophet and the place of descent for your revelation. Therefore bless me by entering it and make it a protection for me from Hellfire and a security from punishment. Make me from the successful ones through the intercession of the Chosen One on the Day of Returning."

He performs ritual bath before or after entering before heading for the visit if he is able to do so. He wears scent and wears his best garment out of veneration for arriving to the Prophet, upon him be peace and blessings. He then enters Illuminated Medina walking if possible having secured his belongings. He enters humbly with tranquillity and reverence taking account of the nobility of the place whilst saying, **"In the name of Allah and on the religion of the Messenger of Allah, upon him be peace and blessings. My Lord, grant me an entry of truth and an exit of truth and, from You, authority to support me. Allah, bless our Master Muhammad and the family of Muhammad ... and forgive me my sins. Open to me the doors of Your mercy and Your grace."**

He then enters the Noble Mosque and prays his two units for greetings at his pulpit. He stands such that the pillar of the noble pulpit is parallel to his right shoulder, being the standing place of the Prophet, upon him be peace and blessings. All that is between his grave and his pulpit is a field from the fields of Heaven. He then prostrates giving thanks to Allah, Exalted is He, for having facilitated this for him and blessed him by arriving there. He then supplicates for whatever he wants.

He then heads towards the noble grave standing a distance of four arm lengths with complete etiquette having his back towards the direction of prayer. He faces towards the head of the Prophet, upon him be peace and blessings, noting that he is gazing happily towards him, hearing his words, responding to his salaams and uttering amen to his supplication.

He says, "Peace be to you, my Master, Messenger of Allah. Peace be to you, Prophet of Allah. Peace be to you, Beloved of Allah. Peace be to you, Prophet of Mercy. Peace be to you, Intercessor of the Community. Peace be to you, Master of the Messengers. Peace be to you, Seal of the Prophets. Peace be to you, Muzzammil. Peace be to you, Muddaththir. Peace be to you, your pure offspring and your pure family from whom Allah removed uncleanliness and purified thoroughly.

May Allah reward you from us the best that He has rewarded a prophet from his people and a messenger from his community. I testify that you are the Messenger of Allah; you conveyed the message, fulfilled the trust, advised the community, clarified the proof, strove earnestly in the path of Allah and established the religion until certainty came to you.

May Allah bless and send peace on you and on the noblest place that has been ennobled by the presence of your blessed body, perpetual blessing and prayer from the Lord of the Worlds according to the amount of everything that has been and everything that will be in the knowledge of Allah, a prayer that has no end to its length.

Messenger of Allah, we are your delegates and visitors to your sacred precinct. We are honoured by being present in front of you. We have come to you from distant lands and far flung places, having crossed plains and rugged terrain with the intention of your visit to be successful through your intercession, looking at your traces and abodes, fulfilling some of your rights and seeking intercession from you to our Lord. Verily sins have broken our backs and wrongdoings have burdened us and you are the Intercessor, the One whose intercession is accepted, who has been promised the Greatest Intercession, the Praiseworthy Station and Wasila. Allah, Exalted is He, has said, "And if, when they had wronged themselves, they had but come to you and asked forgiveness of Allah, and asked the Messenger to ask forgiveness for them, they would have found Allah Relenting, Compassionate." We have come to you having wronged ourselves and asking forgiveness for our sins. So intercede for us to your Lord and ask Him to cause us to die on your way, to resurrect us in your group, to lead us to your basin and to give us drink from your cup without humiliation or

remorse. Intercession, intercession, intercession, Messenger of Allah."
He says it thrice.
"Our Lord, forgive us and our brethren who were before us in the faith, and do not place in our heart any rancour toward those who believe. Our Lord, You are Kind, Compassionate."

He then conveys salaam from those who requested, saying, "Peace be to you, Messenger of Allah, from such and such a person. He seeks intercession from you to your Lord. So intercede for him and the Muslims."

He then blesses him and supplicates whatever he wants at his noble face with his back to the direction of prayer.

He then moves an arm length until he is parallel with the head of the highest saint, Abu Bakr, Allah, Exalted is He, be pleased with him. He says, "Peace be to you, Caliph of the Messenger of Allah. Peace be to You, Companion of the Messenger of Allah, his close friend in the cave, his associate on journeys and his trusted one in the secrets. May Allah reward you from us the best that He has rewarded a leader from the community of his prophet. You succeeded him in the best manner, you traversed his path and manner in the best way, you fought the apostates and innovators, you paved the way of Islam, you firmed its pillars and were the best leader, you maintained family ties and you remained upright in truth, supporting the religion and its people until certainty came to you. Ask Allah, Exalted is He, for us perpetual love of you, resurrection with your party and acceptance of our visit. Peace, the Mercy of Allah and His blessings be to You."

He then moves the same distance until he is parallel with the head of the leader of the Muslims, Umar ibn Khattab, Allah be pleased with him. He says, "Peace be to you, Leader of the Believers. Peace be to you, Exposer of Islam. Peace be to you, Destroyer of Idols. May Allah reward you the best reward. You gave victory to Islam and Muslims, you conquered most of the lands after the Master of the Messengers, you provided for orphans, you maintained family ties and Islam was strong by you. You were for the Muslims an accepted leader and a guided guide. You kept them together, helped their poor and consoled their broken ones.

Peace be to the both of you, Soul Mates of the Messenger of Allah, his Ministers, his Advisors, his Helpers in establishing the religion and the two who took care of the affairs of the Muslims after him. May Allah reward the both of you the best reward. We draw near through the both of you to the Messenger of Allah, upon him be peace and blessings, so that he intercedes for us and asks Allah, our Lord, to accept our effort, to keep us alive on his religion, to cause us to die on it and to resurrect us in his group."

He then supplicates for himself, his parents, those who requested supplication from him and all Muslims.

He then stand at the head of the Prophet, upon him be peace and blessings, as he did originally, saying, "Allah, You said, and Your statement is true, "And if, when they had wronged themselves, they had but come to you and asked forgiveness of Allah, and asked the Messenger to ask forgiveness for them, they would have found Allah Relenting, Compassionate." We have come having heard Your statement, obeying your instruction and asking for intercession through Your prophet to you. Allah, Our Lord, forgive us, our fathers, our mothers and our brethren who were before us in the faith, and do not place in our heart any rancour toward those who believe. Our Lord, You are Kind, Compassionate. Our Lord, Give us what is in this world and what is good in the Hereafter, and keep us from the torment of the Fire. Transcendent is your Lord, the Lord of Might, beyond that they describe, peace be upon the messenger and praised be Allah, Lord of the Worlds."

He adds whatever he wants and supplicates with whatever comes to him for he will be facilitated by the grace of Allah.

He then comes to Abu Lubaba pillar where he tied himself until Allah turned to him which is between the grave and the pulpit. He prays whatever optional prayer he wants. He repents to Allah and supplicates whatever he wants.

He comes to the Field and prays whatever he wants. He supplicates whatever he wants and whatever he desires. He glorifies, praises and asks forgiveness as much as possible.

He then comes to the pulpit and places his hand on the protrusion which was there to take blessings with the trace of the Messenger of Allah, upon him be peace and blessings, and the place of his blessed hand when he delivered sermons to attain his blessings, upon him be peace and blessings. He blesses him and asks Allah whatever he wants.

He then comes to the wailing pillar. In this is the remnant of the trunk that sobbed for the Prophet, upon him be peace and blessings, when he left it and delivered sermons on the pulpit until he descended and embraced it. It then calmed down.

He takes blessings with whatever remains of the Prophetic remains and the noble places.

He strives to worship at night whist residing there, to attain sight of the Prophetic presence and to visit him at general times.

It is recommended to leave for Baq'i and go to the sights and visits particularly the grave of the master of the martyrs, Hamza, Allah be pleased with him. He visits Abbas, Hasan ibn Ali, and the remainder of the family of the Prophet, Allah be pleased with them. He visits the leader of the believers, Uthman ibn Affan, Allah be pleased with him, Ibrahim the son of the Prophet, upon him be peace and blessings, the wives of the Prophet, upon him be peace and blessings, his aunt, Safiyya, the companions and the followers, Allah be pleased with them all.

He visits the martyrs of Uhud, if possible Thursday is best. He says, "Peace be to you because you were patient. How excellent is the final abode." He recites the Chair verse, Ikhlas eleven times and Sura Yasin if possible. He gifts the reward of that to all the martyrs and those believers neighbouring them.

It is recommend to come to Masjid Quba on Saturday or another day. He prays in it and he says after supplicating with whatever he desires, "Helper of those who call for help, Saviour of those who seek salvation, Reliever of the difficulties of those suffering difficulties, Responder to the call of the desperate, bless our Master Muhammad and his family. Remove my difficulty and grief as You removed from Your Messenger his difficulty and grief at this place. Loving, Benefactor, Doer of much good and excellence, Perpetuator of favours, Most Merciful of the merciful."

Allah bless our Master Muhammad, his family and his companions and salute him with a worthy salutation for ever. Lord of the Worlds.

Amen.